AWAKENINGS

AWAKENINGS

*Moments of Truth
from Middle America*

PATRICK COURRIELCHE

&

ADRYANA CORTEZ

INFORM
- VENTURES -

www.RedPilledAmerica.com
www.Inform-Ventures.com

First Edition: November 2019

The authors are grateful for permissions to include the following previously copyrighted material:

Excerpts from Ellen Bukstel's poem Legacy of Love. Reprinted by
permission of the author.

Excerpts from Doug Segal's letter Grow Up and Change the World.
Reprinted by permission of the copyright holder.

ISBN 978-0-578-60571-5

Design: Inform Ventures, LLC

Printed in the United States of America

To our daughter and mothers.

Contents

AWAKENINGS

Introduction

For Patrick, the moment came while watching a seemingly innocuous news report.

Since the announcement of his presidential run, the media had been painting all opposition to Barack Obama as merely an aversion to his skin color. When Joe Biden called the then-senator "clean and articulate," the compliment was seen as the last vestiges of racism. Critics of Obama's longtime relationship with an anti-American pastor were branded as garden-variety racists. Any objections to his Supreme Court Justice nominees were labeled as Republican racial politics of yore. Even an art poster depicting Obama as the Joker from *Batman* was perceived as a creation to stoke racial fears. The media worked to brand each and every instance of resistance to the first Black president as covert or overt racism. So to anyone buying this media narrative – bigotry appeared to emerge at every turn...including in an August 2009 news report. In it, far-left MSNBC introduced video of a man attending a pro-Obama rally – armed with a rifle on his shoulder and a pistol on his hip – as part of a segment discussing racism against the president. "And the reason we're talking about this," opened host Contessa Brewer, "there are questions about whether this has a racial overtone. Here you have a man of color in the presidency and White people showing up with guns strapped to their waist or to their legs." But astonishingly, what MS-NBC artfully cut out of the video was the skin color of the man carrying the rifle and gun. He was Black...a fact discovered and propelled by the emerging independent online media of the time. The blatant fabrication of racism where there was none, was enough to open Patrick's eyes forever to the harmful fiction pedaled by cable news everyday. But that moment was just the trigger – his *awakening* was building for years... with many of those turning points chronicled in the pages of this book.

In the case of Adryana, an awakening moment hit her at a time when she was least expecting it. After a childhood of poverty, working her way through college, then eventually starting a business with her future husband Patrick – Adryana had begun making money, real money, for the first time in her life. The marketing firm she helped found, fueled by the emergence of New Media, was blossoming – hoisting her into the so-called *one percent*. It afforded her all of the accouterments her newfound success offered. Adryana bought a house in the Hollywood Hills, hired a nanny, enrolled her kid in a prestigious preschool, and found herself amongst the rich and famous of Tinseltown – introducing her to an elite segment of society that few people get to witness...especially as the daughter of Mexican immigrants. She'd heard from new friends in this social circle about a kids dance studio frequented by many of the families from the school community. So Adryana enrolled her daughter in one of the afternoon classes. On the first day of instruction, she showed up with her daughter in tow, walked her into class and took a seat in the waiting room...perching herself in front of the glass window looking into the studio. It was a proud moment for Adryana. She'd worked her way out of a pretty deep hole and now had her daughter enrolled with kids who's parents had largely started life on third base. Adryana had made it. As she sat there gleaming at her daughter learning some new dance move, a mother from her preschool turned to her and asked, "So, are you the nanny?" Adryana was sitting next to her brand new Gucci handbag, holding the keys to her Mercedes Benz that was sitting in the parking lot. Despite all she'd accomplished in life, she realized that, living in the sanctuary city of Los Angeles, she was always going to be viewed as "the help" to the liberal elites around her.

These moments of awakening have been happening since the beginning of human culture. But over the past two decades, America has been quietly experiencing a revolution in consciousness – an awakening to the realities of how the world works, largely ignited by an unprecedented proliferation of social media and the unsanctioned information that courses through it. The main beneficiaries of this revolution have been those from Middle America – a realm not grounded by geography, but instead by mindset...and who've been historically barred from traditional media platforms to voice their dissent. When an awakening occurs, at first glance it appears to have been sudden. But in reality it's been an accumulation of small moments that burst to a new breadth of understanding at some critical point. These awakenings can be scientific in nature, or help us see the character of our enemies clearer. They may give us a new perspective on life's most challenging obstacles, or perhaps lead to a new political worldview. But each time it happens, a new layer of the onion is peeled back revealing an entirely new perspective on life to the observer. And that is why the powerful work so hard to control the information that leads to these moments.

Throughout this new awakening, the legacy gatekeepers of information – Hollywood and the arts, the media, the literary industry, Big Tech, and our educational system – have worked collectively to eliminate stories that illuminate inconvenient truths. These corrupt cultural institutions first tried ignoring, then minimizing, then marginalizing unauthorized information. When those tactics failed to contain their spread – the aspiring gatekeepers collectively moved to purge the unsanctioned stories and storytellers from the ranks of polite society. But truth cannot be contained.

Awakenings is a collection of stories presenting themes that America's cultural institutions either ignore or actively work to eliminate, and is an offshoot of Red Pilled America – an audio documentary series with the same purpose. The series first launched on November 1, 2018. We like to think of both this book and the podcast as an autobiography of Middle America – with personal stories from the authors, Patrick Courrielche and Adryana Cortez, weaved throughout. That way, unlike the works of our cultural overlords – the audience is made fully aware of the life experiences and perspectives that go into the stories they are consuming. The firsthand accounts that play out in the pages of Awakenings are a love letter to the American tradition of storytelling and we believe they provide a crucial platform for the forgotten men and women all across our great country. We hope you enjoy it.

- Patrick & Adryana

ONE

David & Goliath
How do the small overcome the mighty?

As we stood there at our kitchen counter listening to the recording of the telephone call, with our two-year-old bouncing
around the house, we couldn't have known what was coming:

> **Yosi Sergant**: "This is just the beginning. This is the first
> telephone call of a brand new conversation…we are just
> now learning how to really bring this community togeth-
> er to speak with the government. What that looks like
> legally?"

In just a few weeks, we'd be caught up in what looked like
a government cover-up, our home would be tracked down
by triggered zealots, property vandalized – and, unthinkably,
we'd be battling it out with the most powerful people on the
planet. And in the middle of it all, as we challenged the behemoth of behemoths, the one thing that kept crossing our minds
was, how are we going to beat this giant?

**

For a husband and wife team just starting a family, with no real history in politics, facing off with the Obama Administration was a surreal experience - and one we would have never survived without connecting with Andrew Breitbart, one of the greatest minds in the history of media...and that's not hyperbole. Adryana and I were faced with a tough decision while standing there at our kitchen counter. We didn't quite realize it in the moment, but the choice we were about to make would change our lives forever. There'd be no turning back – not even if we wanted to – all because we thought we should do the right thing. But before we get to the heart of the story, you need to understand the environment at the time.

It was the summer of 2009, and Congress was heading for their annual August recess...that time of the year when our politicians leave Washington D.C. and go back to their home districts to hear from their constituents. It's typically quiet, even uneventful, but on this particular occasion, the country was in the grips of a national debate...one that had gone nuclear. Obama was pushing for legislation that would require all US citizens to buy health coverage or face a fine. In the young President's brand new world, purchasing medical insurance was the price of being alive. We were being taken one step closer to a government takeover of our bodies...and people weren't having it. At town hall meetings all across the nation, people were rejecting Obama's proposal that would forever change the healthcare industry...and for good reason. Throughout his historic run for the White House, candidate Obama spoke loudly against forcing citizens to purchase health care – otherwise known as the individual mandate. For roughly two years, time and time again, Obama ridiculed his opponents and scoffed at the idea of requiring people to buy insurance. So when he finally won the historic election, everyone, even his opponents, thought the idea had been shelved for the foreseeable future.

But then something happened...Al Franken became the senator from Minnesota. On election night 2008, the former Saturday Night Live comedian had actually, on paper, lost his senate election by 725 votes. But in a race where 2.9 million people voted – the slim margin of victory set in motion an automatic recount. After a seven month legal battle, the comedian had somehow flipped the election in his favor to win by just 312 votes. It was later reported that roughly eleven hundred felons illegally cast a ballot in the race, just about the same number that flipped it. Prisoners voting could turn an election towards the Democrats. Some called foul, but nevertheless, Al Franken was announced the winner on June 30th, 2009. His improbable steal wasn't just any old senate seat – it was the sixtieth...the magic number giving Obama a filibuster proof majority in Congress. In other words, the President had just acquired the power to pass legislation without a single vote from the Republicans. With that kind of leverage he went for the big prize – Obamacare, requiring every breathing US citizen to have health insurance...or else. So shortly after Al Franken's victory, the president, along with his top advisor and friend Valerie Jarrett, embarked on a national campaign to sell the plan he'd spent so long criticizing. It was supposed to be easy...he had the votes. But Obama was about to learn otherwise.

Whenever there is an imbalance of control, when one group is perceived to have too much power, a counter movement arises with the ultimate goal of bringing stability back to the system. With the Democrats in control of the White House, Congress, and now securing a filibuster-proof majority, there was only one way to reestablish balance...and that was to pressure a democrat to vote against Obamacare. Enter the Tea Party, stage right.

Night after night, videos of angry voters confronting democrat politicians went viral. With the advent of social media,
and the smartphone just beginning to infiltrate culture, the
mainstream media were for the first time losing its grip on
crafting the narrative. By August 2009 the spectacles were
so widespread, it became impossible for the media to ignore.
The young administration was desperately looking for a way
to change the narrative, and the Tea Party was searching for
ways to keep the pressure on.

Around this time, an image went viral. A few months earlier
I'd seen a poster a couple blocks from our house that was strik-
ing in that it went completely against the groupthink plagu-
ing the art world. The entire creative community had been for
over two years in a seemingly endless climax over their new
messiah, Obama. From star-studded tribute songs, to PSAs, to
countless fashion spreads, to the famous Obama Hope poster,
artists had become the president's euphoric groupies with a
devotion that seemed to have no end. It was frankly embarrassing. Which made the street art posters I saw while out on a
run through Hollywood all the more stunning. It was an image
of Obama as the Joker from *Batman*, the Heath Ledger version, with a single word below the image...Socialism. I tried
to find an artist name on the poster, but all I could see was an
indecipherable website in one corner. Within no time, maybe
even hours, they were torn down and months went by with
almost no mention of them in the media or online. But when
August 2009 crept up, just as the debate over Obamacare
raged in every enclave of the country with fears that it would
take America closer to socialism, the Joker posters popped up
again...however this time they went viral. First conservative
radio personality Tammy Bruce saw them near the 101 Freeway in Hollywood and posted pictures of the posters on her
website. The images spread – eventually finding their way on

to The Drudge Report. Within days, the media and art community took the predictable route in covering the development.

The LA Weekly declared, "The only thing missing is the
noose." The Washington Post added about the unknown artist, "So why the anonymity? Perhaps because the poster is ultimately a racially charged image." Over the span of years,
this Joker poster was the only substantial piece of street art
that was critical of Obama – and I knew this because I was
steeped in that scene. At the time, I'd been deeply involved
in the art world for roughly fifteen years. The creator of the
famous Obama *Hope* poster was an old business partner of
mine. I thought it was cool what he did, but was nauseated by
the art community's cult-like devotion to Obama...and was
even more disturbed at the reflexive claim of racism towards
anyone that dared criticize the first black president. When the
Joker poster was called racist. I'd had enough. For years I'd
wanted to take up writing for several reasons, but primarily
to convey a theory I'd been developing about how messages
spread and cultures evolve. This was as good an opportunity
as any to give writing a stab. So with Adryana as my editor, I
penned my very first article, chastising the art world for their
blind allegiance to Obama.

We were a bit hesitant to try and publish the piece. We made
100% of our income from the arts and entertainment industry
– a world that seemed ubiquitously liberal. Our family came
from simple beginnings, and as *The Jeffersons* would say, we
were movin' on up...living the good life in the Hollywood
Hills. But in the end, we still considered ourselves democrats.
We weren't the racists or right-wing nut jobs that the media so
often seemed to drum up. I'd been promoting black and brown
artists for almost fifteen years. Adryana and I are of Mexican
descent. Why should we have anything to fear in speaking
out? So I submitted the piece to a libertarian site I'd recently

began reading – Reason.com – and they said they'd print it. I was feeling good about being published on my first try. The art community needed a wake up call. I closed the essay saying, "Most artists would not want to be referred to as tools of the State, but in the case of Obama's administration, that's exactly what they've been so far." But what we didn't know was how quickly that statement would become a dangerous reality.

As we were waiting for the article to go live, an invitation popped into my email inbox. It was from a guy named Yosi Sergant, the new Communications Director of the National Endowment for the Arts, also known as the NEA...a federal agency whose mission is to support the arts all across the nation with our tax dollars. Yosi was the force behind promoting the Obama *Hope* poster...it's why he got the gig at the NEA. We knew of him, on the other hand, as our former employee – a savvy young promoter that should be watched...carefully. The email he sent was an invitation to a White House conference call and it went out to select members of the arts community. "A call has come in to our generation," the invite dramatically opened. "A call from the top. A call from a house that is White. A call that we must answer." The invite listed several art world and media personalities attending the teleconference, as well as political activists – and it invited the arts community to help Obama with his agenda...with health care being at the top of the list. The White House wanted the conference call attendees to show quote "how the arts can be used for a positive change." To a casual observer, it may have looked normal. But it wasn't. It smelled like an extension of the Obama campaign – which is a big no-no once a candidate takes office. The invite came from the largest funder of arts in America, the National Endowment for the Arts – a federal agency that provides financial grants to the very same community being invited to the meeting. The incoming head of the

NEA had announced a desire to give grants directly to individual artists. NEA funding was historically given to arts groups, not individuals. So distributing them directly to artists would be a monumental shift...and anyone paying attention in the art world took notice. The timing of the invite was also suspect. There was a raging national debate over healthcare, the exact topic at the top of the meeting agenda. Was Obama trying to dangle federal grants to get artists to create propaganda about his health care legislation?

To add to our suspicion, on the same day the invite arrived, Shepard Fairey – Yosi's close colleague and the artist that actually designed the Obama Hope poster - penned an article for the far-left Huffington Post entitled *Helping Obama Write the Unwritten Future*. The op-ed urged the art community to help the president fulfill his agenda, closing with a subtle call-to-action, stating quote, "Hopefully Obama and all of us who have stood behind him will do everything we can to fill in our incomplete future the way we've pictured it." At the time, Shepard Fairey was the art world, and the Huffington Post was an outlet of record for that community. As I stood at my kitchen counter reading Shepard Fairey's article, and then the White House invitation - the two efforts appeared to be coordinated. This was no small deal. The National Endowment for the Arts had at the time a massive annual slush fund of over $200 million dollars that it was suppose to distribute to the creative community to promote the arts in America – money that could go a long way in creating political messages. Obama appeared to be politicizing that federal agency - potentially making it into a propaganda arm to change the narrative on the healthcare debate he was losing. If we were right, what the White House was doing was potentially illegal.

My article went live on Reason.com that day and as anyone who's been published can understand, the very first time your words hit the public it is thrilling. I mean, besides college papers and press releases – I owned a publicity company at the time – I wasn't a writer, nor was Adryana an editor. Putting pen to paper wasn't our strong suit. I have a Masters in applied physics – and worked in aerospace designing components for military communication satellites. Adryana had a background in the arts. Writing was something brand new to us. We wanted to get as many eyeballs on the article as possible. So I reached out to a website that could possibly promote it. I heard about this site called Big Hollywood... better known today as Breitbart News. It appeared to publish articles about the entertainment industry and the arts, and it had a marque section where it linked to offsite articles similar to the Drudge Report. So I found the submission email and sent a quick note with a link to the article in hopes that they'd post it. I got a response almost immediately from a guy named Andrew Breitbart with his cell number and a simple note saying, "Call me." I gave him a ring and within minutes I felt like I'd known him for years. Andrew told me he was at some seminar about the Federalist Papers. He thought that if he was going to be talking about the Constitution, he felt like he better know everything about it.

Andrew's energy was contagious. He seemed happy to have found me...and said as much in so many words. My new friend told me he was part of an underground Hollywood community. Some posted on his site and others were quietly part of a secret club. Andrew said he'd introduce me to everyone, set me up with an account to publish on his site. "You'll love it," he said. "There are a lot of people like you. You're not alone," he assured me. We spoke for a while about our backgrounds, and then I told him what was on my mind... fishing for a specific response. "I just got an invite to a White House conference call," I told him. "I'm thinking about calling in." Andrew responded almost reflexively, "You should record it." That had already crossed my mind, but hearing it come out of his mouth was the confirmation I was looking for. Andrew said he'd post a link to my article, and we promised to keep in touch. I got off the phone thinking he was right. The chance that the White House was doing anything wrong was slim. But if they were, and I was going to write about an Obama program that was potentially against the law, I better get every single quote right. And by recording the call, it provided a perfect opportunity to test a theory I was developing about how messages spread.

Adryana and I are partners in running a family and a business. We each have our primary domain of responsibility, but we make every important decision together. Before we could even think about moving forward with writing about the White House, we had to answer two questions. First, should we record the conference call? It was a decision that Adryana and I frankly agonized over. I had a government security clearance in the past and took things like this seriously. After some deliberation, and getting some counsel, we came to the conclusion that since press was going to be on the call – a fact announced on the invite – and the simple truth that it was being organized by federal agencies and the White House, there was no expectation of confidentiality. With a call of this nature, we couldn't even reasonably expect that the White House, or any other participant for that matter, would not be capturing the call. So our minds were made up…we were going to be recording it. But then the second question was, how? How would we record it? Now you have to remember, this was 2009. The iPhone had just come out two years earlier and we as a culture were all just getting to understand the powers of our smartphones. This was long before everyone was whipping out his or her pocket computers to capture every confrontation, embarrassing mo-

ment, and important event. I'd been using the voice memo
function on my cell for a while, but wasn't sure if it would
work over a speakerphone. So Adryana and I began testing it
out. It was clear that my iPhone would do the job.

So on August 10, 2009, I placed it in front of the speakerphone, dialed into the White House conference call, tapped
the record button, and quietly listened.

> **Mike Skolnik**: "This is Mike Skolnik. I am based in New
> York. I am a filmmaker for the past ten years but cur-
> rently serve as the political director for Russell Simmons.
> I have been asked by folks in the White House and folks
> in the NEA, about a month ago in a conversation that was
> had. We had the idea that I would help bring together the
> independent artists community around the country."

In his opening statement he admitted that the White House
and the National Endowment for the Arts initiated the effort.
The meeting organizers claimed that they wanted the people
on the call to get involved with the White House's *United We
Serve* initiative. Then Mike Skolnik stated the goal of the call.

> **Mike Skolnik**: "And so I'm hoping that through this group
> and the goal of all this and the goal of this phone call,
> is through this group that we can create a stronger com-
> munity amongst ourselves to get involved in things that
> we're passionate about as we did during the campaign
> but continue to get involved in those things, to support
> some of the president's initiatives, but also to do things
> that we are passionate about and to push the president
> and push his administration... I wanted to give you all
> the opportunity to hear more about the United We Serve
> from the folks who are running it as well as hear from

the National Endowment for the Arts and Yosi Sergant, who many of us know has been a true champion during the campaign of the arts and as what he's doing over at the National Endowment for the Arts, and how we can all work together to promote and to engage our country in service as well as use art in doing so."

A woman from another federal agency, named Nell Abernathy, stepped in at one point and said the Obama Administration was looking to expand the meaning of "service." The White House's new definition of the word included "to create art"...or what many sane people call propaganda. They introduced the next speaker, a White House staffer named Buffy Wicks who worked directly for Valerie Jarrett, President Obama's top advisor – the woman helping the President sell health care reform to a hostile country. We were informed that Buffy was one of the people who spearheaded this effort. She took the microphone next to add the weight of the White House to the call:

> **Buffy Wicks**: "So I'm at the Office of Public Engagement here at the White House...We have about 20 folks and we work under Valerie Jarrett, she's one of our fantastic leaders"

This propaganda effort was spearheaded by the office of President Obama's top advisor, Valerie Jarrett. Buffy Wicks continued:

> **Buffy Wicks**: "I'm actually in the White House and working towards furthering this agenda, this very aggressive agenda, I'm really realizing that, and I'm also appreciative of the way in which we did win and the strategy that

the campaign shows, which is really to engage people at a local level and to engage them in the process, because we need them and we need you, and we're going to need your help, and we're going to come at you with some specific asks here. But we know that you guys are ready for it and eager to participate, so one, we want to thank you, and two; I hope you guys are ready."

The White House's "specific asks" were delivered by Yosi Sergant of the National Endowment for the Arts:

> **Yosi Sergant**: "I would encourage you to pick something, whether it's health care, education, the environment... My ask would be to apply artistic, you know, your artistic creative communities' utilities and bring them to the table."

He was telling everyone on the call to create art about health care to help support the President's agenda. Yosi told us we were part of a community that knew "how to make a stink" and he encouraged us to do so both locally and nationally... calling on us to tell other producers, marketers, publicists, and artists to do the same. This was a noteworthy request given that Americans all across the country were making a stink about Obama's proposed healthcare overhaul. This was the White House and America's largest art funder, on the phone with the community they funded, telling it to take political action on issues under heated national debate. Was I hearing this correctly? Were we actually being told to create propaganda? Yosi continued:

> **Yosi Sergant**: "This is just the beginning. This is the first telephone call of a brand new conversation. We are just

now learning how to really bring this community together to speak with the government. What that looks like
legally? We're still trying to figure out the laws of putting
government website on Facebook and the use of Twitter.
This is all being sorted out. We are participating in history as it's being made. So bear with us as we learn the
language so that we can speak to each other safely and
we can really work together to move the needle and to
get stuff done."

Artists speaking together with the government? This didn't
sound like a service program, it sounded like a campaign rally,
or Mao's China. A few days later, an NEA grant recipient that
was on the call issued a statement demanding Congress support Obama's health care overhaul. Another call participant
began distributing artwork demanding "health care for all."
It was the beginnings of a propaganda machine...initiated by
our tax dollars!

As we stood at our kitchen counter listening to the recording, Adryana and I began to realize that we were now in a
predicament. I'd published an article just a few days earlier
warning that artists were becoming tools of the White House,
and now we had caught that exact fear on tape. We knew a lot
of the people participating in the meeting. We were the orga-
nizer's old bosses. There were big players from every facet of
the arts on the call. The media was in on it. If we were to be
publicly critical of this meeting, how would it affect our business? And more importantly, how would it affect our family's
future? My hands started to sweat a bit thinking about whether
to go public. We were living a comfortable life...making good
money from the entertainment industry. We knew many of the
people in our world were liberal – but frankly, at the time we
thought of ourselves as liberal. I was still a registered Demo-

crat. We'd even donated to Obama's Inauguration Fund. If we were to speak out now, would we be risking everything? After some deliberation, Adryana and I agreed. Whether we liked it or not, we were now involved...we had to expose the effort. We could not allow a potential propaganda machine to be created from our tax dollars.

So I penned an op-ed, questioning if Obama was attempting to turn the National Endowment for the Arts into a propaganda machine...a machine to take back control of the healthcare debate raging all across the country. I asked readers, "Do you think it is the place of the NEA to encourage the art community to address issues currently under legislative consideration?" This was my first long-form article...and I wrote it in the form of a story...much like our Red Pilled America show. I turned to my new friend Andrew Breitbart to see if he'd publish it. He said yes, and teamed me up with his editor John Nolte, who I'd come to learn that, if Hollywood were a real free market, John would be the head writer of The Tonight Show – he's that funny. Andrew called a few D.C. types and was told that by hosting the call, the White House may have violated the Hatch Act – a law that makes it illegal to use federal funds for political activities. Andrew published my article, entitled *The National Endowment for the Art of Persuasion?* on Breitbart News and the conservative blogosphere began immediately buzzing.

The first to pick it up in the mainstream was Stuart Varney of Fox Business, who had me on the show to discuss the story. "From what you heard, it sounds an awful lot like taxpayer money was, they tried to use taxpayer money to support a specific political position by the Obama team, that what it sounds like," offered Stuart. "Well they are the largest funder of the arts in the United States," I responded. "And they have on this conference call the people that they fund. And in addition to that these are people that were handpicked. They said we were selected for a reason. And they were handpicked basically because they were involved in the Obama campaign. And they used the Hope poster and the will.i.am Yes We Can video as perfect examples of how this community and how this group helped elect this man to office. So when you have this handpicked group, and you are telling them to speak to certain issues, what do you think they're gonna speak to? I mean, it sounds pretty obvious to me." Things were about to get heated.

Earlier in the day I learned a tenacious reporter at the Washington Times, Kerry Picket, started digging into the story. She contacted Yosi Sergant at the NEA to ask who invited people to the call. "The NEA didn't invite," responded Yosi. "We were a participant in a call. It was a third party that did the invitations." Kerry pushed back asking, "I was wondering if you could send me if possible a copy of the invitation." Yosi answered, "Um, it didn't come from us...So, I don't have it to distribute." Yosi had unfortunately made a dumb decision. He lied about not sending out the invitation...I clearly had an electronic version to prove it. But more importantly, by saying the NEA didn't invite people to the conference call, he was suggesting that I was lying. In the new age of Google, that could not stand. What could have been a robust debate over the proper use of a federal agency was now shifting to an attack on my integrity – and the appearance of a government cover-up. The conservative blogosphere went into a frenzy.

As the NEA-propaganda story began to heat up, Andrew Breitbart gave me a warning. He called, sounding like he often did – as if he were doing three things at once – and told me we had a week to get the narrative to break. "I'm working on the biggest story of my life," he said. "We're launching it in about a week. Once it goes live, it's going to dominate the news cycle. You'll have a hard time breaking through," he added. "What story are you working on," I asked. "ACORN," he replied. I'd heard recent rumblings about undercover videos on the controversial community-organizing outfit ACORN. The word was that Andrew was working with a young journalist named James O'Keefe. "Ok, I'll blow it out by next week," I said.

The next day Andrew was guest hosting the Dennis Miller radio show and I went on to ramp up the pressure. "In what you're doing, there's almost no benefit by showing common cause with the political right in this country, with an art community that leans so heavily to the left, and behaves punitively towards those who have rightwing things," said Andrew. "So, as a whistleblower as it were, you're putting yourself in harm's way. What is your motivation to put yourself out there like this knowing that there's a possibility that tomorrow you may wake up being called a racist by Rahm Emanuel's minions?" I responded, "You know, I have a two year old daughter...and I need to set an example for her. And I need to be the kind of father that she will look up to...I think ultimately history will vindicate coming out like this." Later that day, the White House issued a statement to The Boston Globe claiming I misconstrued the purpose of the call.

With both the White House and the NEA putting my credibility at question, it was time to let the world know we had the tapes. We offered Glenn Beck, then a rising Fox News star, the first audio clips. He accepted, and that night his audience was the first to hear the Obama Administration's attempt at politicizing a federal agency.

> **Glenn Beck**: "I'm gonna show you the beginning of something that should scare the living daylights out of you. It is propaganda in America. The National Endowment of

the Arts is now holding conference calls. I want to lay this out for you and then I'm gonna bring a guest in, one of the guys that was on the conference call. Felt awkward about this whole thing. He's an artist and he felt awkward and decided he was gonna tape the conference calls. The only reason why we can bring this story to you with any credibility is because he did the brave thing, probably destroyed his career or at least he'll never get a dime from the National Endowment from the Arts and probably won't speak to any other artist again or they won't speak to him because he has betrayed the movement. I'm gonna introduce you next to the man who received these emails and more of the conference calls and coincidently some artwork that happened within two weeks of this phone conversation."

Glenn was doing something that no other cable news commentator was doing at the time. He was taking deep dives into subjects – sometimes spending an entire show on one topic. Glenn spent three segments on the NEA scandal, dramatically combing through the government's propaganda attempt with Beckian meticulousness. Our story came at an opportune time. The Administration had just announced an upcoming Obama school speech – an act viewed by his critics as an effort to indoctrinate children with socialism. The timing of the two stories helped to amplify the importance of each. The NEA scandal helped define a forming narrative – one of an Administration willing to use propaganda to reshape the nation in their vision. The NEA propaganda story, as it was called, also came at a critical time in Glenn Beck's show. For weeks he had been telling the story of an administration implanted with radicals. Van Jones, then the White House's Green Jobs Czar, had been a favorite show topic. Jones had a colorful past as an admitted communist and advocated for reform through revolution. If journalist skeptics dismissed Jones as just an unvetted fluke in the executive office, the NEA propaganda story would provide another example to label Obama as a radical. Our story even got Glenn's chalkboard treatment, placed right next to Van Jones as another question the Administration needed to address. By the end of the interview, it was obvious that our story had become a potent weapon against the Administration. My iPhone, the same device used to record the call, was blowing up. Life had just gotten a bit more complicated.

The segment had incited many on both sides of the aisle into action. Those that opposed the Administration sent notes of praise and the comment section of the original op-ed swelled to a watershed number for Breitbart.com at the time. Simultaneously, the Glenn Beck interview incited the Administration's grassroots supporters – sending them into organize and attack mode. One started a twitter account inspired by our last name – artfully titled Douchelche. Emails with colorful language littered our inbox. We woke up the morning after the Beck appearance to our car being severely keyed. A few days later a tire was punctured. The hostility got ratcheted up when one attacker tweeted a simple action for his followers to perform - "bang on em!" As the story grew, a leftist writer published an article for the Huffington Post attempting to incite the hip-hop community against us. A Facebook group was even created to organize supporters of the NEA to come after our family. This was all 2009 Twitter and Facebook...before online hate mobs became a cultural norm...so few knew how to deal with this type of aggression.

The story had spread beyond conservative circles to the new social networks. But conspicuously, the mainstream media ignored the controversy. The story had all of the triggers to in affect make it smelling salt for a sleepy newsroom. There

appeared to be a cover-up with a blatant lie by a White House
appointee, federal employees were potentially participating in
prohibited activity, the White House was involved, and it was
all caught on tape. There was even a direct tie to one of President Obama's top advisers – his long-time friend and confi-
dante Valerie Jarrett. All of these ingredients should have sent
the mainstream media news cycle into action. But besides a
piece in the Boston Globe, in the halls of the trusted press, it
was as if the conference call had never happened.

As the story began to enter the radars of mainstream outlets, the reason for the silence became apparent. Anita Dunn,
a top Obama spokesperson, was vigilantly working behind the
scenes convincing the major outlets that the whole affair was
not newsworthy. "The higher ups want to hold the story until I
talk to Anita Dunn," one network news reporter told me. Dunn
wanted to tell them what they were hearing on the audio. As a
result of her efforts, the mainstream media wouldn't yet touch
it.

As the story continued to heat up, Glenn Beck scheduled
me for a radio appearance. But just seconds before I was
about to go live, a major story about Van Jones broke – and
I was bumped. Conservative newsrooms were about to become completely preoccupied. Jones, under fire for jokingly
referring to Republicans as "assholes," was now caught in a
much more explosive story. His signature appeared on a 2004
Truther petition that accused the Bush White House of de-
liberately allowing the September 11th attacks to occur. Van
Jones attempted to distance himself from the inflammatory petition, but it didn't work. In the early morning hours of Sunday
September 6th, he resigned. In the moment, it wasn't apparent
that his resignation had anything to do with the NEA story.
It appeared to be just another affair that could push our story
out of the system. But in reality, the Van Jones' resignation

gave us a boost. The mainstream media was portraying the former green jobs czar as a victim – with Glenn Beck as villain. "Glenn Beck Gets First Scalp: Van Jones Resigns," read a Huffington Post headline. The resignation itself now became a weapon of the left to attack Glenn Beck and characterize him as a right-wing apache riding the beltway pasture in search of new prey. If another Obama official highlighted by Glenn were to fall, the Van Jones resignation would affectively amplify this new resignation.

In the hours immediately after Van Jones stepped down, our NEA story made its first peek onto network television, on This Week with George Stephanopoulos. "Recently there was a conference call arranged by the National Endowment for the Arts, with a representative of the White House for potential grantees or actual grantees of the federal government, getting subsidies," said George Will to the host George Stephanopoulos. "The thing of it was, how the arts community could help advance the President's agenda. Now I don't know how many laws that breaks, but I'm sure there are some." The story was on the brink of breaking through.

With the launch of James O'Keefe's ACORN undercover sting looming, I wrote another NEA article that included new audio from the conference call. Up to this point, both the NEA and the White House were doing their best to block coverage on mainstream media. This was possibly the last opportunity to get a reaction out of them before the big ACORN bomb hit. Probably sensing the urgency of the moment, Andrew stepped in to boost the story. He first added his patented headline flair to the article, pushed it live onto Breitbart News, then while manning the wheel at The Drudge Report, Andrew linked the conservative powerhouse website to the NEA story. That's when the godfather of conservative media covered the breaking news.

Rush Limbaugh: "Now what this is all about is the Obama Administration using the NEA, community organizing efforts, to help propagandize the Obama agenda, all of it."

The following day, Senator John Cornyn of Texas issued a letter to President Obama calling for congressional hearings. This was mind blowing. Two people that started this citizen investigation from their kitchen counter now had Congress pushing for an investigation. It was unreal. Would the White House or NEA respond? Would the story make an impact before ACORN broke? Would the mainstream media finally pick it up? With only forty-eight hours before the ACORN story launch, there was little time.

The day closed with no response from the White House. The next day was again met with silence by the Obama Administration. "Time's up," I thought. We missed our opportunity. But time wasn't up. It was just about to get really interesting. Less than two hours after the ACORN sting broke, I got an email from my editor John Nolte. The subject line read, "Yosi Sergant resigns from the NEA." He continued in the body of the email, "If it's true, it's huge." It turned out to be only partially true. The Huffington Post, initially reporting Sergant resigned, modified his position to "reassigned." The mainstream media could no longer avoid the story. Yosi Sergant: The Next Van Jones? was a headline at ABC News. Glenn Beck had me back on to give an update. "This isn't about Yosi...he wasn't some rogue guy that called this meeting on his own. The White House was on the phone," I told Glenn. "He's the Director of Communications. He takes orders from other people. Those are the answers they need to address...who approved basically putting this art group together?" Glenn was on a hot streak, and he was having fun with this story. He responded, "By the way, the Left blogs are calling this, 'Glenn Beck has another scalp.' I want you to know I personally find that offensive. I think that's demeaning to Native Americans."

The National Endowment for the Arts began to crack. I received a call from its chairman Rocco Landesman almost two weeks after I left him a message. But with the lying, the cover-up, the attempt to discredit us, the vandalism of our property... we didn't trust anyone but our tribe. We sensed a shift. It was time to prepare one final push to prove we were right all along. Up to this point, we'd strategically released segments of the audio. It was time to publish the whole kit and caboodle. Now able to poke his head out from the ACORN story, Andrew assembled a team to help blow it out. He enlisted a young writer by the name of Ben Shapiro, another up-and-comer Dana Loesch, John Nolte, future radio host Larry O'Connor, and others to prepare stories to drop immediately after release of the full audio. Then Andrew called on the big guns. First the godfather put the story on his airwaves:

> **Rush Limbaugh**: "And understandably a lot of people are infuriated about the politicization of the NEA and turning it into an Obama campaign. I don't know why anybody is surprised about this. There hasn't been any evidence up 'til now though of Obama being involved in it, just the NEA. That is until today. Apparently the full transcript here shows the White House orchestrating this through a woman named Buffy Wicks with the White House Office of Public Engagement. Buffy Wicks works under Valerie Jarrett who is at the right-hand of Barack Obama the Almighty."

Then that night, Andrew and I appeared together on the Sean Hannity show. Andrew took the lead:

Andrew Breitbart: "Sean, there is a quid pro quo there. Patrick in his four-part expose, there's a fifth part today where we give the whole context of the conference call and that the White House was involved. But days after this conference call occurred, the net result of that conference call, the 'asks' that the White House talked about, started to represent themselves online. And at Rock the Vote there was a full-scale help the President's healthcare initiative thing. There are multiple, multiple people on the phone call who delivered the goods for President Obama and their desire to politicize the NEA..."

The full court press worked. The context of the full audio left high-ranking White House staffers fully vulnerable – an assistant to Valerie Jarrett was implicated in what some said was a violation of the law. It was time for the White House to cut their losses. ABC News Senior White House Correspondent Jake Tapper reported that, "White House officials say they are enacting specific steps to make sure such a call never happens again." White House spokesman Bill Burton issued a statement to Tapper stating, "We regret any comments on the call that may have been misunderstood or troubled other participants. We are fully committed to the NEA's historic mission, and we will take all steps necessary to ensure that there is no further cause for questions or concerns about that commitment." It was the closest thing to an apology that you could get from the Obama Administration. The White House issued new federal conduct guidelines and the chiefs of staff of the executive branch agencies met to discuss rules and best practices to make sure that such a program would never happen again. Ten senators released a letter demanding the NEA ensure their agency hadn't been corrupted. The story broke big time.

"The National Endowment for the Arts is the largest federal

funder of the arts. It's embroiled in a controversy and it all goes back to a conference call held in August," opened a National Public Radio segment. "Artists as Servants of Power," read a Wall Street Journal headline. "White House to agencies: Don't overstep on grants," read the Associated Press. "Agencies Instructed to Separate Politics from Grant Awards," blazed the New York Times headline. "Administration backs off NEA call," said a reluctant Politico. "My god, Obama has bypassed the bully pulpit, national media, NASCAR, pro football – to use an army of federally subsidized artists to help propagandize his socialist agenda. Brilliant," joked Jon Stewart.

CBS News interviewed us for a primetime network story. But when the White House caught wind…it took extra precautions to end the momentum. That's when I got the call from Andrew. "He resigned," he said calmly over the phone, referring to Yosi Sergant's resignation. "It's a direct hit," he added. And this time, it was true. With this one reported resignation, the story Adryana and I broke gave two of the most powerful conservatives in media – Glenn Beck and Andrew Breitbart – their second and first White House appointee scalps, respectively. Two kids from the wrong side of the tracks, whose credibility had been questioned by the highest office in the land, us two Davids had just beaten the Goliath…with the help of another David by the name of Andrew Breitbart. We weren't particularly happy Yosi Sergant was forced to step down. We thought the Obama Administration did him dirty by throwing an obviously talented arts advocate under the bus for doing what they told him to do. But that's how the powerful roll… they use their underlings as pawns. But in the end, he made an unforced error that made him expendable.

Andrew featured our journey in his book *Righteous Indignation*. He saw the combination of our NEA story and James O'Keefe's ACORN sting, happening at the same exact time, as a quote "breakthrough moment for the New Media." He added, "But in my mind, it seemed that if the ACORN story and the NEA story could be paired and weaponized, maximized and forced into the eye of the American public, they could serve as a case study demonstrating that the New Media could supplant Ye Olde Media."

I continued to write for Breitbart News on and off over the coming years, but eventually took a break to focus on our publicity business. Andrew enthusiastically supported that work as well. When Andrew passed in 2012, it was the first time that my daughter had ever seen me cry. Like so many others, our time with Andrew Breitbart was one of the most thrilling moments of my life. He imparted more in those intense acts of citizen journalism than I'd learned in six years of college.

Which leads us back to the question, how do the small overcome the mighty? The best way to understand how an underdog overcomes overwhelming odds, like taking on the White House from a kitchen counter, is to think of the world as a game of war. The small triumph over the mighty because their ideas, their products, their messages become weapons in this conflict. Our NEA story helped incite an idea that had already taken root in the mind of millions of Americans…the view that the media was silent as the Obama Administration was attempting to make radical changes. It helped reinforce a narrative that the White House was willing to politicize federal agencies to get its way. Our NEA propaganda story became a weapon to resist that effort – it became a social weapon, shared by Obama's critics to battle his power grab. The NEA's propaganda machine was halted in its tracks before it got off the ground…and almost nothing political was heard about that federal agency throughout the duration of Obama's two terms.

But this fight continues to this day. Van Jones, who resigned in disgrace for his involvement in the 9/11 *Truther* petition, has gone on to become a wildly successful CNN pundit. A little fun fact...our kids shared a private school for many years. Even with his scandalous resignation, Van Jones was celebrated on our school campus, while we were reviled merely for voting republican. Mr. Jones now has his own weekend CNN show pumping his ideas into our living room. Yosi Sergant, the man who resigned from the NEA, is largely on the same path as well. He is now organizing huge arts events to push for universal mental health care using the tax dollars of Los Angeles County...and it's all legal.

The Left has massive funding from the government and the billion-dollar funded media to bombard our culture with their ideas. We have you. Thank you for your support through buying this book. Because whether you realize it our not, by backing our work...you are in the game. You are among the few supporting David to fight these Goliaths. The good news is... we are pretty good with a sling.

TWO

Ticking Time Bomb

*Do illegal aliens just do the jobs
Americans won't do?*

You know those expressions you hear so often that you don't
even question their truth? We've all heard them before:

"If you eat a lot of food and go swimming, you'll get
cramps."

"Cracking your knuckles can cause arthritis."

"We only use ten percent of our brain."

"You know Joe Scarborough is a Republican."

Or maybe it's Joe Scarborough only uses ten percent of
his brain. Anyway, there are those phrases we hear throughout
life that get repeated over and over and over again, so often
so that they just become the truth...whether they are or not.
We've been a bit obsessed with one of those sayings, and it
goes a little something like this – *illegal immigrants do the
jobs Americans won't do.*

This idea has seeped so far into culture that Kelly Osbourne
– the purple-haired offspring of famed rock star Ozzy Osbourne – offhandedly delivered a version of the catchphrase
while attempting to dis Donald Trump's early 2016 campaign

rhetoric about deporting illegal aliens. "If you kick every Latino out of this country, then who is going to be cleaning your toilet Donald Trump," Kelly quipped during a segment of the far-left TV show *The View*. Her co-hosts quickly virtue signaled – feigning outrage over the statement. Kelly looked truly stunned by their response, and in a sense her surprise was understandable – because once a version of this slogan enters your radar, you quickly see that it's the media and their fellow travellers in Washington D.C. that have been promoting this idea for the better part of two decades. It has become so prevalent that even we began taking it for granted. But is it true? Do illegal aliens really just do the jobs Americans won't do? We started to do a little digging to find the answer and it led us to some guys from Long Island. What we learned was eye opening because what happened to them could easily happen to just about anyone.

**

Suffolk County is not a household name to people who haven't lived in New York. About eighty miles east of Manhattan in Long Island, the area advertises itself as the leading agricultural county in New York State with a farming community that has survived hundreds of years of development. But as unfamiliar as the name may be to the majority of Americans, the county includes one of the most well known regions in the world – the Hamptons...the vacation stomping grounds for the rich and famous.

Like most affluent neighborhoods throughout the country, the haves are separated from the have-nots by a kind of barrier – and in the Hamptons that barrier is New York 27...a highway that connects Brooklyn to the eastern tip of Long Island. The haves live south of that road. Tom Wedell grew up in an area just north of the highway, in a city called Manorville. A stocky, medium height Long Islander of Scottish decent, Tom is in his late fifties, but with the head of hair of a teenager. Although he lived within walking distance of the well to do, he was anything but. "I come from a family of ten," said Tom. "Five girls, five boys. We come from a farm stand family."

From the time Tom was born until their passing, his mother and father ran a farm stand in West Babylon, a town just north of the highway and west of the Hamptons. His mom and dad would buy fruits and vegetables from local farmers and sold them through their stand. Like many working class families, they would put their kids to work. By the time Tom was old enough to carry a box – he was part of the farm stand crew. "It was one of the biggest on the island," Tom recalls. "And I worked on that farm stand up until the time I was 17 years old and then I realized I could get a job and get paid." Tom got his first paycheck when he caught wind that the father of a friend needed some help doing landscaping out in the Hamptons. At seventeen, he called the guy and got the job. "That's how I started working out East. I started doing landscaping and stuff around houses in a development and I worked my way up. I got good enough at doing what I was doing [so] they let me do some more. I did some carpentry. I did everything. I did what ever needed to be done."

It wasn't long until Tom broke out on his own. He'd become a small business owner – a big step for a guy that came from a working-class family of ten, selling tomatoes starting from the age he could walk. He slowly built his crew, at one point he had up to a team of twenty-five guys working on multi-million dollar estates. "I had a construction company building houses," Tom said proudly. "We did everything right from the ground up. They'd come and pour the foundations and we'd do everything else." Most of Tom's crew was made up of young guys, including George Overbeck – who would handle a specific part of the construction job. "I was a cedar roofing and cedar siding specialist," recalls George. "I specialized in Cedar so I always did high-end work. We're talking million dollar homes and $30K, $40K, $60K roofs or siding." The two became good friends, not surprising given their upbringings. Both were Long Island natives...both from humble beginnings.

"This is where I came from," offers George. "I was six, my sister was four [when] my father had a heart attack and died. The only one that raised me was my mother. At the time, she was just an aide basically working to take care of people. She didn't have a lot of money. We basically lived off the system in a sense. My whole entire life I remember getting free lunch...just hard times from the beginning to the end." George grew up in Hampton Bays – a village just west of the popular luxury vacation spot, Southampton – in a building that he said more resembled a chicken coop than an apartment complex. His family lived the kind of lifestyle where you'd be eating well on the second day of the month, but by the third...things started getting tight again. George never had his own room. He slept on the couch in the living room, which doubled as the entrance room and the TV room. Their kitchen had a bar that was made out of a door...and that was their table. You get the picture.

As a kid George would walk down to the local grocery story, called King Kullen, right before closing time. There was a manager there that knew his family was poor. "And I used to go there like eight o'clock at night when the store's about to shut," recalls George. "He would give me bags of groceries and stuff and I'd go and collect all the carts, and sometimes I would sweep the floors or whatever, but he would give me bags of groceries and I would take them home." When he got old enough – at the ripe old age of twelve – he started looking for a job. George lived down the road from a burger joint in Hampton Bays called Slo-Jacks. It looks kind of like a throw back to the days when you'd drive up and a waitress would walk up to your car and take your order. He locked in a job there cleaning the parking lot in the morning, before starting a full day of middle school. "And then when I became 14, I started working [the] miniature golf course, which [was] in the back, and started as a counter guy."

Living like this grows you up quick. So at sixteen, George decided it was time to get a real job. He dropped out of school and moved to a town called Riverhead, which was on the other side of Long Island, and started working for a landscaping company – basically cutting the lawns of estates. By the time he was eighteen, his younger sister started dating a guy whose father owned a cedar roofing company and was looking for guys to work. He offered George a job, and that was his entry into the construction business. He'd later start working for Tom Wedell, but by the year 2000, for his New Year's resolution, he decided to start his own roofing company.

As the year 2001 came around, both Tom and George – guys who started with nothing, who'd worked manual labor jobs at an age when they should have been riding a bike – had hustled and scratched their way out of poverty to become successful small business owners. George had a bunch of guys working for him. He was a subcontractor to many of the prestigious builders on the east end of Long Island – from East Hampton to Bridgehampton to Southampton. "I was doing quite a few jobs, probably banging out a house a month or something," George remembers. "Everything was possible and everybody was doing the right thing and I was happy about my company and everything was great." Tom was in a similar place. He was busy, and had a ton of guys working for him. "Everything was

good. I really didn't have much problems," Tom recalls. "I'd
bought a lot of equipment, everything was rolling good. My
business was growing. My guys were working hard. Everybody was happy, ya know. The jobs were going good." They
were living the American Dream. But what happened next
would change all that forever.

**

In the classic big screen thrillers, the villain often uses a pretty
sick tactic to control his enemy - he secretly plants a ticking time bomb that threatens innocent lives. This twisted re-
venge seeking monster then sends a warning note that finds
it's way to the desk of a barely sober cop. We watch as this
flawed hero goes from location to location trying frantically to
piece together the puzzle – eventually leading him to maybe a
crowded train station at rush hour. People roam the terminal,
clueless to the potential terror attack, as the now battered hero
sees a beat up leather briefcase through the crowd off in the
distance. As the bomb ticks dangerously closer to zero, this
disheveled, out-of-breath officer shoves people out of the way
in a mad dash against time. The hero first fumbles, but ends up
entering the right code to unlock the latch, and then carefully,
hand trembling, reaches into the bag to pull out the green wire
just in the knick of time. In the end countless lives are saved.
This act of terrorism is demented – but at least the villain gives
his would-be victims a chance to survive.

Back in the real world, many think a kind of ticking time
bomb has been planted throughout America – put there by
men with power…looking to acquire even more of it. But unlike on the big screen, no clue is sent to the hero to find the
bomb. There is no puzzle to solve that saves the day. The villain actually wants the bomb to go off. And when it does, it

destroys American lives. That's what Tom Wedell said happened to him. "Boom, one day, all of a sudden. Your guys are gone. I didn't understand. All of a sudden, one night…I was destroyed in one night. I was destroyed. My government was not supposed to do that to me. That's not right. It's not fair."

The ticking time bomb went off for Tom about a week before September 11, 2001. At the time, he was about halfway through a three-year job on an estate in Sagaponack – a village in Southampton. He remembers that day well. It was in the morning, and his guys had just started showing up to the job site. They usually met at a barn off the driveway to discuss the day's work and divvy out the tasks. "We all met at the barn," Tom recalls. "And I dispersed my guys off. They were doing their thing, working on the various parts of the house. And I guess about two hours after we started, the builder came, his name was Rich, and he had the homeowner with him and he didn't have a happy face on him. And I was like, 'What's going on Rich?' He said, 'We have a problem Tom.' And I said, 'Well what's up?' He said, 'I've got a problem with the homeowner. She doesn't like how much she's paying for these guys.'" Rich explained that the homeowner was going to replace Tom's workers with her own guys. Tom was being fired. He pleaded for them to reconsider. He'd spent about a quarter of a million dollars on equipment to build his company, and had twenty-five guys who thought they had work for the next eighteen months. "I said, 'Rich man, I've been working on this job for a year and a half, there's still over a year and a half left to go on this project. You can't just let me go like that.' He said, 'There's nothing I can do about this Tom. The homeowner wants to bring her guys in here. There's nothing I can do about it Tom.' And that was it. That was the end. I didn't know what to say to the guy…I was dumbfounded."

Since he'd been there for a year and a half, Tom had been

accumulating a lot of equipment that was dispersed throughout the job site. So he thought he'd get a couple of days to remove it from the property. But when he arrived the next day to
pick up his equipment, he was stunned to find that there were
twenty guys on the job, all Latinos, and they were using his
equipment. "It was the most insulting thing I've ever seen in
my life. I couldn't believe it. Not only were they stealing my
job, but they were using my equipment." Tom was shocked
but pissed as well. He started grabbing his equipment away
from the workers. "I was really mad. But I got my equipment
and I put my tail between my legs and I left and I just tried
to carry on, ya know. I tried to keep my guys working. I tried
to get other jobs. I got a couple little ones here and there, but
nothing that could sustain twenty-five guys working. Nothing."

The firing started a spiral for Tom. He struggled for a long
time trying to find enough work to support his guys. He had
twenty-five men working for him at the time – feeding their
families. "I'm struggling. I'm coming out east every day trying to find work, trying to keep me going, trying to keep my
guys going. And over a couple of years I just kept losing guys
and losing guys. It got to the point where I had nobody left. It
was just me, struggling trying to make it. Trying to live. I lost
half of the equipment. It really ruined my entire life." Tom
saw no warning signs that the bomb was about to go off. He
did slowly notice some Spanish-speaking workers on some of
the jobs, but he really didn't pay any attention to it. He was
busy. His guys were busy. But over the course of a few years
after losing that big job, he started to put two and two together.
On his way into Southampton, he'd pass a 7-Eleven everyday.
He noticed a few Latinos standing outside of the place. And
as weeks turned into months the number grew. That's when
he figured out what happened to all of his construction work –

Tom had an awakening. "I'm looking at that 7-Eleven, I pass it everyday. There's two hundred guys, three hundred guys lined up there everyday. Up and down the sidewalks, all looking for work. That answered my question of where all my work went...these guys are stealing my work." The local contractors were hiring the illegal immigrant day laborers standing outside of the 7-Eleven for dirt cheap...cutting every corner possible. "They pay no [workers] comp, they pay no liability. I had to pay all that stuff," Tom said angrily.

Suffolk County had been dealing with an influx of illegal immigrants for a few years. In the late 1990s, when about fifteen hundred Mexicans made there way to Farmingville, a tiny village in Suffolk County, it sent the small community into chaos. Neighbors began seeing twenty and thirty illegal immigrants occupying a single home, and aggregating at the local 7-Eleven looking for work. Local residents complained of harassment and unruly behavior by these new invaders. Then an illegal immigrant killed a single mother while drunk driving, disappearing after making bail. But it wasn't until a few of these day laborers were beaten up that it began to attract the attention of the media. The people of Farmingville were successful in blocking a city-sanctioned hiring hall for the illegal immigrants, but the problem only seemed to spread to other parts of Suffolk County.

Paul Forthmuller, a local at the time, explained why so many illegal immigrants were flocking to the area. "You have a lot of rich people out there, with their park like grounds and mansions and so on, and these people you know they want to have their grounds taken care of, but they don't want to spend the money to employ the correct people, American citizens. So they would always give the jobs to the cheapest guy." After first finding agricultural and landscaping work, the illegal immigrants eventually infiltrated other areas, like painting, carpentry, and general construction. They began to change the economics of the town in other ways too.

Already an expensive place to live – the day laborers made the prices skyrocket. When word of work in the richest enclave in America started to spread, illegal immigrants came out in droves, setting up hubs. First they'd make enough money to rent a house, then bring in fifteen, twenty, thirty guys to live there, each paying say $50 dollars a week. If a landlord had the choice between a small family paying $2,000 a month rent and twenty guys paying much more than that, which way do you think the landlord is going to go? It's not rocket science to figure out the answer. Locals say the illegal immigrants drove up rental prices in the area enough so that a single working-class family – now unable to find work – couldn't afford the rent.

It wasn't long before the illegal immigrants started to enter other areas of construction. That's when the bomb hit George Overbeck. "I specialized in cedar, so I always did high-end work," said George. "It just slowly but surely, every time I put a bid on a job with another builder, they would turn around and try to bunch my price and use [the illegal immigrants] as a wedge. This free, cheap labor." The labor obviously wasn't free, but they definitely worked for cheaper...much cheaper. Their impact on his small business was devastating. "And slowly as I went from fifteen, to ten, to six, to four, to two guys, there was no way to keep up...it was impossible to compete, because the army was vast and I was just a small company. George slowly began to lose everything. "So when I hit rock bottom I contributed it to one factor and one factor only...the fact of free labor, cheap labor. Maybe not free, but cheap labor."

Like many of the local workers, in early 2006 George left the state of New York hoping to find construction work elsewhere. But when he got to Tennessee, he was shocked at what he learned. "It turns out that Tennessee was no different, and then New York or Long Island, everywhere you go it was the same story," recalls George. The so-called day laborers were already in other states. But what was most troubling was that Tom and George were experiencing this work shortage in one of the biggest housing booms in history.

House prices increased from 2000 to the summer of 2006 more than they did in the previous two decades. It wasn't as if there was a downturn in the economy that was forcing a demand for cheaper wages. They also weren't working in a town that was particularly cash poor. In fact, it was the exact opposite. In 2017, BusinessInsider.com listed Sagaponack – the town in which Tom and his crew lost their jobs to day laborers – that village was listed as the number one wealthiest zip code in America, with a median house selling at $8.5 million. The wealthiest zip code, in the wealthiest country in the history of the world, during the biggest economic boom in an industry, had to find cheaper illegal labor.

Illegal immigration has changed the face of working class America…literally – and nowhere is that better illustrated than in construction. California is the canary in the coalmine for how illegal immigration will affect the American working class throughout the country. In 1980, the percentage of Latinos working in construction in Los Angeles County was 24%. By 2015, that number had almost tripled to 70% Latino…an incredible shift in the workforce – and it's largely attributed to illegal immigration. These are the kinds of jobs that have historically lifted Americans out of poverty. And this wasn't the only shift in the industry. From the early 1970s to 2016, American construction workers wages have declined by almost 20%. For all of the talk that immigration creates prosperity in America – the Golden State completely debunks that myth. Even with industries like Hollywood, Silicon Valley, and aerospace titans like SpaceX, California is now the poverty capital of the U.S. Los Angeles has seen a 75% surge in homelessness over a recent six-year span. San Francisco even has maps to avoid the feces of the homeless. And reliable Republican enclaves like Orange County have been faced with this problem as well – with residents of Irvine County organizing to block the erection of tent cities for the homeless in their town. What this massive influx of illegal immigration has done is increase the wealth gap, providing near slave labor to the world's richest populations – all while driving down wages, and in some cities closing off a major pathway out of poverty for America's working class.

This is what Tom Wedell and George Overbeck faced when they came back together in 2006. Around that time Tom protested a chemical fertilizer plant and successfully shut it down. So when George and him started talking about what could be done to deal with all of the illegal immigrants lining up at the Southampton 7-Eleven and stealing their work, it was obvious what they should do. "I went out there with a bunch of kids one day. They said how can we do something about this," remembers Tom. "I said, 'Make some signs up and we'll go protest.'" And so they did. "We went down to the basement, bought a bunch of crayons, a bunch of paint. Made some signs up, went out to protest, just for a weekend."

Tom, like most of us, was taught that if you have any gripe with the government you should peacefully protest. And this seemed like the perfect opportunity. These day laborers were here illegally, right? It was illegal to hire them too, right? The government was doing nothing about the problem. It was a slam-dunk. So they grabbed the signs and headed out to the Southampton 7-Eleven. But when they got out to protest, they learned a new lesson. Instead questioning the illegal immigrants lined up on the sidewalks in the hundreds, the cops turned their focus on the protesters. As soon as the police figured out what they were protesting, they started taking down their license plate number and running background checks on the American protesters. "They were just a bunch of kids," said Tom. "It really made me mad that they were doing that, you know. And here these guys are standing on the side of the road stealing everybody's work. They don't even belong here. Not a one of them could produce identification if you tried. And it just, it makes me mad."

And who wouldn't be? Tom had been trying to do the right thing for years – hiring American workers, trying to keep them busy, trying to put food on their families' tables. When he figured out that the illegal day laborers were stealing their work – he decided to protest for law enforcement to, well, enforce the law. "And here's my government telling me to shut up, you can't do nothing about it," said Tom. "These guys are here that's it, get used to it. It really made me mad. That's when I was determined. Right after that I said that I'm not gonna stop. I guess I've gotta stay out here until people recognize what's going on here." Tom and George became fixtures at that Southampton 7-Eleven. The place was such a hot spot that it received an award for selling the most cups of coffee in the United States. Tom became kind of the poster child for illegal immigration in the area. He took the fight to the businesses and politicians supporting the day laborers.

So many illegal immigrants were lined up on the street looking for work that the city tried something provocative. There was a city-owned field next to the 7-Eleven. So instead of sweeping the area and arresting and deporting anyone in the country illegally – the city decided, unbelievably, to build a drive thru hiring hall on the city-owned property. George Overbeck remembers the city's plan. "They were gonna cut a curb and they were gonna put a U driveway and a couple trailers. And basically contractors like me and all these others guys could walk in and say I'll take four guys or I'll take three guys or whatever, and drive in and drive out…like some type of a work McDonald's." Tom remembers that day. "They tried to dig out the holes and get the driveway built," said Tom. "And one day me and my buddy George pulled up and they were digging it. I stepped right out of the truck and into the hole."

"I'll never forget this," adds George. "They were cutting the curb in the road and they were putting in the U in the hiring hall area, and my buddy jumped out of my car, I mean we didn't even stop to park, he jumped out of the car, he jumped into the hole. And there was this machine, this backhoe, and the backhoe driver turned around and spins around to get another piece of dirt and there's my buddy Tommy in the hole. And he's like you're done here, you're done, you're not cutting this. This is not gonna happen. It's over. You're not doing it." The site ended up getting shutdown for misuse of city property. The hiring hall never opened. But Tom was arrested in the process. It was one of many times.

Tom would stand outside of the 7-Eleven with an American flag and a sign protesting the day laborers. "They arrested me like four times on the word of the illegal aliens. Just saying I was standing too close to them. They didn't like my flag." The illegal aliens became brazen. If his flag brushed up against them, they'd call the cops and have Tom arrested. "It steeled my resolve," recalls Tom. "Every time they did that it just made me have to stay longer. I'm not gonna go anywhere. I'm gonna be out here every day. I had to count up change. I had to count up change some mornings to make it out there with gas. It cost me around $7 a day to make it there and back on gas. Sometimes I'd just coast."

Tom and George did win the battle. They shut down the

hiring hall. But they are losing the war. The illegal immigrants in Suffolk County are now firmly planted in the community. "Basically, nothing has changed," George frustratingly said. "They don't have a location to do their thing except on the side of the road like they'd normally do and they'll always do. But the thing that has changed, is they've come a long way my friend...They're not cutting the grass, they're telling that guy over there to cut the grass. You know what I'm saying. Nothing has changed, except they don't have the steady location, but they don't even need it anymore because the bosses are them!"

With guys like Tom and George and millions of others losing their jobs to these day laborers, how did this phrase – *illegal immigrants do the jobs Americans won't do* – become so widely repeated? Well the day laborers had their own idea, and they shared it with Tom. "They laughed in my face. They told me, 'Get the hell out of here. George Bush already gave us your country. There's nothing you can do about it.' That's what the illegals told me." George W. Bush no doubt played a role in spreading the message. He was one of the leaders that popularized the phrase. But its been used widely by both political parties...possibly more so by Democrats. We are told time and time again – almost like an advertising slogan attempting to sell us something we don't need – that illegal immigrants only do the jobs American's won't do. But the facts tell a different story.

Dr. Steve Camarota, Director of Research at the Center for Immigration Studies, has actually tested the validity of this catchphrase by looking at occupational data captured by the federal government. "We can actually look to find the occupations where there are no Americans working," says Dr. Camarota. "It turns out that you can't find them." Out of the four hundred and seventy-two occupations identified by the

Department of Congress, there are only six that are majority immigrant. And even in those six, forty-six percent of the
workers are still U.S. born. Even in occupations thought to be
dominated by immigrants, both illegal and legal, U.S. born
citizens hold a majority in the field. "So maids and housekeep-
ers in America you might think, well gosh, that must be all
foreign born," adds Dr. Camarota. "It's not. It's fifty-one percent are native born. There are eight hundred and fifty thousand native born Americans who do that job. Fifty-eight percent of taxi drivers and chauffeurs are U.S. born. Sixty-three
percent of butchers and meat processors, sixty-four percent
of ground maintenance workers, and seventy-three percent
of janitors are U.S. born. So the vast majority of janitors are
U.S. born, but we still say things like that's a job Americans
won't do." This is why the claim that *illegal immigrants only
do the jobs Americans won't do* is so sinister. Our politicians
have the data. They know the truth. Tom and George got their
start in the workforce through manual labor. Working in farming. Sweeping parking lots. Cutting lawns. Trimming hedges.
Then getting a break and working their way up in the construction business to become small business owners – only to
have it all taken away by the guys just doing the jobs Americans won't do.

Our leaders continue to allow this ticking time bomb of
cheap labor to enter the country because it gives them more
power…especially in the near future when the new voting
population comes of age. The change in public school enrollment in the Hamptons area highlights this point. In Bridgehampton, public school enrollment went from 6.8% Hispanic
in 2000 to 41% in 2017. In East Hampton it went from 18.5%
to 51%. In Hampton Bays, where George grew up, it went
from 16.1% Hispanic to 55% Hispanic. And in one Southampton school, north of the highway in the land of the have-nots,

the school enrollment went from 10.5% Hispanic in 2000 to 71% in 2017. And this is just one of many towns across America going through the same invasion of illegal immigrants.

Suffolk County sensed the serious problem and in 2016, voted for a Republican for president for the first time since George H.W. Bush. Tom wasn't surprised when it went Trump's way. "Oh my God, if you would have seen all the people for Trump when I held that Trump sign out there in Southampton. I had more support than you could imagine. When everyone was saying he was gonna lose, I knew he was gonna win." Tom stopped protesting three days after Trump was elected, and is hopeful that the president will be able to enforce our immigration laws. Things have not been easy for him since his days of protesting. He's had a hard time finding work, and his living arrangements aren't steady. "I'm renting a house right now that I can't even afford to rent," said Tom. "I'm almost out on this house now. But I've been going through houses that people have been in foreclosure. That's the way I've lived for the last 15 years. I've been going from one abandoned house to another. One foreclosed house to another."

George was forced out of the roofing business, but his painting work has picked up since Trump's election. He is also hopeful that President Trump will be able to enforce our immigration laws – and he's a guy that you can say puts his money where his mouth is. His wife was a Polish immigrant to the United States. They had a son. Then her visa expired. George decided he needed to practice what he preached. He sent his wife and son back to Europe to enter the country legally. But because she overstayed her visa by a month, they couldn't immigrate to the U.S. for five years. So George packed up and moved to Europe with his wife where they had two more boys – eventually coming back to the US after five years. He hopes

President Trump is able to enforce the same immigration laws that were forced on his family. "I voted for Trump and we stopped basically doing what we were doing because of the fact is that we felt like when we voted for Trump that we'd have a leader that was going to take care of this, and he wants to and he's going to but there's so many obstructionists, so many people on the wrong side of this coin that are stopping and affecting us, the American people. Because I'll tell ya, I'm angry still about it. And I'm about to go back out because I don't want to become complacent and say I voted for Trump and that's all I'm gonna do. I'm not gonna be like that." It's probably not a bad idea for guys like George and Tom to give Trump a little nudge because illegal immigrants are still taking jobs from the working class.

Which brings us back to the question – do illegal immigrants just do the job Americans won't do? The answer is clearly no. But if the slogan, because that's what it is, it's a slogan, is repeated over and over again like a well-funded advertising campaign...it can infect even the strongest minds. And if you don't believe me, take a guess at who said the following:

"The biggest problem is that you have some great wonderful people coming in from Mexico that are working the crops, that are working cutting lawns, that are doing a lot of jobs that I'm not sure a lot of Americans are gonna take those jobs."

The answer: Donald J. Trump.

THREE

Cherry-Picking
*Why did Donald Trump claim a lot of
global warming is a hoax?*

Every year, world leaders fly to some exotic foreign land to discuss the global warming "crisis." The topic has been a popular political football since at least Al Gore's 2006 documentary *An Inconvenient Truth*, when the former Vice President claimed that, "Within the decade there will be no more snows of Kilimanjaro." Twelve years later in March 2018, the Tanzanian mountain glacier saw the greatest snowfall in years. A mere twenty-four months after Gore's dire prediction, the issue was so hot, candidate Obama was running on his ability to change sea levels. "This was the moment when the rise of the oceans began to slow, and our planet began to heal," the then-senator from Illinois claimed.

In his run for the White House, Donald Trump would make his own remarks about climate change. "So Obama is talking about all of this with the global warming. A lot of it is a hoax. It's a hoax. I mean it's a moneymaking industry, ok. It's a hoax." The statement enraged so-called climate experts... like far-left MSNBC political pundit Chris Hayes. Once elected president, the real estate mogul took a bold action on the issue. In order to, in his words, fulfill his "solemn duty to protect America and its citizens," President Trump withdrew the United States from the *Paris Climate Accord*. The international agreement singled out the U.S. to immediately reduce its greenhouse gas emissions - but other major polluters…not so much. Trump made the reason for his withdrawal clear. "I cannot in good conscience support a deal that punishes the United States…while imposing no meaningful obligations on the world's leading polluters." But instead of reporting his official reason for pulling out, the far-left White House Press Corps, predictably, locked in on Trump's earlier "hoax" comment – and nagged the head of the EPA, Scott Priutt, during a White House briefing shortly after the President withdrew from the Accord. "Yes or no. Does the president believe that climate change is real," asked one reporter. "Does the President believe today that climate change is a hoax," badgered another. "Shouldn't you be able to tell the American people, whether or not the president still believes that climate change is a hoax," whined still another. And if he hadn't heard the other three times, a fourth journalist asked it again. "What does the president actually believe about climate change? Does he still believe it's a hoax?" Obama thinks he's the god Poseidon…the media is silent. Trump thinks some global warming claims are deceptive…the media pounces.

But President Trump's statement did raise a question that the media would never probe. Namely, why would Trump claim a lot of global warming is a hoax? Global warming is one of those topics – like abortion and gun control – that has become hopelessly politicized. The Left has an almost religious belief in it…and when anyone shows skepticism towards even its most extreme claims, the media labels the person a conspiracy theorist, or worse – a science denier. When Donald Trump said some of global warming was a hoax – the media was incurious as to why he would say such a thing. What could he have possibly meant? To find the answer, we're going to tell the story of how a small group of climate change skeptics battled the global warming establishment – and in the process changed the course of the world's economy.

**

On a cold December night in 2007, Steve McIntyre made his way to a restaurant in downtown San Francisco. A sixty year-old, partly balding, grey-bearded Canadian, Steve couldn't have known that he was about to join the team that would force the biggest science heist in history. Visiting the Bay Area for a climate conference, Steve had recently won an award for best science blog and was grabbing dinner with three locals who were regular readers of his blog Climate Audit. He was quickly becoming a rock star amongst a group of global warming skeptics that considered themselves "lukewarmers" – people that believe humans could be warming the planet, but question the magnitude of the problem and the certainty of climate science. They weren't science deniers, as their critics would say...they were just curious. Steve had become interested in climate science in a very casual way.

In 2002, Canada was discussing joining the *Kyoto Treaty*. Countries that signed onto this agreement had to commit to reducing their carbon dioxide emissions. "And one of the feature arguments of the Canadian government was that 1998 was the warmest year in a thousand years," says Steve McIntyre. "And I wondered in the most casual possible way, how they knew that." Steve wasn't a climate scientist by trade. He was a consultant on mining exploration projects. But he discussed global warming from time to time with a geologist friend who told him that throughout geological history, climate was much warmer in the past than it is today. "And he viewed the climate science alarm as being more or less equivalent to creationism," remembers Steve. So out of curiosity, Steve read the climate studies claiming 1998 was the warmest year. The reports weren't foreign to him. Steve was accustomed to reviewing technical papers for risky mining explorations. When he reviewed the documents, a specific diagram stood out. "And I was struck by the care with which they had made the diagram. When you're trying to raise money, having good diagrams is important. And I noticed that there was attention to the graphics…there was a promotional element to it which caught my eye." The diagram had a distinctive shape. Picture a hockey stick placed flat on the ground, with just the blade of the hockey stick pointing up to the sky. That's what this global warming diagram looked like. The flat shaft part of the stick represented temperature changes over the past thousand years, which looked pretty constant over time, until the 1900s, when the graph dramatically shot up, like the blade of the hockey stick. American climate scientist Michael Mann, along with several of his colleagues, originally created this hockey stick graph. One of the papers introducing the graph was titled *Northern Hemisphere Temperatures During the Past Millennium*. But it was the subtitle that was most noteworthy. It read "Inferences, Uncertainties, and Limitations." Given the admitted uncertainties expressed in the subtitle, it's hard to believe the hockey stick graph would become the poster child of certainty for global warming – but it would become just that. Pay close attention here, because if you understand the following, you'll likely know more about climate science than ninety-nine percent of the people in the world.

This famous hockey stick graph shows the Earth's temperature variations over the past thousand years. The problem is there were no thermometers a thousand years ago spread throughout the Earth to capture the temperatures. In fact, it wasn't until the late 1800s that we have any thermometer-based record of temperatures around the world. So to fill in Earth's temperatures before the 1800s, some climate scientists turned to trees. These scientists believe that some old trees record past temperatures in their growth pattern – picture cutting a cross-section of a tree and looking at that cross-section. What you see are tree rings – those are the concentric circles that start small in the center of the cross-section then get larger and larger as they reach the surface of the tree trunk. You can typically estimate the age of a tree by analyzing those tree rings. The older the tree, the more tree rings it has. We're all pretty familiar with that concept. But some climate scientists believe that you can go even further and calculate the temperature from year to year using these tree rings. Simplistically speaking, the more growth of a tree ring the hotter the temperature – basically providing a picture of past temperatures when thermometers weren't around. So some climate scientists used these tree rings to calculate and find the temperatures before the 1800s.

What was alarming about this hockey stick graph was that the increase in temperature coincided closely with the beginning of the Industrial Revolution, which started at about 1850. If true, the world's temperature increase could be tied directly to the beginning of humans burning so-called fossil fuels. Theories of human-induced climate change had been around long before Michael Mann's hockey stick graph, but his diagram gave the first powerful graphical image of global warming...so powerful that the United Nations used a version of it in their 2001 climate report. This was *the* document that gives guidance to governments on which policies to enact to reduce the effects of global warming. The hockey stick graph became iconic and galvanized environmentalists to call for urgent government action on global warming.

But as history shows, inciting one group often inspires an opposing group to rise up. Such is the story of the hockey stick. Just as quickly as the graph was used as a rallying call for global warming activists, it also gave birth to a camp of skeptics. That's where the Canadian Steve McIntyre enters the picture. The hockey stick graph confused Steve. A well-known *Medieval Warming Period* – where Earth's temperature increased considerably sometime between the year 1000 A.D. and 1300 A.D. followed by a cooling trend known as the Little Ice Age – was widely accepted in the science community, and suggested that the Earth went through natural phases of warming and cooling. But these events were absent from the hockey stick. McIntyre was curious about how the graph was made and as chance would have it, the discipline of reconstructing temperatures using tree rings, largely an exercise in statistics, fit right within his mathematics background. Steve was a math whiz in his early years.

"I studied pure math at university and...I'd stood first in Canada in the high school math contest in the international high school math contest... so it was a form of almost athletic activity for me," Steve proudly remembers. He studied economics at Oxford, and had been offered a PhD scholarship at both Harvard and MIT. But after his university studies he decided to enter the private sector instead of academia. "I hadn't done any math since I was twenty-one or twenty-two," says Steve. "But because I'd learned it well as a teenager...the comparison that I made, it's like you were a Davis Cup tennis player and going in a club tournament when you're fifty-five [years old]...you'd be a tough out. Even if you hadn't played for a long time you could pick it up fairly quickly." His work in mining exploration also prepared him in another way. Like in the days of the California Gold Rush, there are a lot of scammers in the mining exploration business. So successful miners learn to be fairly skeptical of this potential, and are always inclined to analyzing the data and not necessarily believe everything they are told. "And so I have an eye for promotional claims or claims that were not necessarily supported," says Steve. "So while I hadn't spent that time in academics, I spent time with tricky people and learning how to, you know, check things."

So Steve decided to reach out to American climate scientist Michael Mann to get his hands on the data and computer code he used to create the hockey stick graph. He emailed Mann asking for his data, and Steve says Mann responded promptly claiming that he had forgotten where the FTP site for the data was located. An FTP site is an online location where people store data and computer files for colleagues to access over the Internet. "It seemed extraordinary to me that the data was not readily at hand," recalls Steve. The study was Mann's claim to fame. Steve couldn't understand how the information wasn't at his fingertips. But perhaps even more importantly, if the hockey stick data wasn't readily available, it meant to Steve that no outside source had audited the graph for potential errors. This was stunning to Steve. The UN was using the hockey stick graph to argue a reconfiguration of the entire world's economy. Steve couldn't understand how such important data was not readily available and seemingly not being reviewed with a skeptical eye. "And I thought well if none of them have audited it, I will," recalls Steve. "I'll try to figure out what Mann did and I viewed it as trying to solve a big crossword puzzle."

The decision wasn't a political one for Steve. At the time he considered himself to be a Bill Clinton Democrat. He was just curious, and had some time on his hands. Michael Mann's associate eventually got Steve a version of the data that created his hockey stick, and once Steve began reviewing it, he thought he saw some red flags. "I started looking at some of the data and wasn't entirely clear where the shape of the hockey stick came from," recalls Steve. He became suspicious that the climate scientists were possibly cherry-picking the temperature data so that a hockey stick shape would result no matter what data was entered into the climate model. To test his theory, he input random data, called *red noise*, into the climate model and out popped a hockey stick graph. Steve began posting some of his analysis in skeptic chat groups online. His work immediately stood out because his analysis was not based on emotion. Instead it was data driven. And he learned something surprising about the people that liked his work. "A lot of skeptics I guess would be people like me who felt that the climate was an issue but...were concerned that it was being oversold as an issue."

His posts led to a small science journal asking him to write an article. Steve had never written an academic paper before. So he teamed up with an academic he met in the skeptic chat rooms. That person was Ross McKitrick – an environmental economist with a PhD in economics who'd authored a book skeptical of global warming. The two worked on papers evaluating Michael Mann's original hockey stick graph, highlighting what they saw as his errors in using the data. In 2004, some of their findings forced Michael Mann and his colleagues to publish corrections to their original hockey stick paper. However they didn't change any of their underlying results. But the skeptics' work drew blood.

So climate scientists started a blog called Real Climate to debunk their detractors. Steve McIntyre remembers when they launched it. "They begin their existence with a series of blogs slagging me...somebody who was following it sent me an email and said...if you think you can win your disputes...

in academic journals, you're getting killed." Steve had a pretty amateurish website at the time. So someone offered to create a blog for Steve and proposed the name Climate Audit. Steve accepted the offer, and the guy set up the blog for him. "And I started writing and found that I liked it," says Steve. These dueling websites began a daily online battle between climate scientists and global warming skeptics. One of the main contention points between the two camps has been a concept known as divergence.

Some climate scientists noticed a problem with using tree rings to calculate today's temperatures. What they found was that some tree rings showed a decrease in temperatures starting at around 1961 while actual thermometer readings showed a temperature increase – the science and the thermometers weren't matching up...they were divergent. So what climate scientists did in some of the hockey stick graphs was delete the tree ring temperatures after 1961 to hide the tree-ring decline in temperatures, replacing them with the actual thermometer readings. Their rationale was that the tree rings weren't capturing today's higher temperatures. The skeptics thought this was bad science. And why? Because it raised the question that *if the tree rings weren't recording the higher temperatures of today, couldn't tree rings have also missed higher temperatures in the past as well?* Today's spike in temperatures could have also been there one thousand years ago – meaning today's high temperatures were not unprecedented. This divergence appeared to show a serious problem with some of the science behind the hockey stick graphs.

The climate scientists were frequently acquiring new data, then creating hockey stick graphs from that data. So Steve McIntyre asked Michael Mann to provide the data and computer code for these other graphs. But by then, Mann had completely cut Steve off. Their feud began reaching the mainstream media. "So the Wall Street Journal writes an article, and that catches the eye of the House Energy and Commerce Committee," recalls Steve. And in 2006, a series of government hearings began questioning climate science – asking if they were in fact cherry-picking data to create their various hockey stick graphs. One of the people questioned by the panel was a famous tree ring scientist named Rosanne D'Arrigo. "I remember Rosanne D'Arrigo…talked about cherry-picking and said…you have to pick cherries if you want to make cherry pie…and I thought that that neatly summarized the approach of the tree ring people." In other words, it sounded like the scientists were cherry-picking the data to get the results they wanted – a hockey stick. If you are familiar with scientific research, cherry-picking data is typically frowned upon because it's thought of as manipulating the results to get the intended outcome.

Steve chronicled the hearings and his analysis on his blog Climate Audit, and his readership grew. The media typically paints climate change skeptics as toothless, anti-science buffoons. But Steve's actual readers belied that characterization. They were professionals – a lot of scientists from other fields…people from finance, computer programmers, and business executives. "People who didn't have the time to parse the data themselves but were interested in reading about it," adds Steve McIntyre. Readers like San Francisco native Steve Mosher. An open source software developer, Mosher was aligned with most of what climate scientists believed. But when he began questioning some of their work at their blog Real Climate, he got a very negative response. "It kinda shocked me and so I pushed back against that," recalls Mosher. "At some point they were railing about this guy at Climate Audit. And I thought let me go look and see what this is. So I went over to Climate Audit, and he was doing math." Mosher liked Steve McIntyre's desire for transparency in climate science...and became a regular commenter on his blog.

The online feud also drew in Charles Rotter, another San Franciscan. He was drawn to the brewing feud between Steve McIntyre and the climate scientists as well. "It really started heating up on McIntyre's site 2006 and 2007, and it became fun serial drama, like an online community," Charles recalls. Another reader, Anthony Watts, lived just north of San Francisco. Anthony was actually a global warming activist back in the early 1990s. He came up with the idea of doing a series of promotions through television meteorologists around the country to get their viewers to plant trees to offset carbon dioxide emissions. He says the campaign resulted in about half a million trees being planted. Anthony had spent years as a research assistant at the meteorology department at Purdue University. In 2006, he started a science blog called Watts Up With That and began investigating the thermometers used to measure global warming. And what he found shocked him:

> **Anthony Watts**: "It really began to start to take off in around 2007. I started surveying weather stations around the country. And it got quite a bit of attention, particularly from a station in Marysville, California not too far from me that I'd surveyed. And it was basically a thermometer right in the middle of the parking lot at the fire station. The fire chief parked his vehicle in a special parking space right next to the thermometer where the grill of the fire chief's truck was right up against the thermometer a couple feet away. And the city had rented out space for a cell phone tower and there were these two equipment sheds blowing hot air from the air conditioning vents all in this area."

And this thermometer had been showing that Maryville's temperature had been increasing off the charts. But Anthony checked nearby thermometer stations and the similar trends of temperature increase were not at any of those locations. "And it was just another light bulb moment for me," recalls Anthony. "It's like wow, this is where climate science is measuring data, and they consider this accurate? And I put that out, and it got picked up by Steve McIntyre at Climate Audit."

Anthony, and the two other Bay Area gents Mosher and Charles became friendly with Steve McIntyre through his Climate Audit blog. Mosher remembers how he met the guys for the first time. "At one point, McIntyre mentions that he's coming to San Francisco. One of the people on the site...it ends up being Charles Rotter...he says, 'Oh if you're coming to San Francisco Steve McIntyre, why don't we get together for dinner.' And so I chimed in and I said, 'Heck, I'll join you'... Anthony showed up as well." So in December 2007, Anthony Watts, Charles Rotter, Steve Mosher, and Steve McIntyre, four guys that met in the comment section of a climate blog, gathered at a restaurant in downtown San Francisco. Little did any of them know that that dinner would be a pivotal moment in climate science.

Anthony told the table that his skeptic blog, Watts Up With That, was growing faster than he could handle. Charles offered help. "And I basically told him I had tons of experience moderating back from my own site days," recalls Charles. "I also had lots of time on my hands and I worked from home, and I would be happy to give him help moderating." Anthony took him up on his offer. Charles and Mosher hit it off as well, and would become roommates. These four and the many commenters on their blogs would make up a team of climate skeptics that would meticulously audit the work of climate scientists.

The feud between the two camps had been reaching epic proportions – even spilling onto Capital Hill. But what escalated the conflict further was something basic in science – verification of results. The climate scientists refused to allow the skeptics access to their work so that they could review it. Steve McIntyre would ask for the data and computer code used to create the hockey stick graphs, but at every turn the climate scientists would stonewall his requests. With Michael Mann completely cutting him off, Steve looked to audit graphs of a different hockey stick team – the climate scientists at the University of East Anglia's Climate Research Unit, known by its acronym CRU. As with Mann, Steve asked for their data and computer code to verify their work. When politics enters science, the results can only be trusted when qualified people with skeptical eyes verify the work. By this time, Steve McIntyre was a published author on the topic of hockey stick graphs. He'd even become a reviewer of the UN's mother of all global warming reports. None of that mattered. CRU rejected his request, claiming that they had confidentiality agreements with the countries that provided them temperature data, and those agreements prohibited them from distributing that information.

But then Steve discovered that CRU had given their data to another institution, which typically nullifies a confidentiality agreement – so Steve told them they should be free to give him the data. But CRU figured out another way to reject him. They responded to Steve stating that their confidentiality agreements prevented them from giving the data to a non-academic. Steve found this highly improbable. They'd acquired the data twenty-five years earlier. Why would an agreement include that kind of contractual term? "That was just a fabrication," says Steve. "It's that kind of fabrication by the climate community that really undercuts a lot of their claims on other topics. Because that's something that's easily checked, people understand, and so if they're lying about something like that, what else are they lying about?"

So Steve got an idea. Both the UK and the United States enacted Freedom of Information Acts, known by their acronyms as FOIs or FOIAs. These laws provide access to information that was created using tax dollars. Steve decided to use these laws to get what he wanted. He submitted an FOI request to climate researchers asking for the confidentiality agreements they claimed to have with five different countries. Then he turned to his audience. He posted his FOI request letter on his Climate Audit blog and asked readers to also send in FOI requests to the Climate Research Unit. "I viewed it more as a letter writing campaign," says Steve. "If it was just me asking for it they'd just say, 'Oh well it's McIntyre. He's crazy.' Where as, if they got fifty letters, they'd then have to reconsider what they were doing and give it out after all." But Steve underestimated their stubbornness on this issue. CRU rejected his requests again. However, all these attempts at getting data sent Steve McIntryre's Climate Audit readers on a hunting expedition. You see, Steve had been taking these readers on a journey. Slowly teaching his audience along the way – about the uncertainties in climate science, journaling the specific data that he was being refused. Their stonewalling riled up his audience. Getting CRU's data became a game of capture the flag.

At the time of the rejection, many readers began to learn that CRU had an online data storage location – an FTP site. And they began rummaging through it to see if they could find the data that CRU was refusing to give to Steve. "And I remember a couple of them saying that they fell into areas of the CRU website that were unexpected," recalls Steve. Steve's readers were actually finding themselves in private areas on the climate researchers' website. Their data appeared vulnerable – a vulnerability that would change the course of the world's economy.

**

At about 5 P.M. on November 17, 2009, Mosher was heading home from a coffee shop when he got a call. Mosher and Charles lived in an area of San Francisco called SOMA – an acronym for South of Market Street. Mosher was over in the Marina on the other side of San Francisco having coffee with a few friends. He finished up, said his goodbyes, and jumped in a cab heading back home to SOMA. "And Charles calls me," remembers Mosher. "And he says, 'Where are you?' And I said, 'I'm over in the Marina. I'm headed back to the apartment. What's up?' And he says, 'You gotta get here.'"

Since meeting at dinner in San Francisco two years earlier, Charles had become the primary comment moderator for Anthony Watt's skeptic blog Watts Up With That. "I was keeping odd hours," says Charles. "So I might sleep for three hours, and not sleep for three hours. But I was constantly online, approving comments." That afternoon Charles came across a message on the site that stood out. A commenter named "FOIA" posted a link to a Russian server with text that appeared to be snippets of emails. At that moment, his boss Anthony Watt's was out of the country at the European Union headquarters in Belgium. He was there with other climate skeptics to give a presentation. So Charles was manning the site on his own. The comment looked weird so he blocked it from going public and went to the Russian link to see what it was. The link led to a file of what appeared to be documents and emails from CRU – the Climate Research Unit that had been stonewalling Steve McIntyre. When Charles reviewed the contents, his first thought was to be expected. "Holy shit is what was going through my mind," recalls Charles. "It was a real treasure trove showing what was essentially just activist science operating. Not objective, not reasonable. I'm not gonna call it completely fraudulent or a hoax, but it was like activist scientists, as we're now experiencing with activist journalism. Yes, people are still telling facts, but they're telling it from such a skewed perspective, you might as well call it lies. They were actually saying, 'If this guy says this it's not going to be helpful to the cause.' That's not scientific inquiry."

This was a highly sensitive situation. The files were likely either leaked by an insider, or stolen, or perhaps something even more problematic. In an attempt to get some direction, Charles sent an email to his boss Anthony Watts apprising him of the situation and included the link to the files. "And he told me in the email what was going on," says Anthony. "And I got on the phone with him. And this was a couple hours before I was supposed to go into the EU. And I had been forewarned about security and I was going to be searched and all this stuff. And so in seeing what Charles had, and then actually downloading it and looking at it briefly myself, and looking at the timing of it all, I'm thinking to myself, 'Why now? Why right before I'm supposed to go in to the EU and go through security?' And so my concern was that somehow I was being set up." Anthony was getting a lot of notoriety for his climate skeptic blog Watts Up With That, so it wasn't implausible that someone may have been out to get them. They also weren't aware of the data theft and libel laws that existed in Europe. If they were harsh, someone could use them to nail Anthony if he was found with them on foreign soil.

As he looked at the downloaded files, a bit of a panic began to set in. There he was in Belgium, with these potentially very sensitive files in his possession on his laptop. In just a few hours, he was about to go through a big security checkpoint. "So my thought was I need to divest myself of this file," Anthony recalls. "And I purchased a professional file eraser and I told Charles that under no circumstances are you to release this on the blog or anything...because I needed to get back in the United States and I don't want to be listed as someone who's been involved in some kind of industrial espionage or anything like that. And so, he agreed to that."

Charles had strict direction not to publish the files but he was given the okay to talk about them with two people – the others from their San Francisco dinner two years earlier – Mosher and Steve McIntyre. That's when Mosher got the call from Charles in the cab on his way home to SOMA. Mosher was fully versed in the raging feud between the skeptics and climate scientists over access to data and code. And he was the only person that could authenticate the contents without Charles losing control of the files. So as Mosher sat in the back of that cab, Charles proceeded to tell him everything about the files he downloaded from the Russian server. "And so, Charles said Anthony wanted me to look at it," says Mosher. "He was concerned that someone had put it on his site to trap him essentially and that it was fake."

When Mosher walked in the door, Charles was waiting for him with a CD of the files. By that point, he'd already scanned the files for viruses to make sure that they were clean. "So I took the CD, and I put it on my, at that point I had an Apple computer," remembers Mosher. "And I sat on the couch, and I started reading. And I didn't stop reading. And I didn't move and I didn't eat. And I just read everything." What was in the leaked documents was shocking. Climate scientists massaging data and appearing to pressure colleagues to change their results so they wouldn't give ammunition to skeptics. Climate scientists appearing to collude to delete emails, withhold data, and limit the scientific review of their work...and stunning admissions of doubt and uncertainty in their methods. As Joe Biden would say, this was a big fucking deal.

Mosher, Charles, and Anthony all thought that they were the only people that had the files. So they felt they had some time to think about what to do next. And anyways, they couldn't do anything with them until Anthony was back safe on American soil. So their first mission was to figure out if the files were indeed authentic. As they combed through the documents in those first few hours they noticed climate scientists had forwarded emails from Steve McIntyre. So they got on the phone with Steve. "Mosher calls me because he sees some emails from me in it and nobody knows at the...beginning whether it's real or not," recalls Steve McIntyre. "And so he called me [asking], 'Are those your emails?' And yeah, I can confirm their authenticity." Now they knew some of the emails were definitely real, but they weren't sure that they were *all* real. Mosher went nonstop reading the documents for the next day...spending hours on the phone with Steve McIntyre trying to confirm their authenticity. Then they got a break.

A professor at the University of East Anglia emailed Steve McIntyre asking if he knew anything about a hack of their Climate Research Unit. He relayed to Steve that there was some big lockdown at the University. This was the sign they needed. The files were real! But they couldn't go public yet. Anthony Watts was still not on American soil. Mosher was chomping at the bit to go live. Charles had to hold the line. "I was just calmly making coffee in the kitchen and just telling him that if this is as important as we think it is, two or three days is not gonna matter," Charles remembers saying to Mosher.

With Anthony now in a flight pattern heading for Dulles International Airport in Virginia, Mosher had been reading the emails for almost two days straight. That's when they decided to search the Internet to see if the hacker posted the Russian link anywhere else. "At that point Charles started looking and he found the same link," says Mosher. "He found it at Jeff's." Jeff Condon, an aeronautical engineer, had started a lukewarmer site called The Air Vent a little over a year earlier. He initiated the blog to translate some of Steve McIntyre's climate analysis for a non-technical audience. Jeff, like the rest of the lukewarmers, believed that transparency in climate science was key. "The whole purpose of our climate blogs... was to put everything in the open where people can see the information," remembers Jeff Condon. "And there was some efforts on the science community not to allow access." This belief made his website a trigger for this bombshell.

The hacker came to be known as Mr. FOIA. The first time we can see him infiltrate CRUs data server was on September 16th 2009 – just a few weeks after the Climate Research Unit denied Steve McIntyre's request for their confidentiality agreements. Mr. FOIA infiltrated again on September 28th, 29th, and 30th. He was grabbing documents related to the hockey stick graph. Mr. FOIA infiltrated again on October 1st, 2nd, and again the 3rd. He appeared to be looking for something... but what? "It was the data that had been the topic [of a] fight... years before that Mann had refused to provide me," says Steve McIntyre. The infiltrator found it on November 16th. It would be a matter of hours before the files hit the web. The next day, Mr. FOIA gained access to the climate scientists' blog Real Climate, locked out all other users, and uploaded the stolen CRU files to their site. Mr. FOIA then went to their enemy Steven McIntyre's blog and posted a comment with a link to the file he'd just uploaded...and included the text "A miracle just happened." This guy was a prankster with balls.

The administrator of Real Climate quickly regained access to the blog and deleted the file from public view. With the link to the stolen files now gone, Mr. FOIA went another route to leak the files. He uploaded them to a Russian server, and then posted a link to the files on both Anthony Watts' blog Watts Up With That, and Jeff Condon's The Air Vent. As we already know, the comment on Watts Up With That was held in moderation. Jeff Condon, however, had a different philosophy for his site. "In the spirit of openness," says Jeff Condon, "The Air Vent was a site where I literally didn't do any moderation. I would let any comment go on the site. If somebody dropped a comment on there, it was immediately available for the reader."

At the time that Mr. FOIA posted a link to the stolen files on his site, Jeff was practically as far away from the heat of the climate debate as you can be. "I was out in the deep woods hunting deer…up north in Michigan where there was actually no phone service, no cell phone service, no Internet." The link to the stolen files sat in Jeff's comment section for two days while Jeff was in the middle of nowhere. So when Charles told Mosher he found a link to the files on Jeff's site, the game changed for Mosher. He reached out to Anthony Watts, who was now in line at US Customs. "By this point I say, 'The cats out of the bag,'" recalls Mosher. "So I went to Anthony and I said, 'Like hey, I promised you that I would not post them anywhere or send them to anyone or show them to anyone. But now that we know that your place is not the only place… our agreement is off.'" Mosher began posting excerpts of the emails at a small skeptic site, and the lukewarmer community started buzzing. The biggest story in global warming history was about to break.

"I'm in line to go through Customs, and I'm getting text messages from Charles, Steven Mosher, and Steve McIntyre," remembers Anthony Watts. "And they're starting to talk about this. And I remember saying back to McIntyre, 'The whole thing's gotta be a hoax.' And that was just sort of a preemptive in case someone grabbed my phone…[So] I didn't look complicit. And so I got through Customs, and once I got through Customs and I'm back on U.S. soil, the first thing that I did was find Wi-Fi and sat down and I wrote the story." Anthony Watts quickly penned an article announcing to the world the hack of the Climate Research Unit. "And I wrote the story sitting on the floor at Dulles Airport waiting for my flight to depart…I heard them saying, last call for boarding, and I hit send and publish and I'm running for the door…And I got on the plane and I had a four, five hour flight back to Sacramento, California. And that was a time when there was no Wi-Fi on airplanes. So it was kind of a 'what have I done' kind of a moment." With the biggest skeptic blog in the world now covering the story, it went viral. A reader on Watts Up With That dubbed the scandal *Climategate*. The name stuck. And it was a bombshell.

"Climategate they're calling it. A new scandal over global warming and it's burning up the Internet," claimed NBC News anchor Brian Williams. "Have the books been cooked on climate change?"

"Did scientists skew their research to support theories of global warming," asked an ABC News reporter.

"This is a world wide hoax," said Rush Limbaugh. "And it's primary target was you. The people of the United States of America."

"Now that we find out that this institute in fact was hiding from the people of Great Britain and the world that in fact climate change is a hoax, something I've been saying for a long time," touted Sean Hannity.

"Those who doubt that manmade greenhouse gases are changing the climate, say these emails from Britain's University of East Anglia show climate scientists massaging data and suppressing studies by those who disagree," claimed another NBC Reporter.

"One of the most damning emails credits Mann with a trick to *hide the decline* in temperatures," reported ABC News. "In another, the head of the National Center for Atmospheric Research writes a colleague, 'The fact is that we can't account for the lack of warming at the moment and it is a travesty that we can't.'"

The scandal even reached into pop culture...hitting the news desk of Jon Stewart. "Ha. You see it's nothing," Stewart nervously laughed. "He was just using a trick...to hide the decline. It's just scientist speak for using a standard statistical technique recalibrating data...in order to trick you into not knowing about the decline."

The leaked documents didn't debunk human caused global warming, but Climategate did uncover serious issues with climate science – its bias, its attempt to avoid scrutiny, its refusal to show its work to skeptics, its odd massaging of data, and the uncertainties of the hockey stick graphs. This could all be seen in the emails. Mr. FOIA, the leaker of the files, was never caught. UK law enforcement closed its case after two and a half years with no suspects. Apparently Mr. FOIA wiped his trace clean.

For a brief moment it appeared change was coming. The global warming media chastised the scientists involved in the scandal, and called for a new transparency in their work. A few climate scientists even became skeptics – including Dr. Judith Curry, who testified about the scandal. "Prior to 2009, I felt that supporting the IPCC consensus on climate change was the responsible thing to do," Dr. Judith Curry opened in her December 8, 2015 testimony to the U.S. Senate Committee on Commerce, Science, and Transportation. "I bought into the argument...don't trust what one scientist says trust what an international team of a thousands scientists has said after years of careful deliberation. That all changed for me in November 2009 following the leaked Climategate emails that illustrated the sausage making and even bullying that went into building the consensus." But the calls for reform didn't last.

"The establishment managed to put up all its defenses," says Charles Rotter. "Then slowly the establishment crushed it." Several investigations concluded, largely exonerating the climate scientists. After all was done, they proceeded to go right back to the practices that led to the leak in the first place. Steve McIntyre believes that the climate scientist community has become even angrier since the Climategate scandal. "Afterwards, they doubled down in becoming even more insular," Steve says. "Their reaction was not to blame themselves for their language, but they blamed skeptics for putting pressure on them which caused them to write badly...I thought that the people ought to have disowned the practice of deleting data to hide the decline. But they didn't do that. They blamed skeptics for asking questions."

Climate scientists returned to calling skeptics science deniers...a label meant to marginalize lukewarmers like Anthony Watts because the truth of their position is harder to combat. "I believe that carbon dioxide does have an effect on the temperature of the Earth," says Anthony. "The only real scientific question is: How much? And that question has been in flux and unanswered for over thirty years. It hasn't been nailed down. How much temperature increase do we get for a doubling of CO2 in Earth's atmosphere? And the estimates range in science anywhere from a half a degree to eight degrees. There's no actual number where everyone can say, 'This is it. This is the right number.' They've not nailed that down in thirty some years of climate science. And with something that's that uncertain, how do you plan for the future? How do you say we're in a crisis or not? And that is the big question. And so yes, I believe carbon dioxide has some effect. How much, is still the question."

Which brings us back to our question – why did President Trump say a lot of global warming was a hoax? The answer is Climategate.

The hockey stick was considered to be gospel, even with its scientific uncertainties. It was then used as a weapon to try and punish the US while leaving the biggest polluters unscathed. To some, that might look a lot like a hoax – and it was all stopped by a tiny collective of bloggers. What this small group of skeptics did was absolutely incredible. The global warming establishment's resistance to their constant auditing forced the release of the Climategate files. The message that those files delivered eventually planted a seed in the mind of citizen Trump that ultimately blossomed into him withdrawing from the Paris Accord once elected. That decision altered the course of the world's economy. That's how big Climategate was. But you don't have to take my word for it, believe Trump's own words just a few months after Climategate broke.

"I think that the memorandum or whatever it was that they found a few months ago was devastating – by the leaders of the movement of global warming. I think that was devastating, because that basically said, 'You people are a bunch of jerks to follow us and we're just kidding.' I really think that was just the beginning."

According to Trump and many others, this was America's moment of awakening to the climate alarmist hoax…and it can all be traced back to a few lukewarmers.

FOUR

Unity Night
Who will create a post-racial America?

The rise of Barack Obama was a watershed moment for race
relations in America...or so it was sold. His meteoric rise was
propelled by the promise of a colorblind nation. "There is not
a Black America and a White America and Latino America
and Asian America — there's the United States of America,"
the young politician proclaimed. His ascension to the White
House was supposed to be an unequivocal sign that Martin
Luther King, Jr.'s dream had been realized – that we no longer
judged people by the color of their skin but instead by the
content of their character. Yet with all of the hope that Obama
promised – few would say that America is colorblind today.
In fact, many would claim that race relations have deterio-
rated since he took the oath of office. If the election of the
first Black president could not create a post-racial America, is
there anyone that can?

A hint to the answer revealed itself on February 20, 2010 –
barely a year after Obama's inauguration. After a hard fought
national battle, funded by one of the biggest advertisers in the
world, the Sprite Step Off competition entered its finale. The
step tournament, a dance art form practiced almost exclusive-

ly by African-Americans, was billed as the largest ever contest of its kind. Out of almost fifty female teams from all over the country, only six squads remained. One crew was the undeniable underdog entering the finals...the Zetas. "A lot of people don't want us to be there, and they definitely don't want us to succeed," said one member of the long-shot squad.

On paper, the Zetas didn't stand a chance. Their sorority had only been practicing the art form for roughly sixteen years – the other squads had over four decades of legacy under their belt. When the Zetas stepped on the finale stage, you'd be hard pressed to find a single person in the nearly five-thousand-strong audience, aside from their parents, that wanted them to win. But as the underdogs began their final dance, astonishingly, the crowd erupted. Throughout their nearly nine-minute routine, the spectators could hardly contain themselves – jumping out of their seats, screaming, laughing, high-fiving – the excitement was unmistakable. By the end of their performance, little could be heard through the elated pandemonium that filled the theater. "Whoa! Wow," said the event moderator. "Close your mouth. Close your mouth," he called out to the front row, making fun of their reaction. The crowd's ecstatic disbelief seemed to extend for minutes after the Zetas left the stage...making what happened next all the more puzzling.

The festive crowd eventually quieted when the judges' results came in. As the third place team was announced, the Deltas, the air of excitement was quickly erased by the sound of unease. Could the long shots really win this thing? The theater became near silent as the second place team was about to be declared – so quiet that you could hear one errant woman yell in the hushed arena, "come on with it!" As the competition host announced the second place winners, the AKAs of Indiana University, it became apparent who was going to take the first place prize – the underdogs! The room, that was just a short while ago filled with screams of adoration for the Zetas, was now saturated with boos. Audience members began making their way to the exits before the first place team was even announced. "Let me reiterate that this is from the judges' scores," said rapper Ludacris to the almost entirely African-American audience. "They tallied the judges' scores up. They double-checked the judges' scores...so you need to understand that the first place winner, $100,000 in scholarships, goes to... the Zetas!" The sorority from the University of Arkansas, the only White team in the competition, had just won the 2010 Sprite Step Off – and some on the team were disoriented by the swift swing of the pendulum against them. "They gave us a standing ovation and then turned around and booed us. So, I didn't really understand," said Jessica Simmons, a Zeta team member. The winners were understandably confused. But what was supposed to be the end of their journey, turned out to be just the beginning.

With their win, the Zeta Tau Alpha sorority from the University of Arkansas ignited a furious debate within the Black community – with many questioning whether the White girls should have even been in the competition. Some complained of cultural theft. "How are you going to take something that's ours, and give it away," said one critic. Others claimed that the novelty of the color of their skin won them the top prize. The tournament, that was to be aired on MTV2, was accused of being "rigged" to boost the ratings of the broadcast. When someone from the crowd posted the Zetas' winning performance on YouTube, the video went viral – with the view count reaching hundreds of thousands in just a few days...an enormous amount at the time. The remarks posted on the video were so overwhelmingly negative that the poster momentarily questioned whether or not to turn off the comment function – ultimately deciding to leave it on. A radio show in Atlanta,

where the finals were held, heated up with angry phone calls –
prompting one of the competition judges, Chilli of female rap
group T.L.C., to call-in and side with the callers. "The AKAs
from Indiana, hands-down in my opinion should have won."
The uproar was rising to a point that revealed the ugly state of
race relations in America.

**

For the uninitiated, *step* is a blend of cheerleading, military
marching, spoken word, and dance choreography – with signature hand slaps and foot stomps – that's typically performed
by a group rather than a single person. Stepping is unequiv-
ocally a visually exciting art form – and without a doubt a
black-rooted tradition. It traces its origin to Africa and was
first embraced stateside in the late 1960s by the National Pan-
Hellenic Council (NPHC) *Greek* community – a collection of
nine historically Black sororities and fraternities, some formed
over one hundred years ago, and affectionately referred to as
the Divine Nine. The first official step show was said to have
been held in 1976 at Howard University – a historically Black
college. The art form is thought to be a display of unity and
strength – and when witnessed, it's about as fun as it gets in
watching someone else dance. Many college campuses across
the country hold what's widely referred to as "unity nights" to
spread the tradition of the step dance form to the wider Greek
community...this is how the Zetas were first turned on to stepping.

   Around 1994, the University of Arkansas chapter of the Alpha Kappa Alpha sorority, or AKAs, started their own Unity
Night event to help foster diversity on campus. The all Black
sorority would teach non-Black sororities how to step, and
those groups would compete against one another at the event.

Throughout the years, the Zeta girls embraced the art form, placing first or second over the history of the campus-wide competition. At the start of each school year, they'd hold step tryouts and the girls who made the cut trained everyday for two months leading up to their performance on Unity Night. In 2008, the Zetas won with a Matrix themed routine – with the girls all dressing up like the Trinity character from the blockbuster sci-fi film of the same name. Stepping really became a part of the Zeta sorority's identity.

So in October 2009, when the Sprite Step Off competition organized a qualifying round in the Zetas' own backyard of Fayetteville, Arkansas, they decided to enter – and like on Unity Night, the White girls won...taking home the first place prize of $5,500 in scholarships and securing a spot on a documentary series of the competition to be broadcast on cable TV network MTV2. The Zetas were chosen as one of three sororities that would be filmed throughout the rest of the competition as part of the Reality TV style show. This was a big deal. The competition was by far the biggest step event ever created, with $1.5 million in scholarships dispersed to winners all along the way. By taking the qualifying round, the Zetas were set to compete in Houston for the Regional Semi-Finals not only as their first step performance outside of their campus environment, but they'd also be the only White team in a competition completely dominated by Black Greek sororities. "We were obviously a bit nervous about the competition," recalled the Zeta co-captain Alexandra Kosmitis going into Houston. But that nervousness would be short-lived. They again took first place in Houston, this time banking $21,500 in scholarships and advancing to the National Finals to be held at the Boisfeuillet Jones Theater in Atlanta, Georgia. MTV2 couldn't help but set up the racial drama in its trailer for the TV series – depicting the Zeta girls as underdogs that weren't wanted in Atlanta.

When Zeta took the first place title of the entire competition, really no one should have been surprised. They'd already been besting the Black Greek squads for months. But their win unleashed a debate that the Black community wasn't ready to broach, underscored by a judge of the competition, rap star Chilli. It wasn't long after she sided with the outrage mob that an ugly twist to the story hit the news.

Five days after the finale, Sprite made a stunning announcement on their Facebook event page. "After the National Finals Competition this past weekend in Atlanta wrapped, we got together to do our post-competition review and found a scoring discrepancy in the sorority results," claimed the carbonated beverage giant. "After looking at it and looking at it AGAIN, we determined there isn't a definitive resolution." Sprite decided to name the Zetas of the University of Arkansas *and* the AKAs of Indiana University "co-first place winners of the Sprite Step Off," each receiving $100,000 towards their education. It appeared the sponsor had caved to the Black community's outcry. But the company likely received an assist by someone else.

To organize the competition, Sprite turned to the National Pan-Hellenic Council (NPHC) – again, the community of nine historically black sororities and fraternities that popularized step in America. The Council appeared to play a role in the "co-first place" decision. In an interview with the Washington Post at the time, Warren Lee, chairman of the council of presidents of the NPHC, was asked about the initial results of the competition. Lee responded, "We were not so much unhappy as we were confused. We were not sure if the rules had been applied as we understood them. So there was some review, and it's my understanding that one person made an honest mistake in the scoring." Juxtapose that with Ludacris' admission on-stage when he announced the Zetas the winners: "Let me reiterate that this is from the judges' scores…they tallied the judges' scores up. They double-checked the judges' scores." That doesn't sound like a scoring discrepancy. It was pretty clear why the AKAs were being given the "co-first place" status – someone wanted to appease the outrage mob.

It's understandable that Sprite would want to end the controversy and pacify the loudest critics. The entire reason for sponsoring an event of this nature was to connect with the African-American community so that their product was viewed in a positive light. In the noble effort of sponsoring a worthy art form, Sprite found itself in an impossible position. But the act of naming two first place winners after one seemingly won fairly, did much to increase the feeling of a double standard in matters of race – and a few prominent writers from the Black community spoke up in reaction to their decision.

A writer for Newsone, a media outlet "for black America", wrote, "We can't demand genuine respect for our music, our traditions, and our colleges and then expect people merely to worship from afar." Lawrence C. Ross Jr., author of *The Divine Nine: The History of African American Fraternities and Sororities*, wrote an impassioned article to his community. "Can we at least keep stepping to ourselves," asked Ross in his headline. "Nope," he answered. "We've got to share our traditions." ESPN even entered the fray. "Injustice: Coca-Cola changes step show results so African-Americans share title," blazed Jemele Hill's headline. The girls even made appearances on NPR, CNN, and Fox News to address the hubbub. But no one was saying the obvious – that the outrage over Zeta's win conveyed a widespread racism within the Black community.

The truly ironic thing about the entire ordeal was that everyone seemed to forget how the Zeta step team even came into existence. Their squad was literally forged as a part of Unity Night – where Greek communities of different ethnic backgrounds came together to share their cultural traditions. The Zetas even devised their routine with the help of the local Alpha Kappa Alpha (AKA) chapter, an African-American sorority – a fact that stung many when the Zetas outlasted their teachers. The following year, Sprite decided to continue the competition, with the finals going to Washington, D.C. at the Show Place Arena. But for that installment, the Zetas of the University of Arkansas did not enter the contest.

When we spoke to a representative of the Zetas a year after the controversy, it was easy to tell that the sting of the 2010 decision was still present. "I was fascinated by the story of the Zetas winning, I mean co-winning," Patrick started the interview…but was quickly interrupted. "No, you were right the first time," said Christy Barber, Director of Communications for the national Zeta Tau Alpha organization. When asked if they entered the competition the following year, Barber responded, "Most of that team was seniors. They performed their last time in front of eight hundred of their sorority sisters." You'd think that Sprite would have extended an invitation to their sorority for the 2011 competition, so we asked. "I don't believe Sprite reached out to our girls," Barber answered. "I don't think they reached outside of the [Divine Nine] sororities or fraternities. They are trying to reach a specific audience, and it's their right to do that." Sprite claims that they did in fact invite all organizations that participated in the 2010 competition. We asked Barber if Zeta's decision not to enter had anything to do with the co-first place controversy. Her reply: "No." But we received a markedly different response from the 2010 Zeta co-captain, Mary Katherine Bentley. "It had everything to do with the controversy," Bentley frankly answered. "We decided it wasn't worth the scrutiny."

What could have been a unique opportunity for racial unity, a theme that was literally embedded in the Zeta team's existence, was instead turned into an ugly moment of division. "We're hypocrites," said an insightful student to Howard University's The Hill Top newspaper. "The crowd gave them a standing ovation when they stepped, and booed when they won." And this racial animosity all occurred as the first Black president's message of hope was still fresh in everyone's minds.

Which leads us back to the question – if not Barack Obama, who can create a post-racial America? The answer is clear. The ball is now in the court of Black America. They are the only ones that can help us realize Dr. King's dream. Because every time we appear to reach the promise land, Black America moves the goalpost.

Immediately after the Zetas finished their show stopping performance, the event moderator said to the shocked audience, "Steppin' is for everybody." But clearly it's not. When the Zetas ended up winning, the Black community decided to judge them by the color of their skin, rather than the content of their performance...and the African-American outrage that ensued revealed what can only be described as acceptable racism. When the contest outcome was altered, it only underscored that fact. If the tables were turned, and let's say African-American gymnast Simone Biles was forced to share the world all-around title with a White competitor after an outcry by fans of the sport, it would unquestionably be an international scandal. Any attempt at changing the outcome of her gold medal win would be met with a ferocious, perhaps even violent response. The same reaction would come if any Black competitor won first place in a historically White dominated sport, and was then forced to share their earned title with a white competitor after some inexplicable scoring snafu.

Even while conditions are improving within the Black community, as a group they continue to have negative outlooks on race relations. In Obama's final year in office, 63% of those polled said race relations were "generally bad," with a whopping 72% of Blacks agreeing with that sentiment...even with a Black man in the White House. In January 2019 under President Trump, that perception improved by six points to 57% amongst all Americans, but remained steadily high amongst Blacks at 73% – and that's in a year where Black unemployment reached an all-time low of 5.5%. Even after historic gains, our Black brothers and sisters continue their negative perceptions on race relations – and at times behave outright racist...as they did towards the Zetas.

After years of suggesting that his presidency would signal the dawn of a colorblind America, Obama himself downplayed the concept. "No, my election did not create a post-racial society," said Obama in 2016. "I don't know who was propagating that notion. That was not mine." He is now out of the White House. Obama missed his opportunity at creating a lasting Unity Night throughout our country. And there isn't a White man or White woman that can with a media so hell-bent on stoking racial division. At this point, only Black Americans can help us achieve Dr. King's dream of a colorblind nation. But at some point you have to wonder if our Black brothers and sisters are selfishly moving the goalpost just to score a few more points.

FIVE

Mr. Creepy
*Can the #MeToo movement really
clean up Hollywood?*

October 2017 was the birth of Hollywood's #MeToo Movement. Over the years that followed, even while in the midst of one of the biggest scandals in its history, you'd think Tinseltown would've had some shame, and taken a break from its moral lecturing. But you'd be wrong in that assumption. "Like a pornstar says when she's about to have sex with a Trump, let's get this over with," said alleged comedian Michelle Wolf. "I wanna live in a world where an equal amount of white kids are shot every month. An equal world," pondered Chris Rock. "Do something about your dad's immigration practices you feckless cunt, he listens to you," asked Samantha Bee of Ivanka Trump. "It's no longer down with Trump, it's fuck Trump," screamed a belligerent Robert De Niro. The #MeToo Movement may have left a trail of road kill in its path, but Hollywood's moral decay always seems to be on full display. Which has many people wondering – can the #MeToo Movement really clean up Hollywood? To find the answer, we are going to follow the adventures of two Deplorables – your humble authors – and how we found ourselves caught in our own Hollywood #MeToo moment. And in the end, you'll have a better understanding of whether this movement has a shot at cleansing Movie City.

**

We couldn't have known what we were getting into that morning. But there we were – joining a very exclusive Hollywood circle…literally. My wife Adryana and I were sitting on a classroom floor for *circle time* with other kindergartener parents – as part of our first day at one of the most prestigious private schools in Hollywood…Oakwood Elementary. Looking around the room, we saw a few celebrities. Maybe that should have been a sign. But living in LA…it was nothing out of the ordinary. After singing some campfire-esque songs, us parents left our kids and walked through the notably outdated campus to what looked like a performance room where all of the parents gathered to get to know each other. That's when our Spidey senses kicked in.

Each of the parents passed around a microphone to introduce themselves. We eventually met the perpetually smug Adam Scott, then the rising actor on NBC's *Parks and Recreation*. A high-ranking executive at Warner Brothers and several big time talent agents were also in our midst. "Ok, I guess that makes sense. We are in Hollywood," I said to myself. But our entrance into an exclusive club was underscored when the charismatic movie star, and all around nice guy Jason Bateman stepped up and openly expressed his thrill at being a new parent at Oakwood – a place he considered out of reach as a youth growing up in Los Angeles. "Is he serious," I thought. "He was on *Silver Spoons*. He's been a star practically his entire life. Why would he be gushing over this place?" I'd soon learn why.

Jennie Garth, of *90210 fame*, grabbed the mic next and introduced herself. She was fresh off a break-up with actor Peter Facinelli, who left Jennie after he hit the big time with the *Twilight* vampire series. Peter's new squeeze, another young starlet, would often join us in circle time until she dumped Peter after landing the lead in NBC's *Blindspot* – a TV show produced by Warner Brothers, and whose film division was then led by another parent at our school. The gossip among the moms was that the young starlet attended our morning circle time because of the Tinseltown players she'd meet while strutting her stuff on to campus. Linwood Boomer, Jason Bateman's "blind" cast mate on *Little House on the Prairie* and creator of *Malcolm in the Middle*, and Boomer's wife, the producer of the Netflix show *Santa Clarita Diet*, were also parents in our class. Andrew Reich, the head writer of *Friends* during its unfunny years, had kids in our class as well. The co-creator of *Friends*, Marta Kauffman, we'd later learn was the chair of the school Board of Trustees. The future publisher of Variety, Hollywood's industry bible, was also a parent in our class. You see a trend yet? Over the coming years, we'd walk on campus amongst Steve Carell, Van Jones, Mr. Big from *Sex and the City*, Robert Redford's kids, and McSteamy of *Grey's Anatomy*. His wife at the time, former Noxzema Girl Rebecca Gayheart, who in 2001 committed vehicular manslaughter by recklessly running over a nine year-old boy, would go on to chair the school's annual fundraiser. Maybe it's just me, but child killer and charity seem like an odd pairing…but not in Hollywood.

On this Tinseltown campus, school nepotism paid well. Like for producer and school parent Chris Bender, the man behind *The Hangover*, and *Horrible Bosses 2* – a movie that was both green lit and publicized by parents at the school, and starred a father from our class and a former student - Chris

Pine. The list of board members, former students, parents, and grandparents from Oakwood could double as a who's who of Tinseltown…Johnny Depp, Danny Devito, Rhea Perlman of *Cheers* fame, Jason Alexander (aka George Costanza from *Seinfeld*), comedian Melissa McCarthy, Beck, Linkin Park's Mike Shinoda, director Luc Besson, Mick Jagger, The Disney Clan, Bridget Fonda, Danny Elfman of Oingo Boingo, *Punky Brewster*, Johnny Knoxville, the Guggenheims, Bob Dylan, and sometime actor and full-time trustafarian Balthazar Getty. Yes, that "dirty" Getty oil money was spilling into this liberal bastion. And those are just a small sampling of the household names. Adryana and I were quickly learning that we were on the inside of one of Hollywood's biggest secrets… a place completely invisible to Middle America. We'd become members of one of the most exclusive social clubs in the country… and we seemed to be the only ones surprised to learn that little fact. Everybody on campus was very aware of who everyone else was, especially the decision makers. If someone was a writer, and then another person would approach who was, let's say, a studio head – then the writer would all of a sudden become quite witty. We took notice of that…and realized it was happening with abnormal frequency. Unbeknownst to us, but common knowledge to practically everyone else that was entering the school – this was a place where Hollywood dreams could be made…and destroyed.

Movie City's private schools are such an integral part of the Tinseltown system that, in 2017, The Hollywood Reporter started an annual guide for those trying to enter this exclusive social club. Entry is so limited, that just roughly six hundred new members are allowed in each year – and that's in an area with a population of over ten million. The parents in this elite society are the ones that create the hit TV shows that pump messages into our kids' minds, produce the films hostile to

American values, and host the news programs that label nearly half the country as straight up racists...hosts like Van Jones.
A parent at the school, Jones is a particularly amusing character. In TV land he plays a man of the people. But in the real
world, his family includes former president Jimmy Carter. He
also regularly virtue signals on CNN's airwaves:

> **Van Jones**: "Honestly, if a Muslim family moved next door
> to you, you would be the happiest person in the world.
> First of all the chances of your kids getting in trouble,
> just went way down. Ok. Went way down. Because the
> Muslim community has the lowest crime rate, the high-
> est entrepreneurship, the highest educational attainment
> for women in the country, they are the model American
> community."

That's what he preaches in public. But in reality, he sends
his kids to a predominantly Jewish, exorbitantly expensive
private school...almost completely void of Muslims. Perhaps
his virtue signaling was correct...but that's not how he lives
his life. Hypocrisy is an epidemic amongst these people. They
say things like, "Oh my goodness, don't build the wall! Who
would ever say build the wall," when in reality they have walls
built all around their fancy lives. As members of this exclusive
club for many years – we saw this kind of contradiction regularly. Say one thing in public, do the opposite in private. So
when the #MeToo movement was born, we looked at it with
a taint of disgust. Why? Because many Hollywood elites at
Oakwood Elementary either remained silent or actively tried
to silence us from talking about our own #MeToo moment.

**

Getting into Oakwood was kind of an art in itself. It was
thought to be *the* premier school in Los Angeles for creative

types like our daughter. And gaining admittance was important to us. Adryana, in particular, was seeded with the idea that successful people all had fancy educations. Neither of us were Ivy League graduates. We both graduated from a working-class school – Cal State University, Long Beach – for our bachelor's degrees. The most important thing to us was that we provide our child with the best education that money could buy…and at the time, that appeared to be at the schools that were the hardest to gain entry.

The process for getting into private schools in Hollywood is a dangerous labyrinth, where one wrong move can end the entire game. The preschool we were in at the time was considered a "feeder school" – which is a place that increases the chances of a family's admission into the best private schools in Los Angeles. People like Charlize Theron, Benicio Del Toro, Nicole Richie, and Milla Jovovich all had kids at our preschool and were vying for spots at private schools. The competition was fierce and the spots were limited. And many of these Hollywood powerbrokers already had older kids at the top tier elementary schools on our list. So to increase your chances of getting in, you needed to remain on good terms with everyone. For us, that included one parent we'd later refer to as Mr. Creepy.

My daughter's preschool was off of a busy street, and as a result the school administration asked dad's to help guide the cars dropping off kids in the morning. I signed up for Wednesdays – Mr. Creepy ended up on my shift. I noticed early on that he appeared overly friendly with kids - hugging and/or kissing many on arrival. It seemed odd…borderline inappropriate. Adryana was the first between us to vocalize it. Her initial impression was that he was much too friendly with the children. But because I was a new parent, I played it down in my head. "Maybe this is just how some dad's act around here," I thought. During our parking duty, I became somewhat friendly with this dad. He was charismatic. Even funny. But as time went by he made me uneasy. I'll never forget the look in his eyes when one particular nanny dropped off some kids. He despised her. "She used to be a teacher at the preschool, and was fired because she was a horrible person," he said. She didn't care about the kids…was on her phone most of the time. She was disgusting - an evil nanny, he claimed. The disdain he had for her seemed disproportionate to the examples he gave. I took note. Things got weirder from there.

Mr. Creepy started to ask if our daughter could come over and spend the night at his house. From the minute Adryana saw him interacting with children, she was put off by it. And when it came to our daughter, she wasn't going to play coy. You can think of Adryana as the Latina Larry David in a five foot one package. When angry, she's pretty direct…to put it mildly. So when Mr. Creepy started to ask if our daughter could spend the night at his house, and our daughter was only four years old, her immediate response was a clear no. But Mr. Creepy was relentless. He would ask over and over again, every time we saw him. "Hey, does your daughter want to spend the night? Hey, why don't you let her come over and she can have a sleep over?" Adryana just kept saying no. Until there came a time when she'd had enough…and wanted to nip it in the bud once and for all. "Listen to me. It's never going to happen. My daughter is never spending the night at your house," Adryana said forcefully. The problem was, we had to play it cool because Mr. Creepy's oldest daughter was already a student at our first choice in schools…Oakwood Elementary. We were in the process of transitioning from pre-school to grade school. One false move with any parent that was already there, and we could jeopardize our daughter's chance of acceptance…and possibly her entire life trajectory, we foolishly thought. So we kept it cordial. Besides, nothing had really even happened.

Eventually the day came. We opened the mailbox and there they were...our acceptance letters. We'd gotten into every school that we applied to...and we immediately confirmed entry into Oakwood. It was a big day for our family...especially Adryana. "It was really the first time in my life that I felt like I had made it," she recalls. "Like I had done it. And I went on to Facebook and I posted, I made a public declaration, I posted 'today is the greatest day I've ever known.' And then later that night we went to a party with a lot of the parents from that school and somebody roofied us." That should have been a warning sign for what was to come.

In today's world, it's hard to believe the liberal cult let us in. But we were tortilla eating brown people – so in their eyes we were obviously liberal. What no doubt sealed the deal was our ability to pay the full tuition for one of the most expensive elementary schools in America. Typically people from our background needed financial aide to attend the school. So the red carpet was practically rolled out for us. Ethnic diversity in the class was thin. We helped make up for that...along with a black girl that was the only child in our class to receive a full ride scholarship.

Almost from the beginning at our new school, trouble started brewing with The Creepies. Initially, we thought we'd be able to hide in the crowd of new parents. But we were wrong. The school feels designed to maximize parent interactions...a trait everyone seemed to welcome because of the Hollywood connections it fostered. But that meant you had to see each family practically everyday – including Mr. Creepy. He'd typically make a hard push to me for a parent dinner date during morning drop-off. I'd go back to Adryana and tell her Mr. Creepy was trying to schedule dinner with us again. "And I'd say 'No, we're not doing it,'" says Adryana. "And then [Patrick would] go back and he'd have to see Mr. Creepy again and Mr. Creepy would say, 'Well dude, when are we gonna have dinner?' And then Patrick would come back and eventually he would break me down." That was their modus operandi. The Creepies would not relent…and we were in a position where we'd have to see these people every single day because our girls were in the same grade together. "You have to be cordial with people, even if you don't like them you still say hello and treat people with respect," adds Adryana. "And so I thought 'Alright fine. I guess the occasional dinner here and there isn't going to kill me.' But I was not happy about it."

Over the coming months we did our best to avoid them, but the nonstop requests ultimately led to dinner and an evening play date at their house. We brought our daughter's pajamas because we knew we'd be there past her bedtime. "So we go over there for dinner and Mrs. Creepy tells us a story about a play date that they had with another little girl who I'm going to call Tina," says Adryana. Tina was the child that got the full scholarship to the school. Adryana continues, "Tina comes over for a play date during the day. And Mr. Creepy decides to take a nap during the day with little Tina. In the middle of the day, in the middle of the play date they took a nap. And I remember the hair on my arm stood up. And I was so uncomfortable with that. That was so wrong to me. Why would a grown man do that with a child that doesn't belong to him? And, so I asked, 'Was your daughter also taking a nap?' And she said, 'Oh no, she doesn't nap.'" Mrs. Creepy joked about how bad it would have looked if someone walked in and saw her husband spooning with another kid. Our jaws hit the floor.

Before I could fully process what I'd just heard, somehow the topic quickly changed to the *Archie Bunker* TV show, and I said how that show could never be made today and that it was too bad because it brought us all together. Mrs. Creepy started to get hot...claiming it was a racist show. So Adryana stepped in to try and bring down the temperature. "And I said, 'you want to know what's a weird show and what's upsetting? The show *Boardwalk Empire*, where there's a character...a mom who had sexual relations with her son.' And then Mrs. Creepy looked at me and said, 'Well to each his own. They're both consenting adults.'" Adryana and I could not believe what had come out of her mouth. My wife looked at Mrs. Creepy and said that she didn't want to know people like that. It was easy to see that it was time to speed along the process and get the hell out of there. And what happened next has stayed with my wife to this day.

Adryana gave our daughter her pajamas and told her to go upstairs and put them on. So our girl went upstairs. But just a few seconds later, Mr. Creepy went upstairs as well. "And when I saw that he went upstairs I followed him," says Adryana. "It's difficult to talk about for me because my instinct was spot on...it's an image that is burned in my brain. I walked in and there was this man with my five-year-old daughter, and he was taking off her underwear. And I wanted to kick him in his fucking face." It happened quickly – less than a minute. Adryana had found them in a walk-in closet. "He immediately got up and he left the room and I just got in there and I quickly dressed her in her pajamas and I went down stairs and we immediately left." Our daughter was not hurt by this man...but we were.

Adryana wanted to report him to the police. But we didn't have any concrete evidence. He could have claimed anything...like he was just helping a child change. So we decided at that point we would just stay the hell away from that guy. And we were largely successful. But then we got invited to a family tennis lesson hosted by another family at the school...

and when we showed up, The Creepies were there too. "Here we go again," we thought. However, just a few weeks later, the issue would finally come to a head.

Adryana went away to Palm Springs for Mother's Day with a few moms from the school. One morning over mimosas, the group was small talking and the conversation took a turn. "Somebody said that they felt very uncomfortable with [Mr. Creepy]. That he gives them the creeps," Adryana recalls. That mother proceeded to tell a story about how their daughter spent the night at The Creepies house along with another child. "And my friend's daughter...tells her mom, 'Yeah last night in the middle of the night, [Mr. Creepy] came and got in the top bunk with so and so.'" Another mom chimed in and said that Mr. Creepy also shared a bed with her child during a sleepover. Then Adryana told of the time she caught Mr. Creepy in a walk-in closet with our daughter, and how Mrs. Creepy told her that her husband napped with yet another child. "And there was this oh shit moment...this horrible realization that we all had this information that we'd all been carrying. We all felt the same way. We all knew it was wrong. And we knew that we had to say something." Adryana's knee jerk reaction was to immediately call social services. "And another mother there said, 'No, no, no. We just have to keep our children away from him.' And I said, 'No. We can't just keep our children away from him. We have to keep children away from him.'"

It was easy to see that we had to do something, but what? All the wives on the retreat of course notified their husbands about what they'd learned. Two of the husbands thought we should handle the situation discretely. The Creepies were people of immense wealth. Aside for some work as an extra and leasing out their house for shoots, The Creepies didn't make their living in Hollywood. They didn't need to. Their family had generational wealth - the kind of coin that can make bad behavior go away. The Creepies told me how the family's patriarch once called in federal law enforcement on a moments notice when Mrs. Creepy briefly went missing as a child. That's what we were dealing with here. The heavy Hollywood population at the school and its enormous wealth created a warped reality that you have to personally experience to fully grasp. There isn't necessarily right and wrong when people with power are in trouble – especially in Hollywood…it's more a question of what you can and can't get away with that is the driving principle. The town is like a real life version of *Games of Thrones* – where a limited amount of kings control all the work in the city. Everyone is trying to either dethrone a ruler or attempting to be in his or her good graces. Get involved in a scandal, or piss off the wrong person connected to power, and you could be risking all future work in this company town…forever. That's why most people stay quiet.

Our school principal said they'd avoid calling social services, but advised us fathers to confront Mr. Creepy directly about his behavior. The two other dads decided it was best that I not be there for the initial confrontation. I guess I'm too *street*. By the time I got to Mr. Creepy a few days later he sounded coached - repeating the same line over and over again that no one had been harmed under his care. Eventually Mrs. Creepy got involved, talking separately to each of the confronting families. After some iteration, she landed on an approach. Her message? Showing "love" to children was not creepy, shame on anyone who thinks otherwise, and nothing was going to change in their household. According to her, we were the weird ones.

A few days later, The Creepies astonishingly hosted a sleepover themed party for our daughter's six-year-old classmates. Suffice it to say we weren't invited. But up until that point we'd been handling the issue very discretely – discussing the incidents on a need to know basis. But now that The Creepies were hosting a sleepover party, while taking the position that there was nothing wrong with cuddling other people's kids in bed, what were responsible parents supposed to do? We felt an obligation to tell our friends that were invited to the party. That's when the poop emoji hit the fan.

We received a letter from The Creepies in the early summer. They threatened to take legal action if we didn't stop "defaming" their names and spreading what they characterized as false rumors about their behavior (See Endnotes, Letter #1). The whole letter was ludicrous. The Creepies themselves mentioned a time they shared their bed with someone else's kid in front of a group of parents at a tennis lesson. Did they actually think people weren't going to talk about that? We were prepared for, and even expected a confrontation. It was game on.

We responded to The Creepies clearly stating several bed-sharing incidents, reasserted that we would never give up our First Amendment right to speak the truth – and demanded that they confirm an end to their inappropriate kid cuddling (See Endnotes, Letter #2). We may not have had trust funds but we had brains. How'd they think these two poor kids were now roaming amongst the Hollywood elites?

The Creepies responded within 48 hours - apologizing for their behavior and promising it would never happen again. And we got it all in writing (See Endnotes, Letter #3). It was mission accomplished. We sent the exchange to our school for the record.

Throughout the remainder of the summer, we didn't talk much about The Creepies. So by the time we got back to school we hoped the whole ordeal was largely behind us. But it wasn't…it was just getting started. And why? The Creepies went on a campaign to discredit us – and by doing so they helped get the rumor mill churning even further. The news of a man getting in bed with other people's kids was passed around like an intern in the Clinton White House.

For some reason, out of the three families that confronted them – The Creepies targeted us. In Hollywood, contrary to their virtue signaling videos, most of the community is lily white – in our enclave, predominantly White Jewish liberals to be exact. A Jewish friend at the school once joked, "The school is really diverse. We have Sephardic Jews, Ashkenazi Jews…" We were one of the rare Hispanic breeds. Adryana's parents were from Mexico. My father's family emigrated from Mexico as well…and my mother's were largely Irish. Our Jewish friends thought that our having Mexican blood played a part in us being singled out. But we couldn't entirely pin why they targeted us until an ambassador for The Creepies – the wife of a big-time Hollywood agent – approached my wife. Mrs. Ambassador was dismissive – attempting to explain away her friends' creepy behavior. Adryana said the bed sharing was the wrong message to send kids, at best, and something far more nefarious at worst. Mrs. Ambassador played it down. Mr. Creepy was "just a hippie," she claimed. When Adryana explained that she walked in on Mr. Creepy undressing our daughter – Mrs. Ambassador had an answer for that too. "Well, that was after water play. He was helping her out of a wet bathing suit." Now that was a straight up, bald-faced lie… and troubling on many levels. But then Mrs. Ambassador let it slip. "Well, [Mrs. Creepy] did say you guys were conservatives," offered Mrs. Ambassador.

Word was getting back to us that The Creepies were telling everyone that would listen that we were right-wingers. They understood what that meant in Hollywood – we were vulnerable. The tide turned on us almost immediately. Parents that initially expressed disgust toward The Creepies now took their side. One of the fathers that initially confronted Mr. Creepy – Hollywood producer Chris Bender – now began lobbying against us. This is a guy producing Disney's girl-empowerment movie *Mulan* – so he's no bit player. Anyone that knows the Hollywood private school system knows Tinseltown big wigs carry weight…especially against filthy conservatives.

The school headmaster of Oakwood, Jim Astman, who'd earlier supported our position, now summoned us to his office and claimed parents were more disturbed about us than The Creepies' behavior. He demanded we keep quiet. The Creepies hadn't broken any laws, he claimed. When we requested that he mediate between The Creepies and us, he declined. When we asked for a change to the school's code of conduct making a parent getting in bed with someone else's kid an expulsion offense – as was using the n-word off campus – the school would not comply. Weirdly, after the principal advised us not to call social services, the headmaster now wondered if we were so concerned, why then hadn't we called social services? We'd actually already made that call. He eventually threatened to expel our daughter if we didn't stop talking about it – an act that would have surely blocked us from admission into other private schools in the area. The school's priority should have been protecting children. Instead, it appeared more important to them to protect the Hollywood elites. (See Endnotes, Letter #4 & #5).

Several parents eventually stepped forward and told us that The Creepies also had another incident when their older daughter was at our preschool. That daughter was caught describing an inappropriate sex act to her classmates. The classmates' parents asked for a sit down with The Creepies along with the teacher that witnessed their child's troubling words. And who was that teacher? It was the evil nanny. The same horrible person Mr. Creepy claimed was fired from the preschool back when we were on car parking duty together. The Creepies had embarked on a discrediting campaign before and weathered the storm. These guys were pros.

We spoke to a parent of one child that Mr. Creepy spooned during a play date. The father, a struggling actor, expressed anger in Mr. Creepy's behavior, but didn't want to risk their full ride scholarship – so they largely remained quiet. The family astonishingly sent their child back over to The Creepies house. That was probably the final nail in our coffin. In a last ditch effort, we asked to speak to the school board. Surely a group comprised of some of Hollywood's heaviest hitters would see the danger in such behavior. They declined our request. Aside from a few families with rock solid character, including the Batemans that were nothing but friendly, most of the parents in this prestigious Hollywood school completely shunned us. In one instance a parent literally ran away from my wife to avoid the appearance of friendliness. The way we were treated, you'd of thought we got in bed with other people's kids.

Hollywood's response only emboldened Mr. Creepy – who on one occasion followed my wife back to her car after drop off, and bent down to glare at her in the car. On top of being shunned by Tinseltown's finest, my wife now had to see the creep yucking it up on campus with some of Hollywood's future #MeToo advocates. It made our blood boil. We tried to find a school in the area with an opening – but transferring in the middle of the elementary school phase is near impossible. There are just no available seats. Sending our daughter to public school in Los Angeles was not an option. The schools are frankly, a hot mess – plagued by underfunding and overrun by illegal aliens. There were no more strategic moves with The Creepies. We'd ultimately taken our protests as far as we could...and anyways, Adryana had a serious health issue that required our full attention. So we decided to just keep our distance from them and their supporters and find a new school when our daughter graduated from elementary school. Over the next few years we'd become accustom to being the pariah on campus – and learned to navigate the situation with minimal impact on our young daughter's school experience. But with the launch of the 2016 election cycle, that was about to change.

My long-term association with Breitbart News meant the naming of its CEO Steve Bannon as head of the Trump campaign only escalated our isolation. Now we weren't only worse than a kid cuddler, our family was practically members of the Nazi party. We became the only known Deplorables on campus. And our daughter began to feel the heat. Invitations to birthday parties, play dates, and special events evaporated. Classmates taunted her over our vote. At one point, my daughter was tasked with a school project to create a new business. Her assignment partner suggested a startup where customers could pay to torture Trump – it was the Trump Torture Chamber. It shocked my daughter, but when I found out which child it was I wasn't surprised. The classmate's father, actor Adam Scott, proudly pimped his children in a *Late Night with Seth Meyers* TV segment entitled *Adam Scott's Kids Are Anti-Trump* where he talked about why they attended the infamous Women's March:

Adam Scott: "My kids. We didn't make them go to this march. They asked if they could go. Because I think it's important to realize that the things that Donald Trump is doing and saying and the policies he's proposing, or the Executive Orders he's signing, are so kind of mean and unwise and ridiculous on an elementary level that my eight and ten year olds independently can surmise and just go, 'No. No. I want to register my complaint with the US government.'"

It got some laughs on late night. But Adam Scott's family activism has consequences – like scaring our innocent daughter. Adam's wife would later get involved in the #MeToo movement. But she was publicly silent during our ordeal. I guess it wasn't yet a fashion statement when we spoke out.

This stretch among the Hollywood elites became without question the hardest time of our lives – and that's saying a lot with our backgrounds. People rarely discuss ostracization because it isn't a widely experienced phenomenon – and most don't want to admit to having gone through it. But we can tell you that the feeling that it imbues is an overwhelming level of sadness. It's not a short crisis, but rather a long ordeal that seems designed to instill a deep level of shame. For us, it included psychological warfare on our kid…a parent's worst nightmare. The isolation is jarring. And unfortunately, we were in essence trapped in this liberal cult. We were now locked into a school contract. When that ended we could either send our daughter into the illegal alien dominated Los Angeles public schools, uproot our entire life, or try getting her into another private school. So we applied out again. And again, there were no vacancies.

We only saw one way forward. We decided to include an abridged version of our experience in a story we were working on for Breitbart News – entitled *Tinseltown Travelogue* - in hopes that these Hollywood elites would come to their senses. Part of the reason we wrote the article was that it was sort of a Hail Mary. We were hoping that there were possibly people within the community that just didn't know the entire story behind our confrontation with The Creepies. And so we wrote the piece in the hopes that a few parents would come around and we'd ultimately be able to keep our daughter in the school until she graduated. Then just days from its publication – the #MeToo movement was born. What amazing timing. At this

particular moment, if our story didn't open hearts to our situation – and more importantly, to our daughter – then absolutely
nothing would. We gave an exclusive to The Hollywood Reporter to increase the chance of everyone on campus reading
it. Once it went live, we started to get clear indications that
the article was making the rounds. The shunning continued,
maybe even increased with some, but we thought we could
live with it until we were able to find another school. But then
The Creepies started creeping back into our circle.

Our daughter had a group of friends that rarely interacted
with The Creepies' daughter. But then out of the blue, Mr.
Creepy's daughter began to play with one of the girls in our
daughter's inner circle of friends…let's call that friend Tiny.
Our daughter and Tiny had an off campus hip-hop dance class
together. Adryana and Tiny's mom were cordial and would
alternate taking the girls to the class. One day it was Adryana's
turn, and as she was transporting the girls, Tiny tells her that
she was excited because that night she was going to have a
sleepover at The Creepies house. Adryana was shocked. "Wait
a minute. You're going to go spend the night at The Creepies house tonight," Adryana asked Tiny. "Yes, it's gonna be
so so fun," responded Tiny. This was troubling. Tiny's mom,
Laura, had talked about The Creepies ordeal with other school
mom's, including Adryana – so she knew all about Mr. Creepy
getting in bed with other people's kids. But adding to the concern was that in a few weeks, for Tiny's birthday, she was having a sleepover party and she'd invited both our child and Mr.
Creepy's daughter. So Adryana decided that she was going to
talk to Laura about it.

Things were about to get interesting. You see, Laura has
the personality of a bedridden coma patient, which is to say
she has none. Showing emotion is not in her repertoire. Also,
Laura's husband is actor Ben King from Disney's popular kids

show *Liv and Maddie*. And it just so happens that Ben is super Trump triggered. So Adryana decided to call Laura and ask her a simple question. "So I said, 'Listen, I have a question about Tiny's sleep over party...When kids come over to your house Laura and spend the night, does your husband get in bed with them in the middle of the night? Does he do that? Are you ok with that? Does that happen at your house?'" Laura responded, "of course not." Adryana knew she was offended by the question because for the first time in their relationship, Laura actually showed emotion. And that's when Adryana drilled down. "And I said, 'You know what, yeah that's kind of an offensive question. If somebody asked that about Patrick, you know what, I would be offended too. So if you're so offended by that question, why would you allow your daughter to go over to The Creepies house and spend the night... when you know damn well that Mr. Creepy has gotten in bed with other people's children in the middle of the night?'"

Like so many before her, Laura caught Adryana's vapors. She tried to explain her reasoning. Mr. Creepy was out of town when her daughter spent the night at his house. She also made a confession. When her family entered Oakwood, the incident with The Creepies had already happened and the Hollywood parents at the school were forcing her to choose between our family and The Creepies. Adryana recalled Laura's comeback. "You know when we started at the school you have to remember that there were sides being taken," Laura said to Adryana, "and we were being pushed to take a side. And we didn't want to take a side. We didn't want to take anybody's side."

It was a confusing admission. Just a few weeks early, Laura's husband, once again Disney star Ben King, sent out a public tweet supporting the #MeToo movement, saying to the victims that have spoken up, "If your motive in any way lie[s] in protecting the 'next' potential target[,] on behalf of my girls

I say thank you." But in the real world, outside of the public eye, his family told us they didn't want to take a side when we tried to do that exact thing. It was clear that Laura and her husband had taken a side. They had taken the side of The Creepies when they allowed their young daughter to go over to their house and spend the night.

Adryana and I had come to the conclusion that Hollywood was never going to change. "The day that I found out that my daughter had been accepted into this school...I really felt like I had accomplished a life long goal that day," adds Adryana. "And for me, the daughter of immigrants, it felt like the American dream. I never expected to be shunned for the values that got me there."

We ended up leaving Oakwood. The Creepies are still there. We never really wanted to walk away because it felt like running, and that wasn't a lesson we wanted to teach our daughter. But there was another lesson she had to learn – that sometimes a system is so broken that it can't be fixed. And when you come to that conclusion – when nothing you do can change an existing community – it's time to create your own. It was that awakening that led to our storytelling podcast Red Pilled America. Hollywood is so hopelessly politicized that it wouldn't even listen to a story coming from the people that were protecting their kids. So we launched our show to make sure that the people Hollywood ignores had a place to tell their stories.

Which brings us back to the question at hand – can the #MeToo movement really clean up Hollywood? The short answer is of course not...because #MeToo was built on a lie. #MeToo is not about creating a safer environment in Hollywood. If it were, The Creepies would have been expelled from Hollywood instead of roaming amongst their kids and hamming it up with Tinseltown's finest. #MeToo is, and has always been, a political weapon with one ultimate goal… dethroning Donald Trump.

Life is a game of war. #MeToo is just another weapon in that war. Those in Hollywood wielding it are willing to sacrifice some of their own if in the end they can destroy the President. It's just that simple. What decent Americans need to do is see this Hollywood #MeToo movement for what it is – a political weapon. You need to stop funding Hollywood, and join your own in Red Pilled America. Because if you don't, you will be helping Hollywood in its real quest…and that's to settle an old score for a sore loser named Hillary Clinton.

SIX

Learned to Code

Why does Silicon Valley love immigrants?

Silicon Valley is known for its ruthless competition – constantly battling each other to grow ever larger. But one area where they put down their swords and come together with one voice is the topic of immigration. Silicon Valley loves immigrants. "My view on DACA is that Congress needs to fix DACA...and fix DACA to me means allow everyone to stay in the country," says Apple's Tim Cook. "We benefit from immigration...we benefit from diversity," claims Twitter's Jack Dorsey. "Amazon founder Jeff Bezos and his wife are donating $33 million to fund scholarships for undocumented immigrants called 'Dreamers,'" reports the Washington Post. "I hear fearful voices calling for building walls and distancing people they label as others," says Facebook's Mark Zuckeberg. You'd be hard pressed to find a single Big Tech titan who doesn't want to open up our borders to immigration, both legal and illegal.

Silicon Valley is unanimously for increasing immigration to the United States. But as we know, anytime a community walks lockstep in agreement on a subject, something else is usually afoot. What could it be? Why does Silicon Valley love immigrants? To find the answer, we're going to tell the story of two tech industry insiders – one a long-time computer programmer that became a whistleblower, and another...an immigrant to the United States who began his career in Silicon Valley. They'll give a perspective that the masters of Big Tech don't want you to hear.

**

Roger Ross came to the U.S. in kind of a roundabout way. He was born and raised in South Africa after his parents migrated there from Europe. His father worked for the World Bank organization. "It just became a really cozy place to grow up," says Roger, "and my parents never wanted to move back." As a young boy Roger had aspired to come to the States, the land of opportunities, and seek out what he saw as the American dream – or at least what was depicted in the sitcoms and Hollywood movies he watched in his youth. "I really wanted to focus on that end and become part of the American lifestyle," says Roger. "I really valued that lifestyle to the point where I even adopted and started to change my accent to fit in. So I did everything I could to assimilate into the culture."

He went to an international school in South Africa that encouraged its students to study abroad. So in 1999, before his senior year of high school, he made his move to America as part of a foreign exchange program – making a small town of 10,000 people in Northern California his new home. His high school was a predominantly white public school, and his years of admiring America made him fit right in on arrival. He found that the students were very friendly. "They were actually astonished by my level of English," recalls Roger. "Because a lot of the foreign exchange students that they had encountered spoke little English or with a heavy accent, and they thought that I was just someone who had migrated from San Diego and moved up north."

Roger wasn't feeling academically challenged at his new school, so he enrolled at a nearby college to take collegiate level classes while simultaneously finishing high school. He would eventually attend UC Davis, where he got his Bachelor's in Applied Mathematics and a Master's in Economics. The 2008 financial crisis hit while he was in college, but by the time he graduated in 2010, Silicon Valley was already making a comeback. Roger remembers the exciting upswing. "Things started to [boom] in Silicon Valley with Facebook going public and various other tech companies coming into the limelight and showing a lot of great success. So we started to see a boom in the startup industry."

At the time, the message being pumped out by Silicon Valley was that America needed the foreign students graduating from our American universities. Roger found a startup that was interested in a market researcher or market analyst – and the job description fit his wheelhouse. So Roger applied for the job. And that's when the company exposed him to the foreign work visa program. "They were short on funding," recalls Roger. "So they brought me [in] on an H-1B Visa."

An H-1B is a foreign worker visa that purports to help American employers fill job openings for highly skilled workers. They're only supposed to be used if the company cannot find a qualified American worker to fill the job. Its origin goes back to the Immigration Act of 1990. "This bill provides for vital increases for entry on the basis of skills, infusing the ranks of our scientists and engineers and educators with new blood and new ideas," claimed President George H. W. Bush at the Act's signing ceremony. Washington D.C. created a whole host of foreign worker visas that were not supposed to be used to displace American workers or negatively effect their wages. Employers are supposed to pay the foreign worker what is called the *prevailing wage* – which are government published salary levels for jobs within a particular work sector. It's kind of like the minimum wage for a particular profession. This way, the employer can't use these visas to bring in cheap foreign labor. The problem is, many Big Tech firms have been using these visas to do just that.

"If you're paying an American...say a hundred thousand dollars to do a job and then you pay sixty thousand dollars to a foreigner, multiply that savings by two hundred and fifty... that's a lot," says Sara Blackwell – a Florida based attorney specializing in employment law and founder of Protect US Workers. It's a substantial cost reduction, but Sara thinks the ultimate goal for this business model is to eventually send the work offshore to India. "So you take two hundred and fifty American workers who are getting an average of $100,000 and now we're paying Indians in India to do it for $10,000. That's some serious savings," claims Sara. She thinks this windfall cost reduction is why so many American CEOs receive multi-million dollar bonuses. "And that's why the CEOs are making so much money," she adds. "Because they're using the lie of the lack of workers, and globalism, and all of these other arguments for basically using foreign slave labor in my opinion."

For people working in the United States with a foreign worker visa, many refer to this labor arrangement as legal indentured servitude because in order to keep their visas and remain in our country, they have to work in conditions American citizens would not tolerate. H-1B foreign workers need to have a sponsor to keep their visas. If they lose their jobs, and hence their sponsor, they are sent back to their country. So these workers are in a position to be exploited to work a ton of hours at a reduced rate. "So the Americans [that] keep their jobs are left there having to compete with workers who are staying there ninety hours because if they don't they'll be sent back home," claims Sara Blackwell.

Roger Ross experienced this exploitation firsthand when he became a foreign visa worker. When he was initially sponsored for an H-1B visa, his correct job title should have been as an economist, market researcher, or market analyst. But the sponsor saw the government designated prevailing wage for those titles and claimed the salary was to high. So they made a suggestion to Roger. "Why don't we make your job something that we can find a prevailing wage that's much more lower," recalls Roger. "And at the same time we want to employ you on a part time basis but make you work full time and that's how they exploited me per say." Roger says he agreed because he needed the H-1B visa to stay in the country. "I'm just a fresh college graduate. I'm dying for a job. We're coming out of a recession and any job will do because I had loans to pay myself. So I gladly accepted whatever they deemed necessary to get me on the H-1B."

But what Roger learned was that he lost his ability to speak up, because he was beholden to his employer. One false move and he could lose his job and be sent back to his country. "As I got my H-1B, I noticed that there was no way I could retaliate or make my voice heard if I felt like I was being dealt inappropriately with the work, or whether I was not being paid fairly," he says. "I just felt like I didn't have a voice in that, and that was really problematic." Roger had an awakening to the reality of H-1B visas – Silicon Valley was using them to control him and his coworkers.

This dynamic creates serious problems for American workers as well, because this foreign labor not only can take their jobs, but they drive down the wages and set the working conditions for everyone else. If the Americans aren't willing to

work longer hours for a reduced salary, the American is out…
and sometimes they are even forced to train their foreign replacement under incredibly stressful circumstances. That's
what happened with Michael Emmons. "My daughter was
born with spina bifida," says Michael. "She's had about twen-
ty-eight surgeries. I'm training my foreign replacement workers. I'm self-employed so my medical insurance premiums
were nine hundred and forty-seven dollars a month. And to
find out that my trainee salary is fifty-three dollars more than
my medical premium, I mean how does an American compete." He was in a rough position. So he decided to do what a
patriot would do…he decided to fight back.

Michael has seen a lot of America. He was born in Mississippi, and as a young boy lived in Tennessee and North
Carolina…finally parking in Florida around middle school. It
was there that his dad introduced him to programming. "My
father said, 'why don't you try this,'" he remembers. "And I
took one class and I was hooked." Michael did then what so
many people are told to do today…he learned to code. Michael remembers those early days of programming. "One of
my first classes we used an IBM mainframe. The PCs came
in on my senior year. They started having like a PC lab. We
used cards for my first two classes, where you had cards and
you programmed on the cards and you ran them through a card
reader."

He'd eventually graduate from the University of Florida
in 1984 with a degree in computer science and began solving
people's problems through coding. He worked for the Florida
Department of Revenue, creating an application to accept revenue through checks at remote locations. He left there for a
small company that created a crime laboratory tracking system. Michael built an application for jails to handle all the
money that an inmate receives. "So when [someone] was ar-

rested, they took everything from [them] and they put it into our system and gave the inmate a receipt," recalls Michael. "I was working eighty hours a week and they were paying me about forty, and I asked for a raise and they didn't want to pay me. So that's when I decided I'm just going to go do this on my own."

He went coding in South Carolina, Texas, and Harrisburg, Pennsylvania. He ended up at the Church of Scientology in Los Angeles, working for the groups Sea Org division. Michael remembers the kind of programming he did for the organization. "Writing...I call it a book selling application, because to me it's not really a church." Then a guy he worked with left the Church of Scientology and got a job in Silicon Valley with Siemens. So Michael took a contracting gig there as well, working on voice over IP phones. He was thrilled to be living in the epicenter of the coding industry in the 1990s, smack dab in the heart of where everything was happening, was thrilling. But he now believes Silicon Valley has completely changed. "It's overrun with foreign workers," says Michael. They'd soon overrun him as well.

After the dotcom bubble burst in 2001, Siemens merged two of their businesses into one. They had an office in Florida and offered Michael a contracting job at that location. He jumped at the chance because now he'd be able to actually live in his house instead of being on the road. But it was short lived. In mid-2002, the employees in the I.T. department were brought into a room and told that they were being let go...and that the company wanted them to train their replacements. "I wasn't an employee, I was a contractor," says Michael. "So they didn't bring me into the room. But some of the employees had told me this is what's going on. About thirty days later, in [come] about thirty or so mostly young male Tata India employees...our trainees." Tata is a huge Indian company that, among other things, provides a foreign Indian workforce to corporations on American soil. At the time, Michael can't recall any foreign visa workers at Siemens in Florida, and remembers only a few while he worked in Silicon Valley. "The group I worked for in Sunnyvale they had about two or three on H-1B's," recalls Michael. "And I knew who they were, and they were friends of mine and it was no problem. We worked together, we taught each other, we learned from each other." But now Indians were replacing the entire I.T. department. The company assigned them people to train, and then watched over Michael and his co-workers as they instructed their replacements.

Michael was floored. There was no worker shortage. Their foreign replacements didn't have high-skilled training that the IT staff didn't already possess...the incoming foreign workers were being trained *by* them for God's sake. They were being replaced by H-1B visa workers simply because they were cheaper. It was a rough time for Michael. His daughter suffered from spina bifida and needed surgeries to deal with her condition – so Michael's health insurance was a lifeline. Having to train his foreign worker replacement stung in a way that sparked something that he didn't even know he had within him. He decided to fight back. Michael, a programming wiz, began digging around on the company servers and found some interesting documents. The company had set up a shared drive for Tata India – and on that drive, Michael discovered what's referred to as knowledge transfer documents and staffing paperwork related to the incoming Tata India workers. "And what was interesting in the staffing document is all but about one or two of the people were on L-1B visas, not H-1Bs," says Michael. "L-1Bs are called intra-company transfer visas. So Tata India transfers their employees from India to Tata America. Then they sell them out to businesses in the U.S."

L-1B visas are rarely discussed but they're particularly harmful to American workers. This visa was originally created to allow a foreign company to bring in their employees with quote "special knowledge" to help set up a branch in the United States. But in practice, L-1Bs are predominantly used to replace American workers with cheap foreign labor. Foreign companies, primarily from India, set up shop in the United States then bring their countrymen into the country and shop them out to American corporations. Unlike H-1B visas, there are no numerical limits on how many L-1B visas are issued and there are no restrictions on paying the foreign worker a prevailing wage. In other words, the American corporation can pay them as little as possible. So L-1B workers become very attractive. When the corporations hire them, they make their outgoing employee train them. This process is known as knowledge transfer. And if an American worker refuses – they receive no severance package. Also, as a condition of receiving a severance, the corporation shuts them up by making them sign away their right to speak to the press. These foreign visas are so often used in the I.T. business that insiders won't speak out about them for fear of being blacklisted from the industry. That's why we seldom hear about this morally reprehensible practice.

We are constantly sold by the Big Tech industry that foreign workers are needed because of American worker shortages. But they are lying. "The argument is they're high skilled and that's why we need them and we don't have enough American workers to do the job. That's the argument," says Sara Blackwell. "But obviously we have high-skilled American workers if the American high-skilled workers are teaching the foreigners how to do their job."

Sara represented former Disney employees in a high profile case. In 2014, two hundred and fifty of the company's I.T. employees were forced to train their replacements – which was a large group of Indian nationals with foreign work visas. She filed a RICO lawsuit, reserved for cases where unlawful acts are performed as part of a criminal enterprise. "These corporations have a lot of money," says Sara. "And they paid some really smart attorneys to figure out how to break immigration and employment laws without breaking employment or immigration laws. So basically what Disney did, if they would have just done on their own they would be violating employment law, because you can't take two hundred and fifty people and then replace them all with one race and one national origin... that's race and national origin discrimination. And if that contracting company had walked in and had fired two hundred and fifty of their American workers and replaced them with H-1B workers, they would have been violating immigration law. But the way they do it, they come together and set this business model up so that neither one are violating either law."

So they find loopholes to legally replace their employees, take advantage of the desperate foreign workers, and gag their outgoing workforce so no one knows what's going on. And they do it all with the help of our politicians in Washington D.C. That's why what Michael Emmons did in 2003 was so important. He was a pioneer in blowing the whistle on this despicable corporate scam. When Michael was forced to train his replacements he wasn't an employee – he was a contractor, and corporations at the time were not yet hip to shutting people up. Michael wasn't going to take this abuse sitting down. He was a highly skilled programmer that kept up-to-date with the industry's new technology – continuously learning new coding languages and techniques throughout his career to stay proficient in the industry. So Michael approached a former customer and said he was looking for work. They scooped him up – but at a sizable salary decrease. Nonetheless, that freed him up to blow the whistle on the entire foreign worker visa scam. He contacted a local reporter at WKMG Orlando. Stations outside of New York, Washington DC, and Los Angeles are typically focused on more local news – like a small business cheating the folks around town. But Michael brought WKMG Orlando a big story with international implications... so the reporter was excited. It took them a few months to put it together, but when they finally released their investigative report, Michael was at the center as the whistleblower of the whole sorted business practice:

> **WKMG Reporter**: "What if I told you that when you go to work tomorrow, [there would] be someone there to take your job? What if I told you that you had to train that person to do your job? Sounds rather far-fetched, don't you think? Well it isn't."
>
> **Michael Emmons**: "Americans across the country, hundreds of thousands of Americans, have lost their jobs and can't get work."
>
> **WKMG Reporter**: "Mike Emmons and James Granberry were working at Siemens in Lake Mary and they both claim the company has replaced them with cheaper foreign labor."

At the time, there was no Facebook. There was no Twitter. There was no YouTube. But Michael was a programmer, and he used that skill to distribute the story over the web. To bring awareness to the investigative report, he captured the WKMG segments using a video camera, then transferred the files over to his computer, digitized them, then served it up on the Internet. "I had a little Linux box in my office here," recalls Michael. "That was my server and I had 30,000 hits a week at times." Eventually the national news caught wind, with immigration legend Lou Dobbs covering the story:

> **Lou Dobbs:** "We've been reporting for weeks on this show
> about the massive loss of American jobs to foreign coun-
> tries in our series of special reports – Exporting America.
> What is less well known is how tens of thousands of for-
> eigners take jobs in this country every year under special
> visa programs. Incredibly, some American workers are
> training those foreigners to take their own jobs."
>
> **Michael Emmons:** "They held out a carrot for the Ameri-
> cans - a severance. Stay on and train your replacements
> then you'll get this severance when you leave. I stayed
> on in November until I landed another job. But what I
> learned about these H-1B and L-1B visas is very discour-
> aging for American workers."

The story even reached the national news desk of Peter
Jennings, anchor of ABC World News Tonight. What drove
Michael was the simple injustice of it all. Our leaders in D.C.
were actually allowing and helping corporations replace
American workers, its own citizens, with cheaper foreigners.
"To use visas and say there's not enough Americans – to ac-
complish their goal to get cheap labor – it's just wrong," says
Michael. "The U.S. Congress created visas that allow corporations, that line their pockets, to get rid of their employees." We
often hear how illegal immigration devastates the American
worker by flooding the labor force with cheap labor – driving
down wages and taking our working-class jobs. But it is not
just illegal immigration hurting the Americans. It's legal immigration as well. Michael blew the whistle in 2003 – and yet
here we are over a decade and a half later and it's still happening in America.

Worsening the problem is the White House's positioning

on this topic. In what Trump has even acknowledged as a re-
versal from his previous position, he's called for a record increase in immigration to the United States. "I want people to
come into our country in the largest numbers ever, but they
have to come in legally," Trump adlibbed in an off-script moment during his 2019 State of the Union address. Roger Ross,
an economics expert who once benefitted from a foreign work
visa, sees a real problem with the White House's position. "I
truly think that there's no difference between illegal and legal
immigration when it comes to labor supply economics," says
Roger. "It's all about getting the cheap labor. And as long as
that mantra is propelled on, we're going to see more devastation of our economic conditions in this country."

Which leads us back to the question, why does Silicon Valley love immigrants so much? It's simple – immigrants are
cheap labor that they can exploit. Silicon Valley pushes both
legal and illegal immigration because it helps their bottom
line. "You know people often talk about two parts of the issue – high-skilled H-1B is the issue that tech companies have
and full comprehensive immigration reform – as if they're two
completely separate issues," said Facebook's founder Mark
Zuckerberg. "But anyone who knows a Dreamer knows that
they're not." Silicon Valley is only worried about continued
growth – and they're willing to find that growth at any cost,
including replacing the American workforce.

We are living in unprecedented times. Americans are losing
jobs to automation, new technologies, and offshoring. Some
are predicting driverless cars will eliminate over four million jobs. Illegal immigrants have flooded construction, landscaping, farming, house cleaning, factory, janitorial, and the
childcare industries – lowering wages and replacing American
workers. And throughout all of this, Silicon Valley is constantly making a push to increase foreign work visas. A 2016 report

showed that nearly three quarters of Silicon Valley techies are foreign born. Three quarters! How many more do they need? The Big Tech billionaires are not being altruistic – they're being greedy. They love the cheap labor. It's just that simple. The situation has become so dire, that it has even triggered Roger Ross, a man who once benefited from a foreign worker visa, to speak out.

Roger married an American. He is now a permanent resident with a green card. And he's using his insider knowledge to the abuse of H-1Bs to inform the public on this issue. "I'm just seeing a total destruction of our economic conditions and that's why I'm beginning to panic," says Roger. He's alarmed that our future leaders and Congress, including Donald Trump, are going about the whole immigration reform concept in the wrong direction. And he believes that's why we're not seeing any meaningful progress. Roger thinks the economic devastation that has happened over the past few decades is why Trump was elected President. "You are seeing a total stagnation of our wages," says Roger. "You are also seeing the labor participation rate, which is the true measure of people employed in the labor force, is declining. But President Trump and a lot of the White House [staffers like] to tout on the unemployment rate, which is [at] an all-time low, but it's not a true measure of how the economy is doing. And I think that these kind of steps are misguided and we're pretty much headed to a cataclysmic condition of our economic situation, exacerbating to where you're going to have a lot of our college graduates not being able to find jobs, they're inundated with student loan debt and it's piling up each day."

Roger sees Silicon Valley executives' claims that there is a shortage of workers – while many high-skilled American workers are not finding jobs – as an attempt by Big Tech titans to line their pockets. "What we're seeing is that there's a standard discrimination of workers who are either American or are at higher age. There's this whole ageism discrimination that's going on where if you're...past the age of 30 years old, you're not as valuable to the company because they know you would warrant a higher pay based on the experience that you have, and they don't want to pay those salaries. So that's why they would rather hire someone who's a younger...international student or a younger H-1B [foreign worker] who will happily accept the wages in exchange for immigration benefits." Roger thinks that Donald Trump has given too much credence to the claims of Silicon Valley titans. "Donald Trump has changed his tune, and said I don't like illegal immigration but I like legal immigration – and we need more legal immigrants because Tim Cook from Apple is telling me so, that we need these high-skilled engineers."

When coal workers were losing their jobs during the Obama Administration, journalists suggested they should learn to code to find employment. Well, Michael Emmons actually did just that...long before that helpful tip came from our thoughtful media. But in the age of the Big Tech titans, learning to code is hardly a fail safe when those same titans continue to push for more and more cheap immigrant labor. Silicon Valley is pulling a con job on the American people by claiming we need more foreign workers. We don't. And if we continue to let Big Tech dictate our immigration policy, companies like Google will alter the American dream forever. "If you think your living space is cramped, take a look at this truck," stated Matt Lauer during a 2015 Today Show report. "It looks like any other, right? Well it's not. This truck is actually home to a twenty-three year-old man who works at Google. It's actually parked right outside the headquarters of Google." American dream? Sounds more like a nightmare.

SEVEN

The Minority

*What does the Black community need to do to
finally overcome the legacy of slavery?*

In the classroom, on the big screen, and in the media, Americans are constantly lectured about the lasting effects of America's original sin. "This country was founded on white supremacy, and every single institution and structure that we have in our country still reflects the legacy of slavery," said Robert Francis O'Rourke. "America has a history of two hundred years of slavery," posits Kamala Harris. "We live in a country now where the president is advancing environmental racism, economic racism, criminal justice racism, healthcare racism," lists Elizabeth Warren. The topic of racism in America has become a constant motif in our daily lives. What does the Black community need to do to finally overcome the legacy of slavery? To find the answer, we're going to follow the story of a family that faced years of racist attacks, and what they did to overcome them.

**

This may sound odd today, but a Mexican man dating a Caucasian woman was once relatively rare. When witnessed, it even raised the suspicion of law enforcement. "Rudy and I were stopped on numerous occasions just to be stopped," recalls Nancy. "Nothing. No headlights out, no tail lights out." Her new love interest Rudy, looked indigenous Mexican... with very dark skin. Nancy is Irish...and as an 18-year-old young lady, she was lily white with light reddish brown hair and hazel eyes. In the late 1960s, interracial couples weren't a societal norm. The two met at a local dance club called *Baby Huey's* in Gardena, California – a suburb roughly fifteen miles south of downtown Los Angeles. Once they met, Rudy and Nancy quickly began dating. In those early years, when the cops saw them driving down the street on their nights out, they'd pull them over to make sure Nancy was okay. The interrogations occurred so often, that she says it became a bit of a routine for Rudy. "I would like to sit back and say how many times it happened, but God...I'm going to say at least a dozen times." When they were pulled over, Rudy knew exactly what was happening and what he had to do. He'd typically have to get out of the car, they'd check his I.D., perform a minor search of the vehicle, ask Nancy if she was okay, and when she responded yes, the police would send them on their way. For whatever reason, the interrogations didn't seem to bother Rudy. "I think that [the police] seeing me sitting in the car with an obviously Mexican guy just you know, it was an alert thing to them. It was like driving while black. It was just one of those things."

Rudy grew up in a slightly rougher neighborhood, served in Vietnam and respected law enforcement. But the constant inquisition infuriated Nancy because it was something entirely new to her. She came from the predominantly white suburb of Torrance, which bordered Gardena and stretched all the way to the Pacific Ocean. At that young age of eighteen, Nancy was naïve to the ways of the world. She spent her early years in Catholic School, then by fourth grade transitioned to public school. In her day, society self-segregated and largely kept to their own neighborhoods – it was just the way things were at the time. "You had your own community and you had everything to do in your own community," she recalls. "It was such a fear of having...any kind of other culture than your own. You were looked at. And...you'd have to categorize everybody – Black, White, Mexican – everybody as a racist in those days...because they all did the same thing." And if some outsiders tried to make inroads into a neighborhood populated by people that weren't of *their* kind, the locals made moves to stop them. Nancy remembers one of those instances. "Manhattan Beach, there was this big plot of land that's still there, and they were going to build brand new houses on that land. And they had some black families that were interested, wealthy black families that came in – [maybe] not wealthy, but [they] could afford it. A bunch of Manhattan people got together, bought the property, donated it to the city to use as a park, and it's still there."

By the time she'd met Rudy, this kind of behavior already left a bad taste in her mouth. So when the cops repeatedly interrupted Nancy and Rudy from getting from point A to point B on date nights, over time it began to leave a mark, even making her a bit protective over the issue. The racial profiling felt like an injustice that shouldn't exist. Whether you were Black, White, Mexican, Asian, or whatever...if you weren't bothering anyone, in her estimation, no one should be bothering you. The two forged through the profiling, continuing to date even as it ruffled some feathers in their respective families and communities. "In those days, all I thought of was how great this was," recalls Nancy, "and how much love, I was falling in love...[for the] first time ever."

In 1969, Rudy and Nancy married. A few months later, they had their first son – me, your humble co-author Patrick. And two years after that, my sister Denise was born. We were a pretty happy crew. Dad was gregarious...always wanting to go out on excursions. Mom was shy and perhaps a bit of a homebody...so the dynamic worked out for both of them. The young couple hardly had two nickels to rub together. We first moved to dad's hometown of Gardena, and then bounced around to a series of apartments in my mom's hometown of Torrance. The two scrimped and saved for a couple of years. In those days, it wasn't unheard of to get into a mortgage with a few thousand dollars. By 1975, they'd pocketed enough to start looking to buy a house. So they turned to a realtor friend of my father's, George, and he began showing them properties. They looked at a ton of places. But, in hindsight, mom doesn't think he had their best interests in mind. "He just wanted to sell us a house."

The realtor was using a technique of that time – and that was, first show the client dump after dump after dump. "And I mean, places in Gardena that you couldn't have a dog live in," mom remembers. And then once they saw those, the realtor would take them to the house that they really wanted to sell them. The Internet wasn't around at the time, so you couldn't pop onto Zillow, or Trulia or any number of the other real estate sites to get a lay of the land. So for most people in the midst of this grift, it was hard to get a handle on what was happening. "So...we told him what we wanted," recalls Nancy. "I wanted a community with kids. It just was really important to me that we lived in a community with kids where you could play outside." So they looked at a bunch of houses, and they found one in Carson, California – a suburb of Los Angeles, just south of a little known town at the time called

Compton. "A new community…new homes. Lots of kids in that neighborhood," mom fondly remembers. "There were kids everywhere. And we were still young enough and everybody else was still young enough to have children." With so many young families, the neighborhood felt up-and-coming… with lots of culture. There were Samoans, Blacks, Whites, and Asians. For our family, the home was perfect. It was only two bedrooms, but had a family room, a living room, and a big kitchen. It was also a relatively new community. The city had only incorporated a few years earlier in 1968. The yards were well kept. It looked like a solidly middle-class neighborhood. "To me, it was like this utopia," recalls mom. "As a young family, here I am in my mid 20s or so, and I'm just thinking this is like perfect. It's [the] kind of neighborhood I grew up in without the farmland…lots of kids, kids riding bikes in the street, playing ball and all of this kind of stuff. And we just, we fell in love with the house."

So mom and dad brought a few people to come check it out. "Before we moved in, my brother-in-law, Terry, he came over and he said, 'Don't do it.'" She brought her dad and oldest brother to the house. And they warned them against buying it as well. The neighborhood was about fifty percent Black with a smattering of everything else. Everyone that advised her against moving in expressed that they were worried they wouldn't fit into the demographics of the area. But having grown a bit sensitive to the racial profiling just a few years earlier, mom was a bit protective over the issue. So any attempt to dissuade them from living in an ethically diverse community was quickly discarded. "A lot of it was because it was a minority neighborhood," remembers mom. "But to me that should not have mattered…we were friendly people that didn't care what color you were. So how much more perfect can it be? Because if I don't care what color you are, you're not going to care what color I am, right?"

So mom and dad purchased the house. It was a proud day. We took the classic family picture in front of our new home. But what the young couple didn't realize at the time was that this area of Carson was going through a major shift. Within a matter of just a few years, our four-person crew would be the only "white" family in the neighborhood. By the second week, troubling signs started to show. The weekday routine was that when mom got off work, she'd scoop us up from our babysitters and we'd head home. But on one particular day when we pulled up to our driveway, the police were at our house. Someone had broken in.

The robber had gotten into the garage through a backyard access door and tried to kick in a door leading into the kitchen...you could still see the footprint. When that didn't work he came around the backyard and threw something through the window. "I can say I was more pissed off and angry at the mess that they left. I mean it looked like they picked up the house and shook it. It was beyond ransacking." They took anything of value – which wasn't much. Everything we moved into the house with was secondhand. "We just had no money," says mom. "The bed that we slept in was my mom and dad's." The thief was brazen. He hit up a few houses on the block all at once. Someone heard him and called the cops, and they nabbed the scum as he was robbing the place across the street. For me, it was a coming of age moment. The criminal had a big black Glad trash bag and filled it with whatever he could from the homes he robbed. When the police brought the bag into our house for the stolen items to be identified, I locked in on something that is still burned into my brain to this day. The bag was tied shut with my red bandana. The thief used my favorite piece of cowboy gear to secure his ill-gotten gains. It was the first moment where I realized that there were people out there that wanted to take what I had. As unfortunate as the situation was, it could have been chalked up to a fluke. A bad seed made his way into the neighborhood – but it was hopefully an anomaly. However, another red flag was about to go up.

A few months after moving in, our parents threw a house-warming party. They invited friends, family, and the realtor that sold them the house...who showed up carrying a gun "for protection" he said. "And I immediately thought to myself, 'You've sold us a home in a neighborhood that you feel compelled to arm yourself when you come to visit us for a house-warming,'" recalls mom. "But again, I'm still so young and naive. I just, I wouldn't let it sink in."

By the time that we'd moved in, my mom had been using a babysitter near her work to watch my sister and I during the day. So to make sure I had someone to come home to once I started elementary school, mom arranged for us to use the babysitter's address to attend the public school there. The area was made up predominantly of Hispanics, Blacks, and Asians...with a sprinkling of Whites. It had the feeling of an elementary school version of *Welcome Back Carter*...if you understand that reference.

As we settled into our new home in Carson over the first few years, houses were going up for sale throughout the neighborhood. The Samoans, Asians, and Whites were putting their houses on the market...and the properties were eventually scooped up exclusively by Black families. The process happened over just a few years. By the time I'd become old enough to play outside by myself, roughly seven years old in the 70s, we were the only so-called "White" family in the neighborhood. Everyone else was Black. And I mean every-one. But honestly, I didn't notice, and neither did my sister Denise. The local park had a modern dance class for kids, and my mom signed up my sister. My mom remembers a time that

Denise performed at a local fair in Pomona. "I remember one time somebody saying to Denise, 'Are you the only White kid performing?' And she thought, 'I don't know.' She didn't even think about it. I thought, 'Okay. This is good.' And she was the only White kid."

My sister and I had two good friends in Carson...a brother and sister duo named Maurice and Heather Simms. Maurice and I would play pick up football games on the street with the neighborhood kids. All the guys would take out their BMX bikes to a local vacant lot that had huge hills to *drop in*, and mounds of dirt we'd use as jumping ramps. On the weekends, Maurice and I would run the streets with the rest of the local boys. Denise was too young to be outside without supervision, but she'd play with Heather either at our place or at the Simms' house right down the street. For a few years everything was relatively normal. We got some looks around town for sure, but we were largely left alone. My baby brother, Casey was born, when I was about nine and a half, and around that time the atmosphere oddly began to shift. An animosity towards our family began to brew. It seemed like overnight, my name went from "Patrick" to "Honky"...and my friends pretty quickly dwindled down to just Maurice. A few years ago I was having dinner with a prominent Hollywood TV writer and somehow the topic of the racial slur "honky" came up. He laughed at how un-scary it sounded. "Well, the word takes on a whole new meaning when you're surrounded by five or six Black guys yelling it at you," I responded. The idea was so foreign to him he didn't know how to respond. But that's what I was going through as 1980 arrived.

Being the only sibling that was allowed to play outside by myself, I got that slur regularly thrown at me. Denise, who'd just reached the proper age to start playing outside without constant supervision, began to feel the heat as well while trying to enter a game with the neighborhood girls called *Double Dutch* – a method of skipping rope with two long jump ropes turning in opposite directions. The game takes at least three players, typically girls – two who stand at a distance apart from each other and a third, the jumper, stands in the middle. Each girl on the outside holds one end of the ropes in each hand and quickly whip them around in opposite directions, and the jumper has to time their jumps to avoid being hit by the rope. When the neighborhood girls were playing the game, Denise only felt comfortable walking up to the group if she was with Heather. "I was terrible at it," says Denise, "and they didn't like when I tried to jump in because I would mess it up." But her and Heather were inseparable at the time, so Denise would join in if Heather wanted to play. Denise continues, "I would only walk up to these girls if Heather was by my side and they would only hand me the ropes. I was only allowed to be the spinner of the ropes." Denise and Heather never saw each other through the lens of color. But over time, Denise remembers that the other girls did – and they began to vocalize it. "And there is one time that I remember that I was going out to the car to get something out of the car, and across the street [were] a lot of the neighborhood girls and they start singing this song to me. 'Black is beautiful. White is funky. If you don't believe me, ask a White honky.' And they said it really loud. And I thought, 'Oh, my gosh, some of those are my friends that I play jump rope with.'" Denise was scared, and embarrassed. So she jumped in the car and hid. She didn't even know what a "honky" was – no one ever called her that before. But she knew it wasn't good.

The confrontations began to escalate, but one encounter in particular pretty much ended any chance of playing outside again. I was turning eleven. So I invited my elementary school friends over for a sleep over birthday party. Everyone wanted to go to the arcade, so my mom dropped us off down the street at the Carson Mall. We dumped a bunch of quarters on *Pacman*, *Asteroids*, and *Space Invaders*, and then went outside to wait for my mom to pick us up. But as we were waiting, an older black teenager must have seen us as easy prey...and pulled a knife on me, demanding we give him money. "I remember I was with mom," Denise recalls. "And we were going to pick you guys up in the front of the mall, but you guys were waiting in the back. So there was a miscommunication." But because there were no cell phones at the time, they had to either wait, or come up with some other plan to find us. So mom decided to drive around the back to see if we were there. Denise continues, "I remember coming around the corner and the looks on your faces was just complete fear...it was just terrifying. Then you weren't allowed to go to the mall anymore." From then on, we were largely confined to the house. "I don't have a lot of memories of playing outside," recalls Denise. "We really weren't allowed unless mom maybe sat outside with us."

One of the few times Denise was allowed to play outside unsupervised was when she got a new bike and one of her good friends Shannon spent the night. The two begged mom for Shannon to ride my BMX, and Denise would give her new Pink Panther bike a spin. Mom said yes, as long as they stayed within eyesight of the house. "And we were just riding around the front in circles in the street," remembers Denise, "and we put the bikes down on the grass, then ran into the house to get a drink of water and come back out and the bikes were already gone."

We were now restricted to indoors, but things were getting so bad that just making our way between the front door of our house and the car created opportunities for confrontation. On one instance, we were outside in the car ready to go inside the house, and a neighborhood teenager that was pretty friendly had an unfamiliar boy playing basketball with him across the street. "The friend...started making the white comments and the honky comments," recalls mom. "Then he came over and I rolled the window up and he spit on the window." I'll never forget that. It was a big healthy loogie from a guy pushing the age to vote. We couldn't get out of the car until he was out of sight. The attacks shifted from verbal to a bit more aggressive. We'd have wine bottles thrown on the porch, and beer cans thrown on the front lawn like it was some kind of vacant lot where people discarded whatever trash was in their hands. People would yell "honky" through their laughter as they drove by. "And then when I went out one time," says mom, "we had two cars with locks on the gas caps...they were crazy glued shut. We had to have somebody come out and pry the gas caps off." It became open season.

No longer able to get to us on the street, they started to break down the boundary of our home. That's when the break-ins started up again...in full force. It'd been years since someone had broken into the house. But then we came home one day and our front door was open. We'd been robbed. Then the next month we came home...again, the front door was open. Robbed. "I felt like it was like a monthly thing there for a while," recalls Denise. It was happening so often that it became hard to keep track...one ransacking of the house just bled into the next. If I had to guess, I'd say twelve to fifteen times over the course of the next year and a half. We'd come home and the house would be completely torn apart, in the bedroom all of the clothes pulled from the drawers, mattresses flipped over. My sisters favorite *Little Twin Star* pencils all over the grown...stepped on and broken. "Our house was so ransacked," says Denise. "And then I remember one time they kicked the dog... and Benji was just laying there, couldn't

move and was just whining and crying." It was traumatic to
see our beloved dog Benji cowering in the corner in pain.
Coming home to that month after month was such a violation.
"It's like you lived in a glass house, and after a while that's
what it was like," adds mom.

It was obvious we were being targeted because we didn't
see the police rolling up to any of the neighbors' houses, just
ours...the only non-Blacks in town. Our place was not even
remotely the nicest in the area either. It would be fair to say
that it was on the lower value end of the neighborhood spec-
trum. The cars in our driveway, an old beat-up Mustang and a
Toyota pickup, also didn't scream money. After a few times,
the invaders weren't even taking anything anymore...it was
just a complete annihilation of the interior. "There was nothing to take. Because it was a monthly thing and they saw that,
why did they continue coming back,' says Denise. "If you're
not finding anything, what is the point? It's harassing."

After a while, with the number of break-ins racking up and
no one getting arrested, reporting the robbery to the police
became a big waste of time. At times, Mom and dad didn't
even bother calling...they just cleaned it up. But Denise and
I, maybe out of exasperation, just left our room ransacked.
Why bother when they'd just be back in a few weeks. On one
occasion when our parents did call the cops, I remember an
officer coming into our bedroom and asking, "Oh, did they
do this to your room?" and I responded, "No, that's how the
room has always looked." We just gave up and submitted to
the ransacked look. I asked my mom for the first time recently
why we didn't leave the neighborhood. "Rudy did not want to
move," she said. "He just didn't want to go through the trouble
of doing it all. Even with the robberies, that kind of stuff just
did not faze him." Something was obviously brewing within
my father. Something abnormal. His sister would later tell me

that he returned from the Vietnam War a different man. The experience somehow scarred him. That may have been part of the issue, but not all of it. As a father today, I see that it's the man's job to keep the family safe. And dad was failing miserably in that regard. "He didn't like change," adds mom. "He was not going to move. I could move if I wanted to, but he was going to stay there in that house until everything blew up." And everything was about to blow up...even further.

With "honky" becoming our de facto nickname, it wasn't hard to tell that we were being targeted because we were white. Thankfully, all of the break-ins occurred during the weekdays when we weren't home. But it was only a matter of time before our luck ran out.

**

It was December 1982, just a few days away from Christmas, and I woke up at the regular time in the morning...but to my surprise mom wasn't there. That never happened. I mean never. "She went to visit Aunt Maryann," was the explanation I got from my dad. Even as a pre-teen, I knew something was off. My dad followed our same weekday ritual...he dropped my sister, my little brother, and I off at our babysitter's in Gardena. Then later that morning, while my sister Denise and I were walking with a group of friends to a park across the street from our elementary school, I asked her where she thought mom went. And that's when she told me what happened.

I've been thinking a lot about how to tell this story and, perhaps more importantly why I'd even want to share such an incredibly personal, and trying time for our family. It can be emotionally taxing and make one feel exposed...even vulnerable, as this story admittedly has at times. I discussed it with Adryana, my mom and sister, and also dug through some of my old journals to review my thoughts on this era throughout the years. And what I gathered is that for as long as I can remember I've wanted to tell the story of what our family endured over that nearly decade long span of my childhood in Carson. The first real short story that I ever wrote was in my ninth grade English class...and the story I told was about this very phase in my life. So why, since my freshman year in high school, have I felt compelled to talk about our Carson experience? The conclusion I came to is that it's a story that is rarely told.

The number of movies about white racism against blacks seems endless. *Mississippi Burning, To Kill a Mockingbird, Hidden Figures, 12 Years a Slave, The Help, Get Out, Django Unchained, The Color Purple, 42, The Butler, Fruitvale Station, Driving Miss Daisy, Selma, The Birth of a Nation, Blackkklansmen.* The list goes on and on and on. But can you name one movie that addresses the reverse? Try to come up with a single film that tackles black racism towards whites in a negative light. Go head and name one. Just one. You can't. Why is that? Why have Hollywood and the mainstream media and our literary industry stayed away from that topic? I think I know the answer, and we'll get to that before the end of this story. But I knew from a very young age that this lived experience was incredibly important to share because of the powerful lesson that can be extracted from it...a lesson that our cultural gatekeepers do not want Americans to contemplate.

What we lived through in Carson – the racial slurs, the property damage, the terrorizing – was too much for any family to endure. But what happened on that night in December 1982 was something different...something even darker. To this day we only refer to it with two words: the incident.

On that night my dad went out to celebrate his birthday, leaving my mom, sister, baby brother and I home alone. Us kids were asleep, when a man broke into the house. "I just remember waking up to hearing mom like just scream really fast," recalls Denise. "Like she got scared."

"I just remember him running up behind me and slamming me from behind," describes mom. "Almost knocking the wind out of me and now I'm off the ground."

"And I just open my eyes, and I remember our bunk bed was facing the hallway and there was a light on in the living room," says Denise. "So it lit up the hallway. And then I see mom get dragged to her room by a guy. He had [an] afro with a hat…and it wasn't completely sitting on his head very well." It was a surreal moment for a half asleep, little girl. Denise thought she was dreaming. She continues, "So I just kind of laid there and I could just hear her crying. And I just remember lying there and I was terrified. I was in shock."

My mom's yelp didn't wake my baby brother or me. For years I wished it had. The guilt over that issue stayed with me well into my adulthood. But as a father now, knowing the difference in strength between a man and a pre-pubescent boy… well, perhaps it was a good thing that I didn't wake. I was twelve, my sister ten, and my brother three. We didn't own a gun. I was probably in no place to challenge that savage. At least, that's the way I like to think about it now. "That was my biggest fear, is I didn't want him to hurt the kids," recalls mom, "and so…then we got to the bedroom. And I thought, 'Fuck. This is not going to happen.' I said, 'My kids are in the other room.'" It didn't matter. So she tried a different tactic, "My husband just went to the store. He's gonna be right back," she told him. That got a reaction. He picked her up, dragged her to the front door, deadbolted the door, and then returned to the room. "Goes back in and does his thing, and then left," says mom.

"And then I saw him again run out…of the room," recalls

Denise. Mom could hear him running down the street, so she knew he didn't have a car in the vicinity. When it was all over, she just wanted to crawl up in a ball. "As a young woman to me, I was going to fight it off," says mom. "There was nobody ever gonna be able to do that to me because I was going to fight it off. I'd die first. But when it's happening and your kids are in the other room and the fear and the paranoia sets in... and your body locks. And that's how I pretty much was when [Rudy] got home." It wasn't long after that dad got home. "He came to the door and knocked on it and wondered why I had locked it," recalls mom. "And then I told him what happened." Denise remembers the moment. "As she's telling him about it, she's closing our bedroom door. But she's telling him what just happened, how she was raped," says Denise. "And then I thought, 'Oh my gosh, this really happened.'"

Mom was, of course, shook to the core. So she left that night to stay at my Aunt Maryann and Uncle Randy's place. She was in no shape to be around us kids. The next morning, when I asked my sister where she thought mom was, she told me what happened the night before, and I was devastated. Denise hadn't yet told anyone what she saw. So when mom returned home a few days later, I let her know that Denise got a good look at the guy. After some time mom went down to the police station with her friend Suzanne to report what happened and learned that they'd already had a profile on this monster. "I was the 13th victim," says mom. "One woman had been raped twice. Her husband would go out of town for a week or two weeks at a time." Carson had a serial rapist on its hands.

After talking to all of the victims, the police department created a profile of the sicko. He was a young Black man of average height. Because he ran away on foot – they suspected he didn't have a car, or was local. He also had a unique characteristic...he had Asian looking eyes. I guess it's in our blood to be proactive, because I remember mom searching for the guy herself, venturing into previously uncharted areas of the neighborhood. Denise recalls this as well. "We lived there our whole childhood, for years, and we were driving down streets that we had never been down. You know, we were starting to get deep." In hindsight, it was understandable. She wanted to catch the animal. And given the experience that we had with police in Carson, we didn't trust that they'd find the guy.

But in parallel, the police began to hone in on a potential suspect – a young black man in his early twenties living in our neighborhood...only a few blocks away from our home. Just a few weeks into the New Year, law enforcement began to stake out his house – carefully watching the property. At some point, they decided to make a move and bring him in for questioning. But coincidently, just as they swarmed the house, his younger brother, an eighteen year-old young Black man, was riding up on his bike. He had Asian looking eyes. When he saw the commotion, he thought the police were in fact coming for him. So he turned around and bolted down the street on his bike. The police took chase and caught him. And once they did, they began drilling down, not on the initial twenty-something guy at the residence, but instead his eighteen year-old brother. It wasn't long after the arrest that my mom got a call from my aunt. "Mary Jo called and she said they arrested somebody, it was in the Daily Breeze. And she read me the article."

The police eventually called my mom and asked if her and my sister would come down to try and identify the sicko in a police line up. Denise was terrified. Aside from maybe seeing it on some cheesy TV show, she didn't know what to expect. Was the guy going to be in the same room with her? Would he be able to see her? Is he going to yell at her? "I had no idea what to expect, so I was terrified," admits Denise. "I just couldn't eat that day and I just did not want to go. But mom was just like, 'Do this for me. You're gonna be fine. We're safe. We're going to be at the police station. We'll be fine.'" So mom and Denise went down to the station with the twelve other women that were assaulted. "All I remember is he was number four," recalls Denise. "They took turns stepping forward and then when he stepped forward, I just said, 'Oh, my gosh, it's number four. Number four.' And so apparently, mom and I picked out the same guy."

But it wasn't over for them...they still had to testify in court. Denise recalls having to sit right across from the monster. She was tongue-tied with fear. "I remember the judge had me say my name. And I sat there for a minute and I'm like, 'What is my name?'" The prosecutor asked Denise to point out the guy. But she didn't want to have any eye contact with him. She was hoping that she could just spot him with her peripheral vision and point in his general direction. She wasn't so lucky...Denise had to look directly at him and identify the animal. "And that was just terrifying, because after that...I don't remember walking out of the court. I don't remember anything I said after that." She wasn't on the stand long. The prosecutor asked her a simple question. "What do you recognize about him," he asked. Denise said he had Chinese eyes. "And the prosecutor was Chinese or Asian of some descent... that kind of like cracked everybody up," remembers mom. When it was over, Denise just wanted to get the hell out of there. She wanted it to be over.

The man was convicted and sentenced to a little over a decade in prison...what seems like a paltry amount for a clearly incurably sick young man. Does anyone think that someone capable of viciously raping thirteen women can ever be rehabilitated?

After the incident and through the trial, the status quo remained. We were still prisoners in our own home...largely unable to go outside other than to get into the car and leave. Everyone wanted to move – that is, everyone except my father. "He didn't want to move," says mom. "He wanted to stay, period. That was all there was to it." Weeks turned into months until dad slipped right back into his old ways...frequently leaving us home alone at night. As desperately as my mom tried to keep the family together – this couldn't go on any longer. Something had taken hold of our father...the beginnings of a very long, dark journey with addiction. My mom had had enough. She kicked him out and immediately put the house up for sale.

Mom began looking to move us back to her hometown. "I remember going house hunting in Torrance and just being so excited," says Denise. One of the houses that we looked at was a cute three-bedroom in North Torrance. The backyard had a playhouse, with carpet and a working light. It was modest, but larger than our Carson home. And compared to what we'd endured for nearly a decade, it was like a little slice of heaven. So mom bought the place. I remember our Uncle Pat helping us pack up and move out of the Carson house. It was sad that we were leaving our friends Heather and Maurice behind, really the only bright spot of that neighborhood. But we were all ready to put that place behind us forever. Denise recalls the moment we left. "I just remember just saying to myself, 'I'm never going back there again.'"

The day that we moved into our new Torrance home was incredible. We'd finally be able to go to a school within walking distance and play outside again! Mom didn't have to sit outside to watch us while we were playing. No longer did we have to walk around in groups for safety. We could roam the streets on our bikes, and leave them sitting in the driveway without them getting stolen in thirty seconds. "I just remember it being glorious," says Denise, "and just so happy to get out of there, and just have a normal life like my friends did when I would go to my friend's house and go play outside." The first thing I did in our new home was jump on my GT BMX bike and cruised the neighborhood...making my way to the adult school down the street called Hamilton, checking out the Little League baseball field in the back, riding through the parking lot behind the church next door. To most people, this little trip would seem mundane. But for me, it was the first time I can say that I truly understood the meaning of the word "freedom."

As incredible as it was for Denise, Casey, and I, it was a struggle for mom. She was now going it alone – with a mortgage payment triple what it was in Carson. She worked every single minute she could to make ends meet. When she wasn't, she picked up side gigs babysitting. When winter came around, she employed her crafting skills to make octopus dolls that she sold as Christmas presents. Mom would grab used socks and clump them together to form a head. Then she'd wrap yarn over this makeshift cranium, braid the excess strings into tentacles, and glued eyes, a nose, and lips to the head – topping each octopus head with a tiny beanie. Those things sold like hot cakes every year. "I did everything I could to make money," mom recalls. "We drove old cars. We ate cheap. We never took vacations except camping. Think about it. Never."

As the years went by, we had our struggles, including with our father. But we weren't under siege like in Carson. Torrance was ethnically diverse – Hispanics, Japanese, Koreans, Filipinos, Hawaiians, Whites and Blacks – that's what made up our group of friends. Mom always instilled in us the idea that our experience in Carson was not representative of the Black community as a whole. Even with the brutality of the

situation, prejudice never took hold of her or her kids' souls. I
asked mom about how we were able to avoid forming any racial animosity after our experience in Carson. "I think because
you had enough good people in your life, and good Black people in your life, and good minorities and good majorities and a
mixture of cultures…going to school in Gardena, you had all
the mixture of cultures there." Largely because of our mom,
we were able to isolate and compartmentalize our experience
in Carson as just a series of incidents in a bad neighborhood.

Mom continued to teach us to reach out to the Black community…and stay connected to it. Unlike most non-Black
families, in many ways Black American culture was our culture. In our formative years we lived in an all-Black neighborhood. Taking in the music, the attitude, and the energy. Even
though we were shunned by the neighborhood over time, we
understood the African-American experience. Throughout
the years people have told me, oddly, that they thought I was
Black. One Black man I met said that he sensed, "a hint of
tint" in me. Carson was in the rearview mirror, but it wasn't
totally out of sight. However, one event in particular seemed
to bring our entire Carson experience to a close.

The LA Riots hit in 1992. It was a surreal time. The week
that followed gave a quick glimpse at how quickly society can
breakdown into complete chaos. With the dust barely settled,
mom wanted to do her part to help the Black community recover. About a week after the tragic events it was Mother's
Day. "We were like, 'Where do you want to go,'" Denise remembers, "And she wanted to go to South Central." Mom's
job as a technician for the phone company meant she had to
drive through a lot of the burnt areas for her work. She also
had work colleagues that were familiar with the neighborhoods and helped mom identify a good church for us to bring
donations. "I felt comfortable because I had to drive through

those neighborhoods to work," explains mom. "I knew where you had to be careful. And I knew you don't go down an alley unless you have to…those kinds of things. I felt very comfortable in the neighborhoods as a general rule driving up and down the streets." And having lived in Carson for all of those years, it prepares you a bit for tough areas.

So mom wanted us to take the money we were going to spend on her for Mother's Day, and instead, buy groceries to donate to the church. So we went to the local market, bought canned foods and other odds and ends, bagged it all up and headed for the church mom identified in South Central. But when we arrived, there was a bit of unease. We weren't sensing animosity, but rather the organizers at the church had a hint of concern for us in their eyes. The area was not yet safe. So they hurriedly showed us where we should place everything for it to be divvied out later to the community – then they sent us on our merry way. They were concerned for our safety. But all in all it was an unforgettable experience. "And it just felt so good," recalls Denise. "And it felt like, wow, this is something we should do all the time and not just for a Mother's Day gift, because it just felt so good to help people." It was an incredibly rewarding experience. For some reason, it felt like through that moment of giving back on Mother's Day, we were ceremonially forgiving Carson for what that neighborhood did to us. "You would think after something so traumatic like that, that happened to mom," says Denise, "you would think that maybe sometimes people end up being, you know, a little racist after that or harboring some serious bad feelings. And [mom] didn't. We went to the root of it. We went to the heart of South Central there. And we were all exposed. And it was just a wonderful experience."

Which brings us back to the question, what does the Black community need to do to finally overcome the legacy of slavery?

Throughout my life, I've often thought back to our time in Carson and wondered why my name went so abruptly from Patrick to "Honky" with the neighborhood kids. In the moment, I just didn't understand it. At my elementary school, no one ever called me that...and I'd say roughly 25% of the student body was black. But for some reason just one city over, amongst kids I'd known for years, my name became a racial slur. Then about ten years ago, Adryana and I began touring elementary schools to send our daughter to, and at one school we dropped into a second grade class in session as part of the tour. I was immediately struck by what they were being taught. The kids were learning about the water fountain for the "colored" people. "Why in the hell are they teaching kids about this at such a young age," I thought. It reminded me of a time in my elementary school years when we too were taught about racism.

In 1977, the miniseries *Roots* aired. Although it claimed to be a true story at the time, it was later discovered to be a fictional drama about the journey of Kunta Kinte, a man who was enslaved in Africa and brought to America. The series was a brutal and graphic depiction of slavery, and debuted at a time when a popular TV show was watched by literally everyone. Many teachers began using the show as part of their lesson plans in elementary school...including in one of my classes. There may have been some other affects, but I don't recall it creating any animosity on campus at the time – likely because we were an ethnically diverse school. Everyone had relationships with people from other races. It felt like we were all on the same playing field...we were all poor. But in an all black neighborhood like Carson, I could see how watching *Roots* could have a completely different affect. A few years ago, Adryana and I spoke to YouTube stars Diamond & Silk and they brought up this same lesson plan:

Diamond: "Okay, so I may not have paid attention in school but this is what they would do, they would play this show called *Roots*. They would play that show, and that's how you learned the history of what was going on, and it's really the truth. And now, that kinda stuff would outrage people. But what they did not do is they did not tell us who sold black people into slavery, because really it was other Africans that sold other Africans into slavery. They didn't give you the details. They took a story and sensationalized it and that's how you learned it."

Silk: "And the more that they continued to play that story *Roots*, over and over and over, and more stories like that, what it did, it kept you stuck in the pain of your ancestors. You begin to believe that that's you. And that's happening to me and my people right now, even though you've never picked cotton a day in your life. Even though you [were] never a slave under any slave master a day in your life. And that's being implemented into the new generation that they feel like, 'Oh I'm so in pain, I've been whipped with many strikes, and the white man is the one that's out to get me.' That's taught mentality."

I'd eventually have an awakening on the issue of race relations – coming to the conclusion that slavery and the Civil Rights Movement should not be taught to students until well after their elementary school years because young minds simply aren't prepared to process that information without extremely negative effects on them and society as a whole. I believe it's a big part of the reason why we have the racial divisions that exist today. Racism is seeded in us. We're taught it. And our so-called leaders just use it to inflame the masses and retain or regain power.

So I'd like to give some friendly advice to my Black American brothers and sisters out there. I'd like to humbly suggest that to overcome the ugly legacy of slavery, you need to forgive those few long-dead Americans that actually owned slaves... forgive them and move on. Don't fall into the trap of victimhood created by Hollywood, the media, and our educational system. Our family was directly attacked for many years by Black people within our community because of the color of our skin. We were attacked...not our ancestors, not our grandfather's grandfather's grandparents. We were attacked. And we never held the entire Black community responsible for what we endured, as our cultural elites want you to do against White Americans...for slavery that you never endured. We could have easily let the victimhood mentality infect our soul. We could have blamed an entire group. We could have conflated the vicious attack against our mother with all of the other neighborhood attacks on our family...even though that Black man didn't attack her because she was White. He attacked her because he was a monster. We could have let the racism that we endured stain our view of the world. But we didn't. We let go of the terrorizing and the pain and the anger and the fear... and chalked it up to just a series of bad apples.

To my Black brothers and sisters out there, many of us Hispanics and Whites and Asians understand your suffering. "When you look at me and you see this Caucasian woman," says Denise, "if a minority looked at me and said, 'She would never know what I've had to go through.' But I know. I know what that feels like to be the minority."

It's time to let go of the suffering of your ancestors, because holding onto that ugly history only allows power hungry opportunists to exploit that pain intentionally seeded in you at a very young age...opportunists like Elizabeth Warren. "I believe it's time to start the national, full-blown conversation about reparations in this country," said Warren at a 2019 CNN town hall. Warren and her ilk have no intention on delivering reparations to Black Americans. She just wants to use ancestral pain for personal gain – as Warren did when she claimed to be American Indian when she clearly was not…to advance her career. My Black brothers and sisters out there, don't let anyone continue to frame you as a victim, because when they successfully do, it's a mental prison that only extends the legacy of slavery to no end.

EIGHT

Sanctuary

*Do illegal immigrants commit less
crime than American citizens?*

Our mainstream media has made something abundantly clear
- immigrants outperform American citizens in just about
every way possible, except for perhaps in one area...com-
mitting crime. "Immigrant teens are less likely to do drugs,
commit crime, and engage in violence," said one MSNBC
report. "Immigrants are disproportionately unlikely to be in
prison," claimed a PBS report. "Immigrants are less likely to
be criminals than U.S. citizens," offered Fusion TV. "In the
cities where you have the most undocumented immigrants,
you have the least amount of crime," argued another media
pundit. This narrative is constantly pumped out to the public
by the mainstream media. But is it true? Do illegal immigrants
commit less crime than American citizens? To find the answer,
we're going to tell the story of an immigrant and a veteran...
and what we learn in the process may completely change your
view on law and order.

**

Sabine Durden wasn't born in America. She came into the world in Nuremberg, Germany in 1957. By her own summation, her childhood had a few hiccups here and there, but all in all it was pretty easy. She had loving parents and a sister ten years her senior. In 1978 she met a young soldier stationed in Germany serving in the U.S. Army. A year later they were married, and by 1982 they had a son. "I gave birth to my best friend…to the love of my life, Dominic," recalls Sabine. "He was born January 22nd, 1982 in Nuremberg – the same hospital I was born in."

The young family remained in Germany when Dominic was born. Sabine wanted her son to be bilingual because she knew eventually the family would have to move to the States when her husband's station assignment changed. So when Dominic started elementary school, over the course of a week he spent three days in German kindergarten and two days in American kindergarten. Dominic's nickname was "German Chocolate" – he was half black, half German – and Sabine remembers people being drawn to her son because of his compassionate nature. "He would sit with the snotty-nosed kid that nobody wanted to sit next to at lunch," she recalls. "He would play with the kids that were left alone on the playground. And so I noticed him already establishing this social behavior of truly caring for others."

When Dominic was ten, his father got orders from the military. He was going to be stationed in California. The family was of course sad to leave their friends and family behind, especially Sabine's parents that had become a big part of Dominic's life. But Sabine was equally excited about the family making its way to the Golden State. "At that time, I was a little naïve. I thought, 'Okay we're probably close to Beverly Hills and Universal Studios, Disneyland, and to the beach.'" So when the family arrived in California, Sabine's husband showed them around – taking them to those signature spots as well as the Hollywood Walk of Fame. She was a bit star-struck by the tour of the area. But after a few days of spoiling the family, Sabine's husband said it was time to go to where he was stationed. So they started driving northeast. And they drove a little more…and they kept going. Day turned into night as they drove over the El Cajon Pass – a highway be-tween the San Gabriel and San Bernardino mountains. As any-one that has traversed that roadway for the first time knows, leaving the Los Angeles area over the El Cajon Pass is a clear indication that you are entering a remote area – something that wasn't familiar to Sabine.

"And it was getting darker," Sabine recalls, "and I could barely see any light. So now the tears started running but I didn't want to alarm my son. So I just kept myself together. And then we arrive in Victorville and I thought that was it. And no it wasn't. We drove another hour and I arrived in Bar-stow, and stayed at a hotel. And the next morning when I woke up, I was in the shock of my life." They were in the desert. Just about as far away from the glitz and glamour of Hollywood as you can get. They spent a few months in Barstow, then moved to Fort Irwin, another half an hour drive into the desert. Sabine was a bit shell-shocked at first, but quickly learned a lesson – that she can make home wherever she's at. "I can't just cry for Germany you know…I got to make where I'm at the best place to be. And Fort Irwin became that."

Dominic went to school there with other kids that spoke German, but by then he spoke fluent English. They lived there for a few years. After some work, Sabine became a legal U.S. citizen in 1993, and then her husband left the service and the family moved to Moreno Valley, right next to Riverside, Cali-fornia. But Sabine and her husband's marriage started to fall apart and so in 2004 she filed for divorce. By then, Dominic was grown. He had high school behind him – and grown to a six foot three inch gentle giant. Dominic was heavily involved in community service with the fire department, volunteering and in emergency relief. That year he received an award for Volunteer of the Year. When asked at the time how he felt about receiving the award, Dominic responded, "There's no words that can describe it. I'm still in awe that I was even nominated...not something that I ever expected. Not something I'd ever been working for. Just with all the work I've put in...happy to be recognized." It was a proud day for the humble young man.

After the divorce, Sabine and her son became roommates. Dominic eventually found work as an editor and producer for a Moreno Valley TV outfit. But he got bored with things easily and was always looking for more. He learned how to fly and became part owner of a Cessna. But it was his joy in law enforcement that became his main driver. He began studying to become a motorcycle cop with hopes of one day being a helicopter pilot for the sheriff's department. Then in 2006, he entered law enforcement by becoming a 9-1-1 dispatcher for the Riverside Sheriff's Department. It was a perfect fit for his calm demeanor. Dominic had developed into a bit of a prankster, looking to get a laugh out of the people around him. He could be telling a joke to his coworkers, but if a call came in, he'd flip the switch and become dead serious. "He had I think three ring tones," recalls Sabine. "And so the police officers knew it was Dominic that was on the other line...and many told me they knew when they heard those three rings that they were in good hands and they would get home to their families."

By 2012, Dominic enjoyed what he was doing. He loved his coworkers...and they counted on him as a colleague and a friend. Him and his mom were best friends, and they were enjoying everything life had to offer. Sabine had also fallen in love again. Anthony, a San Diego post office worker, found his way into her heart and Dominic approved. "[Anthony] would come up on the weekends on his motorcycle and the three of us would ride our motorcycles together," says Sabine. "And so Anthony became a part of our life. And Dominic told me I would walk down the aisle with that man."

On July 11th of that year, Anthony and Sabine were getting ready to fly to Atlanta for Anthony's family reunion. Dominic took them to the airport in Ontario and Sabine can still remember every detail of this simple little trip to her flight. They stopped at a new restaurant called Miguel's. Dominic said he wasn't hungry, but Sabine wasn't having it. "Well, you sure you don't want to split a burger with me," Sabine asked as they got to the counter. "Sure mom. Okay, so I won't starve to death till you come back, I'm gonna have a half a burger with you," Dominic joked, as he rolled his eyes. This dynamic played out often between the two – Sabine worrying about her only child...Dominic ribbing his mom for her attentiveness. They continued their route to the airport. When they arrive at the passenger drop off area, the three popped out and Dominic pulled their bags from his truck. In the commotion of the unloading, Sabine stumbled over the curb and fell into Dominic. "And he picked me up and he twirled me around and he kissed me all over my face," Sabine fondly remembers. "And told me to have a good time. 'I'll see you in a week.'" Anthony thought their long goodbye was cute. "Man you guys act like you're gonna be gone for a year," Anthony joked, "And by the way Dominic, we got cameras up in the house so in case you have a wild party, we will watch everything." It was one of those brief little moments that make the love of family so fun. Sabine and Dominic hugged, she kissed her son goodbye, the two told each other how much they loved one another, and she watched as Dominic walked back to his truck and drove off.

Sabine and Anthony took a redeye flight to Atlanta. They were going to stay with his cousin but by the time the two arrived it was too early...they didn't want to wake him up. So they decided to go to a waffle house for breakfast. They ate, paid the bill, and as they walked back to the car, Sabine suddenly dropped. "I lost all feelings in my legs. It was like somebody unplugged me and Anthony didn't know what it was," recalls Sabine. "He thought I felt sick or jet lag, but that was weird."

They arrived at Anthony's cousin's house and the place was huge – with a home theater on the top floor. Sabine and Anthony set up their bags in the guest quarters on the bottom floor, but she couldn't keep her eyes open, so Sabine decided to laydown and get some rest while everyone else watched a movie. But as she tried to nap, her cell phone kept buzzing. For some reason she couldn't pick it up. She was feeling nervous. Something was off. "And I saw one text, it says, 'Please call me as soon as possible right now. This is Elaina, Dominic's best friend.'" Sabine got up and, unfamiliar with the house, began frantically looking for Anthony – running through a few rooms until she found him. "I yelled at him," she recalls, "I said, 'something happened to Dominic. We got a call.'" So she called the number, flipping the phone to speaker mode so Anthony could hear. A young lady answered the phone and began stuttering as she talked to Sabine. "And I said, 'Just let me talk to Dominic. Let me speak to him.' And she said, 'Well ma'am can, can you hold on a minute. I've got to get the Chief.'" Sabine was confused. Why get the Chief, she thought. "Just let me speak to Dominic, just let me talk to him," Sabine responded. The Chief suddenly jumped on the phone, Sabine recalls, "And those words that you hear on TV, in movies. I heard that all of a sudden when he said,

'I'm so sorry Ms. Durden, but Dominic got killed this morning.'" As Sabine heard the horrifying message standing in the kitchen with Anthony, his family members were parading into the room to meet his new girl. "He wanted to show me off proudly and so they started coming in," she remembers. "And all they find is this horrific scene of Anthony and I screaming in the kitchen on the floor."

Anthony and Sabine got the first flight back to California – crying the entire way. Part of her still couldn't believe what was happening. Maybe it was all just a bad joke, she thought. Dominic was a prankster. "I'm gonna kill him," she said to herself. "He played the worst prank ever." Sabine was in shock. She arrived back home and exited the plane. But as she walked down the stairs, Sabine saw three of Dominic's best friends standing there in the terminal and she just lost it. "I broke down. I passed out," Sabine says. "They dragged me to the car. And by then, I needed to see…I needed to know that it really happened. So I asked them, 'Please take me by the spot where he was killed.'"

So they took Sabine to the location. It was just three miles from their house. One of Dominic's best friends, a police officer, met her at the scene – still in shock. When they arrived at the intersection, Sabine could see marks on the street. "And then I see a spot and then I looked at Chris, the police officer, and he just nodded his head. And that's where my son took his last breath. So you stand at a spot and you know that your family has been wiped out. You never get to hug, kiss your child again. I'll never ride motorcycles again with him or get pranked by him." Dominic had been on his way to work when Juan Zacarias Lopez Tzun turned his truck in front of Dominic. He was on his motorcycle, and hit the car so hard that it killed him instantly. The impact threw Dominic into a wall on the sidewalk. Two marines driving behind him witnessed the horrific accident. One stayed with Dominic's lifeless body on the sidewalk, while the other took chase after Juan because he tried to flee the scene – ultimately catching him and holding him down until law enforcement arrived.

In the coming days Sabine was in shock. She came home to a house full of people, everyone crying. She was on autopilot. "You go through the [motions]. Your body tells you, okay… breathe. Blink. We didn't eat. We didn't drink." Sabine and Anthony had to remind each other of the most fundamental tasks. "I told Anthony, 'If you take a bite, I'll take a bite,'" she remembers. Slowly but surely Sabine started to come out of it. She initially thought the death of her son was just an accident. But she'd soon learn otherwise. Everyday they'd go to the spot where Dominic was killed and the wall was plastered with notes to her son. The entire sidewalk was saturated with flowers, candles and hundreds of people standing around just wanting to be as close to Dominic as possible. "And I remember one cop walked up to me," says Sabine, "and he said, 'I know they're telling you it was an accident. But you need to ask the D.A. to stop lying to you'…I had no clue what was to come."

**

Around the moment Sabine was learning the details of her son's death, Chris Odette, was facing an uncertain future. His wife had received a devastating health diagnosis. At the time, Chris was serving in the National Guard in Afghanistan. His eleven-year-old daughter Chrishia had noticed that there was something wrong with her mother, and so she tried to encourage her to see a doctor to get checked out. Mom finally scheduled an appointment – and without giving her a detailed diagnosis, the doctor told her to get her personal affairs in order.

"That's what had her so scared," remembers Chris. "She sent me an email asking me to call her as soon as possible." Chris immediately flew home to Coppell, Texas from Afghanistan and learned that his wife, Shiomara, had a rare form of cancer known as triple-negative. The doctors gave her two years to live. Chris' daughter was in Puerto Rico with family for a summer vacation and decided to come home early. To her surprise, her father was unexpectedly home with her mom. As the two tried to sit her down to tell her what was going on, before they could get anything out of their mouths Chrishia said, "Mom's got cancer, doesn't she."

This eleven-year-old girl was incredibly bright. Chris was deployed in Iraq when he and his wife enrolled Chrishia into a private elementary school. "And they said that she was so ahead of her class that they wanted permission to have her in first grade for half the day and in kindergarten for half the day just to keep her challenged," says Chris. It wasn't long before she'd be on the radar of colleges. When Chrishia was in fifth grade, her parents received a letter from Duke University. It turns out that her reading interpretation scores on the state assessment tests were so high that the renowned college wanted to offer Chrishia a scholarship when she graduated from high school. They already saw promise, and it shouldn't have been surprising to anyone. Chrishia had a knack for language and music. She spoke Spanish, was teaching herself Japanese, and would later enter German class. She also played the piano, violin, and guitar. Suffice it to say, Chrishia was one smart cookie. So even at eleven, she could read her mom and dad when she got home from that summer vacation in Puerto Rico.

Chrishia shared the news of her mom's progress with her friends, and handled it like a champ. "I just want to share some not so good news with you guys," she said at the time in a YouTube video she posted. "I've been blessed to have the most beautiful and awesome mom ever. Unfortunately, exactly one year ago we found out she has breast cancer. Throughout this entire year she has had several surgeries to remove the cancer, but the sucker keeps coming back." The doctor's prediction was accurate. Roughly two years later, on their thirteenth wedding anniversary, Shiomara Odette passed away. Chrishia was only twelve. When her mom passed, Chris had the difficult task of breaking the news to his daughter. A year later, the two would move to Rockwall, Texas. "I didn't know of course at the time, never heard of the term sanctuary city," says Chris, "and didn't know that Rockwall was a sanctuary city."

Because of her early scholastic abilities, Chrishia entered high school at the age of thirteen, a year younger than her peers. A little over a month after entering high school, Chris got a call that all parents of teenagers are familiar with. Chrishia had gone to school that day like any other day and later called her dad to ask if she could go to a birthday party for one of her classmates. Chris was excited his daughter was making new friends, and said yes – just asking for the location of the event. Later that same evening, Chrishia texted her dad and asked if after the party she could spend the night at her friend's house for a girls' night. "I told her initially no, because I hadn't met the parents," remembers Chris. "And I thought about something my wife had told me…not to be so protective over her. And just to let her have fun." And so Chris changed his mind. He told Chrishia that as long as she cleaned her room, she could have a sleepover at her friend's house. She agreed, and Chris said he needed the parents' contact information because he'd never met them. "You can meet them when you drop me off," said Chrishia.

So Chris picked her up from the birthday party and brought Chrishia home. "She was supposed to clean her room and the little turkey didn't clean her room. She kind of picked it up but of course, being a teenager and being excited...she didn't really clean it all the way." Chris took Chrishia to her friend's house where she'd be having the sleepover, arriving at about nine at night. But when he got to the front door, he realized he'd forgotten his cell phone inside his truck. The mom answered the door without her phone as well. So Chris told the mother that he'd have Chrishia text him the mother's phone number so the two could coordinate a pick up time the next morning. He said goodbye to his baby girl and left...happy that his daughter was finding her way in a new community.

Chris hadn't eaten yet, so on his way home he grabbed take out. The entire trip took maybe thirty minutes. But by the time he walked in his front door, another parent from his daughter's school urgently called Chris saying that another school parent was trying to get a hold of him – the same mother he'd just left his daughter with – and to call her as soon as possible. Apparently Chrishia had been in an accident. "And it didn't make any sense to me because she was supposed to be in this lady's house," says Chris. "So I couldn't understand. I thought maybe they went for a drive or something. And I called my daughter's phone and my daughter did not answer. It was the girl that she was with that answered the phone and she was frantic and said that the police could not find a pulse on my daughter."

Chris quickly jumped in the car, but in route to the accident, he tried to run a red light to get to his baby girl quicker and hit a car. By chance, the person he hit was an off-duty police officer. Within minutes the police arrived. Chris explained to them that he ran the light trying to get to his daughter that was in an accident. He asked if they could please call on the radio to find out the status of Chrishia and whether she was okay. "And they just kept telling me they need to get my information and they would go from there." The police took his driver's license and shortly after told him they were taking him to his daughter at the hospital. "When I got there, they took me in to a room and asked me her name and I told them. And they told me that my daughter was pronounced dead at the hospital." In just the amount of time it took him to get home, Chrishia was gone.

Three days later, a police officer came to Chris' house to get a sworn statement from him on what he knew – and that's when he found out what happened to his daughter. According to law enforcement, the mother of Chrishia's friend allowed the girls to walk to a grocery store a quarter of a mile away to buy some soda. They crossed at an intersection in front of a hospital without a crosswalk and successfully made it across. But in route, Chrishia dropped her cell phone in the street...so she went back onto the road to retrieve it. When she entered the street, all of the cars stopped...but one. Apparently, the driver didn't see Chrishia until the last second when he hit her. The officer told Chris that they believed she died instantly. But Chrishia's death certificate says that it took minutes for her to die. "My daughter," Chris struggles to say, "my baby girl was gone 30 minutes after I dropped her off."

Initially the accident report said the driver was at fault – but was later amended to place blame on Chrishia for crossing the street in a non-crosswalk. The police officer told Chris that the man who hit his daughter was a thirty-four year old that didn't have a driver's license. His name was Ramiro Tolentino Guevara. Chris asked the officer how a thirty-four year old man was driving without a license. "I am not allowed to officially say this," answered the officer, "but we believe he may be here in the U.S. illegally." Chris did some digging and learned that when Ramiro hit his daughter, he had an outstanding warrant for both driving without a license and speeding. "He had been in the U.S. illegally for 15 years," says Chris. "[From] whenever he got his initial tickets four years prior…they knew already the night of the accident that he was here in the U.S. illegally."

Chris couldn't help but think that if this man had been deported when the city initially found him to be in the country illegally, and committing crimes, that his only daughter, his only connection to his wife that passed away just a year earlier, might still be with him today. Chris asked the officer if Ramiro was going to go to jail for killing his little girl. "He told me that it's probably not likely because in the city of Rockwall, unless someone commits a violent felony, they don't check their immigration status. And he ended up not being charged with a violent felony. They gave him a ticket for driving without a license…they just let him go. They did nothing about it." Chris says he tried to contact his state representatives to press the issue of deporting Ramiro. The only one that would help was Texas Congressman Michael Burgess.

A congressional inquiry was opened to find out why the Department of Homeland Security never went after Ramiro – and they learned that the City of Rockwell never reported Ramiro to immigration. "So Congressman Burgess gets DHS involved," says Chris. "DHS goes out in 2016 and arrests Ramiro Tolentino Guevara for his citizenship status. If it hadn't been for him killing my daughter, DHS wouldn't have even gotten involved. But because he was a repeat offender and he'd actually killed a child this time, they were requesting he not be given bail." However, a Dallas immigration judge didn't agree – and Ramiro was bailed out a month after he was arrested on ten thousand dollars cash bond. Chris continues, "So while I thought he was in jail he wasn't."

According to Chris, Ramiro ended up losing his immigration battle. The judge ordered him to return to immigration to collect his bail money and be deported. When Ramiro never showed up, immigration went to arrest him and he was gone. "Ironically the flight risk actually ran," says Chris. "Who would've thought?" Ramiro is now considered a fugitive from the Immigration and Customs Enforcement agency, or ICE, but because they're overwhelmed and understaffed, they're not actively looking for him. "And now the only way he's going to be stopped," he says, "is if he commits another crime in a city that isn't sympathetic to illegal aliens." Chris had an awakening – ultimately coming to the conclusion that sanctuary city policies are in place to protect criminal illegal aliens. What really bothered him is that it appears Ramiro began driving almost immediately after killing his daughter. His sister found Romero's address from the accident report and drove to the house to see where he lived. "And she got a picture of him working on the truck that he killed my daughter with," claims Chris. "So he'd already been given back the vehicle he killed my daughter with, and was already driving it again within weeks of killing my little girl."

**

"I remember one cop walked up to me," recalls Sabine, "he said, 'You know, I know they're telling you it was an accident, but you need to ask the D.A. to stop lying to you.' And I said, 'What?' And he said, 'Yeah, because the killer of Dominic was an illegal.'" Sabine remembers thinking that she was familiar with illegal immigrants in the area. They worked as day laborers outside of the neighborhood Home Depot. Sabine continued, "And then it hit me that, right above where Dominic was killed is a Home Depot. And that's what happened. The guy was trying to drive into the side street to park because there was an American contractor picking up illegals." Sabine got the license plate number of the contractor picking up these day laborers, and gave it to the D.A., but she says he wouldn't look into it. He asked her to trust them that justice would be served. "[They] just continued lying to us," says Sabine, "and not really giving us the details that...they knew the killer. They had him before, when he had a felony of armed robbery and a felony of grand theft in 2008 [or] 2009 I believe it was. And they gave him a deal so he only had one felony on his record and he was deported." But according to Sabine, he came back. He drove drunk. He got probation. He drove drunk during probation and got probation again. And five weeks later, he killed Dominic.

**

The tragic stories of Dominic Durden and Chrishia Odette are unfortunately not unique. There are countless angel moms and dads throughout America, who's kids were killed by illegal aliens who were known to be illegal aliens to local law enforcement, shouldn't have been driving, and should have been deported long before taking the lives of American children. How has this senseless loss of life been allowed to continue? It's largely because of sanctuary policies.

Many city, county, and state governments prohibit local law enforcement from working with federal immigration agents, or ICE, when they detain a suspected or known illegal alien. These same local governments prohibit law enforcement from even inquiring about the immigration status of those they come in contact with. Because of these sanctuary policies we don't have good statistics on the illegal immigrant crime rate. And the reason why law enforcement doesn't capture this data is perverse. "Well the main reason that we do not have good statistics on the public safety impact of illegal immigration is because very few jurisdictions or local, county, state governments track crimes of illegal aliens or non-citizens in general," claims Jessica Vaughn, Director of Policy Studies for the Center of Immigration Studies. Law enforcement tracks all kinds of information about people who commit crimes. Jessica continued, "They track crimes by race and ethnicity. They track crimes by age and other kinds of demographic data, but they don't usually track the citizenship or immigration status of people who get arrested or who are convicted of crimes. And sometimes this is deliberate that they just don't want to know." And why don't they want to know? Because proponents of illegal aliens don't want any data that will go against their narrative that immigrants are less crime prone than American citizens. "Crime rates among immigrants are lower than those born in this country," claims Jorge Ramos. "Native born Americans unfortunately commit crime at over twice the rate of undocumented immigrants, so if we're gonna kick anyone out, it would be us," claims Cenk Ugyur. It's a narrative that is constantly peddled by the open border types in our media.

Some government officials have gotten so radical that they're even willing to help criminal illegals escape deportation. Officials like Oakland Mayor Libby Schaaf, who defiantly asserted that she was willing to go to jail over protecting criminal illegal immigrants from ICE raids in her sanctuary city. The policies that create these havens for illegal aliens are not only disturbing because of the crime they help perpetuate, but also because they block collecting the very data that would show that sanctuary policies lead to more crime in our communities. Thankfully though, federal law enforcement does collect non-citizen crime data. And what do those numbers show? According to statistics from a 2017 U.S. Sentencing Commission, non-citizens account for 22% of federal murder convictions, 18% of federal fraud convictions, 33% of federal money laundering convictions, 29% of federal drug trafficking convictions, and 72% of federal drug possession convictions. The non-citizen population is roughly 7%. That's a stunning level of crime that shows, at least at the federal level, that non-citizen are far more crime prone than Americans for many very serious crimes. Jessica Vaughn thinks that law enforcement agencies everywhere should be tracking the immigration status of people who they arrest so that they can be found by ICE and sent back to their home countries. "It's really common sense I think for most people and for most law enforcement agencies," says Jessica. But politicians, activists and the media want to continue the narrative that illegal immigrants are more law abiding than Americans. So they do what ever they can at the local and state level to block law enforcement from capturing the data and working with ICE to enforce our immigration laws. Jessica continues, "It's a false narrative that they've created, and the result of it actually is a threat to public safety."

If these sanctuary policies weren't in place, and we actually had effective immigration enforcement to block reentry once deported, both Dominic Durden and Chrishia Odette would likely be alive today. Chris Odette thinks this dangerous lack of enforcement of our immigration laws must stop. "My 13-year-old daughter never got to graduate high school," says Chris. "She would have graduated this year, would have started college. I never got to finish teaching my daughter how to drive a car. Everything that I had in my life, that I had built with my late wife…the last connection I had of her with my daughter is gone." Chris launched a website called Justice4Chrishia.com to get the man who killed his daughter deported. When he's not working, Chris spends all of his spare time trying to locate his whereabouts, and posting information online and on Twitter in hopes that someone will identify him so law enforcement can deport him once and for all. "It seems like it is an absolute impossibility to get media to talk to me about my daughter's death," says Chris.

The man that killed Sabine's son was deported. But then she got word from law enforcement friends of her son that the man returned, and is somewhere back in California. Understandably, Sabine was broken over the loss of her boy. "I got so distraught that I wanted to kill myself," confesses Sabine. "I lost my only child. I knew I would never be that incredible grandmother I wanted to be. I would never spoil my grandkids. I would never get to see my son again." She couldn't take the loss. So she began planning how she would take her life. "I knew how and when," she says, "and my poor fiancé had no idea what I was planning. And then that day…Donald Trump came down the escalator." Sabine watched the screen and thought Trump was potentially starting a new TV show. But he wasn't. He was running for President of the United States…and promised to enforce our immigration laws:

Donald Trump: "When Mexico sends its people, they're not sending their best. They're not sending you. They're not sending you. They're sending people that have lots of problems, and they're bringing those problems…"

"And I stopped and I broke down," says Sabine. She looked up to the sky, and felt God was sending her a message. "And I said, 'Okay. If that's your sign, I'm not gonna take myself out.' I didn't know what was to come from there." Sabine met Donald Trump on the three-year anniversary of the last time that she saw Dominic alive. The presidential candidate gave her a platform to tell Dominic's story. She went on to speak about her son's death at the Republican National Convention:

Sabine Durden: "The killer was from Guatemala and was previously deported with felonies for armed robberies and grand theft. After returning to America illegally again, he was caught drunk driving. No license. No registration. No insurance. And he got probation. Another DUI...another probation. Five weeks later, while barely under the legal limit of being drunk, he killed my Dom. He was given a misdemeanor and served just thirty-five days in jail. I have been talking about illegal immigration since 2012, since he got killed, and no one listened until Donald Trump."

Which brings us back to the question - do illegal immigrants commit less crime than American citizens? Even with our leaders trying to hide the statistics, it is clear that noncitizens vastly outpace American citizens for many serious crimes at the federal level. The narrative that illegal immigrants commit less crime than U.S. citizens is fake news. But really, it doesn't matter. Because if we were simply to enforce our immigration laws, many of our beautiful citizens would be alive today – and America would be a true sanctuary for freedom lovers instead of a land struggling to keep its identity under an onslaught of foreign invaders.

NINE

Tested

How should we view life's greatest challenges?

So you're going through life. Trying to make the best of it. Treating others as you would like to be treated. Carefully making decisions. Raising a family. Trying to get ahead. And then out of nowhere you're hit with a bombshell, something so unexpected that it takes your breath away…and you may begin to think, why me? Why is this happening to me? I think we've all faced this moment, including Adryana and I.

The nightmare started for us on December 28, 2009…we just didn't know it yet. That Monday morning had actually been a victory lap of sorts. I'd just got off of guest hosting the Dennis Miller radio show with rising conservative star Andrew Breitbart and Larry O'Connor, a big time theater man who'd just came out as conservative. We were filling in for the former Saturday Night Live comedian during the Christmas vacation break. Andrew's team of renegade citizen journalists had had quite a stretch of breaking stories, Andrew himself had become a national figure, and we were all using the guest hosting spot to celebrate Larry's coming out as well as the end of a year full of accomplishments. It was an exciting time. It seemed like the start of something new. But it's funny how sometimes in those moments of triumph…big trouble lurks just around the corner.

I was scheduled to co-host again the following day and then that night a few of us were going to head off for dinner to celebrate our stellar year. But my plans were about to drastically change because by the time I got home, something was happening with Adryana. "I started to get a very sharp pain in my abdomen," she recalls. "But it was almost as if I could not locate exactly where the pain was. But it was incredibly intense. I was doubled over in pain." At first I didn't take the situation seriously. Adryana sometimes has a flair for the dramatic. But as a few minutes went by, and another wave of pain hit her, I could see that something serious was happening. So her mother stayed with our little girl, who was just a baby at the time, and I rushed Adryana off to the hospital. "We went to the emergency room. I was experiencing a ton of pain and they could see that so they took me back right away," recalls Adryana. "They didn't have a room for me, so…they just put me in the hallway. And by this point, I was definitely starting to become a little incoherent from the pain." It was hitting her in short episodes, but they were coming frequently. And from the building intensity of her voice, you could tell that the pain was increasing. "When it would hit me, all of a sudden, I would get a very, very, very sharp intense pain…I was screaming in agony."

We felt a bit helpless because they couldn't get a handle on what was going on. It was like we were living a scene from Aliens…where the person is belting in excruciating pain as a creature tries to force its way out of the victim's body. They gave Adryana morphine, but astonishingly it wasn't working. Eventually they performed a scan on her abdomen to see if they could get a visual on what was happening. "And I mentioned to the doctors that I thought maybe it was a ruptured cyst on an ovary because I had had those before," says Adryana. "And so that's what they were looking for. But what ended up happening is that they didn't see anything." She spent the next few days in the hospital. The doctors tried a few different meds and the pain slowly subsided. We thought they'd gotten the episodes under control, but we'd later find out that that's not entirely what happened. The unsettling thing was that, at the time, they never identified the problem. It was a big mystery, and it wasn't like we were at some dump of a facility. It was Cedars-Sinai Medical Center – thought to be one of the best hospitals in Los Angeles. A good friend was a surgeon there, and he made sure we were being taken care of. It was baffling to everyone. We reluctantly went home hoping that the pain episodes wouldn't spring up again.

Fast-forward to a couple weeks later and Adryana went to go see her gynecologist, Dr. Frankel. "When Dr. Frankel looked at my scan, he said, 'I don't think it was a ruptured cyst because there was no fluid in your uterus,'" she recalls. "I guess typically when there's a ruptured cyst in the uterus, you see fluid. But in my case there was nothing there. So he too was unable to pinpoint exactly what had happened." He had an old school approach to healthcare. Dr. Frankel was a very practical man. He figured that Adryana seemed fine. The episode was behind her. He advised that if it happened again, she should just go back to the emergency room. Adryana thought then, and still thinks today, that Dr. Frankel was a great gynecologist. But roughly two years after that visit, he passed away from cancer. He was pretty old, and was likely already sick. So at the time, he perhaps wasn't at the top of his game. "And I looked good to him. I looked healthy to him. But it still just, it didn't sit well with me. And I didn't feel great. I felt tired."

Ever since we had our daughter, Adryana was plagued with

fatigue. I didn't think much of it. Anyone that knows Adryana knows that she loves to sleep – and that I frequently get in the way of her favorite pastime. There's even a family legend that she was born napping. I actually used to poke fun of her on this topic because aside from being married, we've always worked together – so when she was too tired to deal with work issues, I'd give her a good ribbing about being "lazy." But this unsolved pain mystery was something different. So a friend turned her on to a concept we weren't familiar with in medical care, but is quite common in elite circles...Adryana was turned on to something called a *concierge doctor*.

The concept is just like it sounds...you have a doctor at your disposal all the time. Unlike the doctor you have via your insurance, where you have to go through their practice, when you pay a concierge doctor directly, you have real access to that physician. You have their personal cell phone number. You can email them. Basically, there is no middleman filtering access. You can reach them at anytime. "I have a very sensitive system and for a long time after I gave birth, I just didn't feel 100%," says Adryana. "So I sought out a concierge doctor because I just felt as if I needed better care. We never really discovered why I'd gone to the hospital in 2009. We never came to a conclusion." So we thought this was a good avenue to pursue. A concierge doctor was recommended to her and for several years he was her primary physician. We paid him a yearly fee, she saw him as needed – including a once a year exam – and any tests that need to be done were done through our insurance. But when the effects of Obamacare hit, her concierge doctor saw an opportunity to go even higher end...and his fees skyrocketed. He was basically looking for less patients for more money, and according to him, he was going to give his patients even better care. "He ended up going to very high end concierge service," says Adryana, "which we were not willing to pay."

So around the end of 2013, he in essence sold the group of patients that couldn't make the jump to another concierge doctor...Dr. Chang. Adryana decided to schedule a meeting with this new physician to get a feel for her. She sat down with Dr. Chang for an hour to review all her medical records and the two immediately had a great rapport. "So we're sitting there in the doctor's office," recalls Adryana, "and she's looking through all of my paperwork. And all of a sudden she said to me, 'Did you know that you have a lesion on your liver?' And I thought, a lesion? When I think of a lesion, I don't know why, but the first thing that entered my mind was a scab. It must be like some sort of a scab on my liver. And she continues to ruffle through the papers and she said, 'And it's grown.' And then I sort of perked up a little, and immediately said, 'Wait a minute...what do you mean a lesion? Do you mean a tumor?' And she said, 'Well, I don't know. We don't know what it is.' And I said, 'Could it be cancer?' Immediately my heart is beating. I'm nervous. I have something in my liver that's growing and I don't know what it is. And she said, 'Let's get an MRI of this right away.'"

By chance, a few years after the 2009 pain incident, Adryana had some scans done of her abdomen for another reason. That scan also showed a spot in her liver, and the spot appeared larger than the one in the earlier scans. "You could see from the images alone just by looking at the liver that it had grown," recalls Adryana. "It had grown a lot." The fancy concierge doctor, the one that went to serve higher end clientele, completely missed it. But in their first visit, Dr. Chang caught the issue.

After leaving her first visit with Dr. Chang, Adryana started the trek home, wondering how she was going to tell her husband. "I was so worried about myself. I thought, 'Oh no! I'm definitely dying...how am I going to tell my loving husband about my impending death?'" For the rest of the day she contemplated how to break the news to me. That night when we were getting in bed, instead of coming up with some artful way of telling me, she just let it out. "I said, 'Honey, I have a lesion on my liver,'" she quickly said, waiting for my shocked reaction. But apparently, I was nose deep into my iPad. "And you just kind of nodded, you just sort of ignored me. And of course I immediately got hot. I was furious because here I am, you know, near death and you're ignoring me. And I said, 'did you not just hear what I said? I have a lesion on my liver!'" And I snapped out of my daze and responded, "Well, what does that mean? You mean like a tumor?" And Adryana said she didn't know, that the lesion had been in her liver since at least her pain incident in 2009 and that it's grown since then. I responded, "Well, it's probably not cancer, because if it were cancer, you would probably be dead by now." My thinking was logical. We know it's been there for roughly five years, Adryana is still here yelling at me – so it's likely not a big deal. "And that sort of did make me feel better," remembers Adryana. "Of course, I then called Dr. Chang and I said, 'Well, if it were cancer, don't you think I'd be dead by now?' And she said, 'Yeah, if it were cancer, you'd probably be very sick by now. I agree with that.'"

At the time, we had a lot going on. We'd just come off of a long struggle with parents at our daughter's school. A creepy father was getting into bed with other people's kids and we called him out. That turned into a nearly nine-month long ordeal. We'd done everything we could possibly do with that particular situation, and now that we knew Adryana had a potentially serious health issue, it was time to move on from the conflict with Mr. Creepy.

We also had some unprecedented struggles with work.

Shortly after Adryana's pain incident, business began to pick up for our small marketing firm. We stepped away from citizen journalism to take on the incoming projects...but were still involved in the culture war. Instead of taking center stage breaking stories, we played a behind the scenes role producing a national touring global warming debate...working with our friends in media to open up the discussion and tone down the apocalyptic rhetoric. The campaigns had been so successful that by the beginning of 2013, we'd sold our biggest project ever to an enormous global brand. Our business model was a bit abnormal. We were kind of creative hired guns. When a client needed an out of the ordinary marketing idea, they'd come to us to develop something. And if they signed onto the project, we made a percentage of the overall budget...what's considered a creative fee. It was always a bit of a gamble. You could put hundreds, even thousands of hours into a proposal and nothing would come of it. But with the right project it could be very lucrative...and this was one of those times. Our client was one of the largest companies in the world, and the project we sold to them became so hot that they were gearing up to put an extraordinary amount of money into it. Our idea was becoming a mega project for one of the biggest brands on the planet. And as a result, our fees were going to be life changing. But amazing projects are few and far between. And there was a bit of a power struggle over who was going to run it – which was new for us because 100% of the time, over a decade long relationship, our company managed the projects we sold to our clients. In the end, they promised we'd run it and we'd sort out the details later. But when it came time to announce the project to the world – they refused to follow through on their promise. An ambitious young brand manager wanted to control the production for this sexy new concept. So they terminated our involvement in the project. The problem was, they still owed us our creative fee – and by this time the project had grown exponentially...think blockbuster movie size budget. So what did they do? They denied they owed us anything. Large global brands know they can pull this off on the little guy for obvious reasons. Going up against a behemoth is an uphill task...whether you're right or wrong. So we began politely negotiating with them in hopes that we could come to an agreement and avoid any legal process.

This was all in play when Adryana's new doctor found the spot on her liver and so she was hesitant to take on any additional stress. So she put off the MRI scan of her abdomen for five months. But every single day it haunted her. "And I thought, 'You know, I'm a mom,'" she remembers. I have a responsibility to get to the bottom of this. But the truth is, there is a part of me that didn't want to deal with it. I just, I knew in my gut that it was not good. I really, I believe so strongly in an intuition. And, you know when something's wrong with you and I just, I knew it." So finally, five months later Adryana went to get the MRI. And when she did, life became drastically more complicated.

Adryana took her mom Gloria with her to get the results of the scan. Dr. Chang confirmed that it was a tumor, and that it had grown – taking up an entire side of her liver. They also found a second tumor. "So at that point, Dr. Chang said, 'You have to go see a liver specialist,'" remembers Adryana. We all remember those big traumatic moments in life – the first time you broke a bone, or your first car accident, or being suspended from school. They are forever seared into our minds. When Adryana walked in from the doctor's office, this was one of those moments. Our young daughter was in the kitchen with me, and Adryana came in shaking her head and looking me dead in my eyes while mouthing, "Not good. Not good." Up until then, the whole thing was theoretical. We actually tried to play it down as much as possible. We were young...too young to be dealing with a life threatening illness. This spot had been there for years...and most of the time she was still just her normal Adryana self. But the look she gave me changed all that. Her difficulty getting pregnant, the pain incident that sent her to the hospital, the fatigue she'd been experiencing for years, my ribbing her about being lazy – it all came rushing back. You can imagine the guilt I felt. This lingering unease that she'd been feeling going back at least seven years was because of this foreign object growing inside her body.

Dr. Chang connected us with the most celebrated surgeon in this arena - the man that pioneered the liver transplant. When any major health concern develops, physicians typically pull up the entire medical history of a patient looking for the first signs of the problem. And ultimately we learned from an image Adryana had done during her pregnancy...that the spot first showed up on her medical history in 2007. Needless to say, we were incredibly nervous. I'd recently lost a childhood friend, Louis, to pancreatic cancer. It was stunning to everyone that knew him. The doctors explained that just because a tumor started off benign, that didn't mean that it was going to stay that way. They'd also deduced that, during her 2009 incident, the larger of the two tumors had mutated and the pain she experienced was due to a spontaneous tumor rupture. Apparently, she was extremely lucky to have survived that episode.

So we decided to see the doctor that pioneered liver transplants. "He looks at the scans," Adryana recalls, "and he says to us, 'This looks sort of like an FNH tumor to me.'" An FNH tumor is a benign tumor of the liver...not yet cancerous. However, the specialist said that he could not be sure because there was a portion of the larger tumor that looked a little different than what he typically saw. "It looks benign to me," claimed the specialist. "But I can't tell you it is for sure...we know it's been there since 2009 and you're still alive." He suggested that we just sit back and not do anything and wait to see if the tumors continue to grow. The surgery she would need was a liver resection – they'd need to cut out approximately a third of Adryana's liver. And he made no bones about it. "This surgery can kill you," said the specialist. "You're young, you're alive, you're fine for now. Let's just wait and see what happens." Adryana didn't like his answer. She didn't want to sit around and wait. "From the very beginning, I knew that I wanted to get the tumor out," remembers Adryana. "I felt like I was young. I was healthy. I could survive the surgery. So I said, 'we're getting a second opinion.'"

We went back to Dr. Chang and told her what the specialist had said and that Adryana wasn't happy with his approach. If it was as big and as serious as everyone claimed, she wanted this thing out of her body immediately. So Dr. Chang connected Adryana with another doctor, this time a specialist from Cedar-Sinai in Los Angeles – Dr. Annamalai. We set up an appointment with him and he saw Adryana right away. He had generally the same diagnosis on the tumor itself…he also thought it could be a benign FNH tumor. But there was a portion that he couldn't be sure about and the rupture in 2009 concerned him. So the two specialists were aligned on the nature of the tumor. However, Dr. Annamalai had a different approach to dealing with it. "Listen, if you were my wife," Dr. Annamalai told Adryana, "I would advise you to get it out." So many people had advised Adryana against the surgery. But she figured that she'd given birth, so what could be harder than that? What we didn't know until learning about the surgery was that the liver is the only organ in the human body that can regenerate. Once a portion is cut out, it grows back to its original size. As we probed more about how the surgery would be done a picture of the path ahead began to appear. This was not going to be a walk in the park. The surgeon illustrated with a marker the incision that would need to be made to open up her body to get access to the organ. It was a large reversed L shape that started at her rib cage, down her stomach, then to the side along her waistline. They'd then flap over the skin to gain access to the liver and do their thing. With the full picture largely painted in, we began to see that this looked a lot harder than giving birth.

Ultimately we decided we were going to move forward with the surgery. But because of the serious life risk associated with the operation, we figured it'd be prudent to get everything in order. We made sure our will was entirely squared away. And we also wanted to get a plan in place to make things as easy as possible for our daughter during the surgery, and God willing, the recovery. We wanted life to go on for her as normal as possible because as an early grade schooler…she was just too young to feel the weight of these events. She also wasn't going to be able to visit Adryana while she was in the hospital. So we asked the parents of our daughter's friends to set up play dates…and they really came through for us. For roughly two weeks our little girl had a full schedule. We also enlisted our moms to help. The plan was, my mom would watch our daughter…stay with her at night and get her to summer school and her play dates. And Adryana's mom Gloria and I would alternate - one watching Adryana in post-operation recovery and the other relieving my mom as needed. Our daughter's play dates kicked off at Disneyland with her best friend's family. "I wanted her to be at the happiest place on earth," recalls Adryana, fighting back tears. "If I was going to die in that moment, I wanted her to have a good memory at that moment, to remember that day just being…her being in a good place." We had everything ready. The date was set for early July to get this thing out of her body.

The morning of the surgery, we arrived at 5 A.M. so that they could prep her for the procedure. Melissa, Adryana's good friend, came to give us moral support. I was nervous. My mother-in-law Gloria had been handling the situation pretty well throughout the process, but come that morning she understandably started to crack a bit. Adryana, on the other hand, was cool, calm, and collected. "They took me back. They prepped me. I remember sitting on the gurney. They gave me something to relax." By the time Gloria, Melissa, and I walked into the surgery prep area to see Adryana off, whatever they gave her to relax seemed like it had kicked in. The doctor told us the surgery would be about three hours. To keep us abreast of the progress, they'd give us an update every hour. Everyone left to give us a moment alone. Adryana and I kissed, said our goodbyes, and I quietly prayed. Her life was now in his hands.

We went back to the waiting room and were joined shortly after by a friend of my mother-in-law's. I must have been driving everyone crazy because I could not stop talking…that apparently was my coping mechanism. There wasn't a thought that came to my mind that I didn't verbalize. The first hour came along and the surgeon gave us an update as promised. Things were progressing. Then the second hour came…and again they updated us with a simple, "things are going fine," kind of message. But it was the third hour where things began to unravel in more ways than one.

You may recall that our former client owed us a nice chunk of money for a creative fee that they were now trying to stiff us on. Well the negotiations had been dragging on right up until surgery day, and they weren't going well. If you've ever been drawn into a legal dispute with an enormous Fortune 10 company, you know that they have extraordinary power beyond mere mortals. Disputes like ours become a long methodical chess match, one that they have perfected over decades.

They're not only in the business of selling whatever product or service they offer – they're also in the business of winning legal fights. Our former client was so adept at the game that they pulled strings to force our lawyer of ten years to step away from representing us in the dispute because of an alleged conflict of interest. Apparently someone in our lawyer's firm represented our former client in the past, giving them the option to disqualify the firm from representing us. They wanted Adryana and I to start over with new counsel. So we relied on a lawyer friend, Devon, to get us through the hump until we could secure an alternate counsel. In the weeks leading up to the surgery, we'd reached an impasse with our ex-client. They were still claiming that they didn't owe us a creative fee, so the only way to remedy the situation was to start the legal arbitration process.

Well, as Adryana was on the cutting board in hour three, our former client pulled a fast one, claiming, through some twisted reading of our contract, that we had to file paperwork that day to start the legal process to resolve our dispute. If not, they were going to file a motion that would block us from ever pursuing our payment in the future…and our creative fee would be lost forever. So as an enormous section of my wife's liver was being removed, I was forced to make the decision right then and there on taking one of the largest companies on the planet to court. This was not the type of major business decision I made without my better half. After some guidance from Devon, for who I'll be indebted to for life, I decided to file the paperwork to initiate the arbitration process. But as this decision was being made, the third hour came and went with no update from the surgeon. As the fourth hour approached, there was still no word…and by now the surgery was supposed to have been done. I asked for a status and there was none…the surgeon was busy, was the response. Then the fifth and sixth hour came and went. Still nothing. What I didn't know was that Adryana was fighting for her life.

Apparently the tumor was in the worst possible spot. What the MRI scans didn't show was that it was almost blocking the main artery into her liver – called the portal vein. So to cut out the mass, the surgeons had to carefully shave away at the liver to avoid cutting the main artery – an act that would have led to almost certain death. In fact, on three separate occasions, they had to stop the surgery, pack her with ice, and give Adryana blood transfusions. As hour seven arrived the tension in the waiting room became almost unbearable. I'd shifted from chatty to complete silence. But then finally, as despair started to seep in, the doctor came out of surgery. Adryana survived…barely. And the initial word was that there was no cancer. However, due to the uniqueness of the tumor, they wanted to have some lab work done to be sure. Adryana was moved into intensive care, and the anesthesia slowly started to wear off. "I remember I couldn't open my eyes, but I was happy to be alive," remembers Adryana. "I knew that I had survived the surgery and that was step one…just survive the surgery…because there was a chance that I wasn't going to live. And I actually came very close to dying on the table. So I was like, 'Yeah, I'm alive, I'm alive, I'm alive!'"

I finally got to see my beautiful wife. And, to my surprise she was jovial. We'd dodged a bullet. If Adryana hadn't gone with her gut and instead listened to the original world-renowned doctor – the tumor would have likely blocked her portal vein, or just as bad…mutated to cancer. In fact, the doctors informed Adryana and I that lab work revealed the tumor had been full of clear cell – and had it been left in, it would likely have mutated very soon. With Adryana now in recovery, and the initial word was that there was no cancer, we thought the rough patch was behind us. But little did we know that the ride was just getting started.

When they took Adryana into the ICU recovery room, she was having a hard time swallowing. So she periodically called to the nurse, and in a whispered tone because she could barely speak, she told him she couldn't swallow. "It's just because your throat is dry," answered the nurse, "you had a tube in your throat." Adryana turned to me and said something was wrong, but the nurse interjected and said that he sees this all the time. It was just the anesthesia talking. That's when Adryana told me to get her mom on the phone. So I called Gloria, to come help out. Adryana's mother, who I typically call mom as well, had been through major surgeries herself, and by now was slightly more rested than both Adryana and I who'd been up for roughly 24 hours. Gloria was by far more equipped to deal with the situation. She arrived within thirty minutes and saw immediately what was happening. "She's having an allergic reaction," Gloria told the nurse. And she was right. Adryana was having a reaction to the morphine – which was making her throat swell shut. So the staff immediately took her off the drug. "And it scared all the nurses," recalls Adryana. "It was a big deal." At this point, the nursing staff didn't know what to do. It was around four in the morning when they took her off the painkiller. "And within a couple of hours, I was in the most excruciating pain that I had ever been in," says Adryana. "The doctor came in to do his rounds very early morning, probably 7:00 in the morning, and I couldn't speak from the pain. And when he realized that they had taken me off of all the pain meds, he was furious." The doctor tried a different medley of pain meds, and within several hours he was able to get the pain under control.

We had a major hiccup, but now everything seemed to be back on track. My mom dropped our daughter off at summer school that morning. And the doctors had finally figured out a cocktail that lowered the pain enough to get Adryana to sleep. As I looked at her lying there, a sense of comfort rolled over me. Things had stabilized. She was now on the road to recovery. But at around noon, as I sat there with my mother-in-law watching Adryana sleep, my cellphone rang. It was my mom. I didn't know this in the moment, but apparently she'd become concerned when my brother, who suffers from mental illness, wasn't answering her calls. So after dropping off my daughter at summer school, she went to check on him. And when she did, she found him unconscious in the living room. Apparently, he'd attempted to end it all…and was now clinging to life in an emergency room. I can't imagine what my mother must have gone through when she found him, but in the midst of the worst moment in her life, her voice was calm…almost comforting. She must have known it was an extraordinary moment for everyone. She told me she'd have to stay in the hospital with him. We said goodbye and hung up.

The news was devastating. As my wife was in one hospital recovering from major organ surgery, my baby brother was clinging to life in another. It was a surreal moment. The kind of thing that would be unbelievable if put in a Hollywood script. I couldn't help but feel some guilt for pulling my mom away from her son to help me with my daughter. I gathered myself and re-entered the recovery room and asked Gloria to join me in the hallway. Adryana was asleep. When I told her what had happened, it was the first and only time that I'd ever seen her cry. After we allowed ourselves a few moments to grieve, Gloria and I quickly turned to the problem at hand… we were down a man and needed to come up with a plan. We agreed that there was no need to tell Adryana what had happened. She was in no shape to take that on emotionally. I would have to pick our daughter up from summer school and Gloria would call my brother-in-law, her son Jay, to see if he could briefly babysit my daughter so that I could rush to the ICU to comfort my mother and potentially say goodbye to my brother.

If all this wasn't enough, as I was walking my daughter out from summer school I receive an email notification. To my disbelief, a recently acquired client was suing our company over a contract dispute. Early in the year we'd signed an agreement to execute a brief marketing campaign for a relatively young company. But as we were producing the project per the contract, the client wanted to make material changes to the campaign...ones that would substantially change the budget of the project. When I informed them that this would increase the cost, they declined the budget increase and swiftly terminated the contract – demanding we pay back the initial fees. We of course refused. So they decided to sue us in hopes of getting their money back. It was shocking. After almost twenty years of business we'd never been in a single lawsuit nor even been close to entering one. Now, in less than 48 hours we'd been forced into two during the most trying personal time in our lives.

I took my daughter home and was met soon after by my brother-in-law who came through when we needed him. I went to the hospital to check on my wife, and she was sleeping...with my mother-in-law by her side. Once I knew her situation was stabilized, I jumped back in the car and began the trek to the other hospital. To say I was a wreck would be the understatement of the year. I was practically drunk with grief and exhaustion. The weight of the situation was overwhelming. Driving that car, I never wailed so hard in my life. Why us? Why was this happening to us? What did we do to deserve this? Why were we being tested? As I drove down the 405 Freeway desperately trying to stay on the road, that last word "tested" repeated in my head, and I said out loud,

"You're being tested. You're being tested right now." I had an awakening. As bad as that moment was, if I didn't keep it together while I was flying down the fast lane, things could even be worse. I could crash and die right now. "Get it together," I thought. "Your brother is still alive. Your wife is still alive. The lawsuits mean nothing." And in that despair I had a moment of clarity. Why is this happening to me? In those trying times, you're being tested. Things can always be worse than they are right now...even in moments of great despair. I pulled myself together and was thankful for what I had. I was blessed we were all still in the game.

In the end, my brother survived. He's still struggling with mental illness...but he's alive. It was a long battle, but we also won the lawsuit with one of the biggest companies on the planet. It didn't turn out quite as we hoped, but they were still forced to meet their obligations to our tiny firm...but that's a story for another time. After a few months of back and forth, the second company that sued us smartly decided to drop their case. And most importantly, my Adryana, as you know, is still here with us today. Her struggle went on for quite some time. After about ten days she was released from the hospital, but about a month and a half later she was readmitted. She'd gone septic, which is a life-threatening illness where the body fights off an infection that's spread through the bloodstream. However, my little fighter survived that as well. And honestly, we may be facing this health struggle for the rest of our lives...but right now, we're still in the game.

We tell you this story because if you too are going through a rough patch, and it feels like the ceiling is caving in, like your world is coming to an end – please realize that you are being tested. As bad as the moment may seem, you are blessed to have what you have. Find solace in that undeniable fact. Look around you and hug everyone a little harder, tell them you love them, and apologize for any mistakes you may have made in this short but fantastic journey we call life. Don't let the despair take you out...because you have the strength within you to pass the test.

TEN

Unfriend Me Now

How do you handle a triggered Leftist?

America has had a lot of gate scandals. First of course was Watergate, then Climategate, Deflategate, Gamergate, Pussygate, and probably my personal favorite…Weinergate. My love of witnessing these train wrecks was bound to one day engulf me in my own gate controversy. And in fact, it eventually did…albeit not a very famous one. I called it *selfie-gate*, and it had all the makings of a proper scandal. It was set in La La Land amongst the rich, famous, and virtue signaling Hollywood elites. The story is rife with rumors, gossip, outrage mobs, racism, cyber-bullying, and intolerance. But unlike most scandals, getting embroiled in this one was productive. Why? Because it helped me answer the question – how do you handle a triggered Leftist? Break out your notepads Red Pilled America…because class is in session.

**

It was July 25th, 2016, and the day started off like any other beautiful sunny summer morning in Southern California.

I woke up and read my emails, made some coffee, checked out the new filters on Snapchat. Reviewed my friend notifications. "Oh…Goop followed me back!" Then dropped my kid off at summer camp and went to work. We all take quick "social media" breaks throughout the day – it's become part of our "normal" daily routine. So sometime mid-afternoon I peeked into Facebook. Truth be told, FB had been on a steep decline for me. Self-indulgent political diatribes had replaced the things I loved about the site – namely, cute animal videos and clips of laughing babies. What was different about this day though was that it just so happened to be Day One of the 2016 Democratic National Convention – what was supposed to be a well-choreographed event to anoint Hillary Clinton as the first female nominee for president on a major party ticket. The problem was that massive news had recently hit everyone's social media feeds. Wikileaks had dropped the mother load of document dumps – a batch of Democratic National Committee (DNC) emails that showed without question that Hillary Clinton and the DNC had colluded to screw Bernie Sanders out of the nomination. Within hours of the news, the Hillary camp, oddly, had already assessed how the emails had gone public. In their telling, the DNC email server had been hacked by Russia to help Donald Trump win the election. They must have had the greatest forensic I.T. team ever assembled to come to that conclusion so quickly. Or maybe it was just bullshit because if they did have that kind of computer muscle in place, the emails would've never been released in the first place.

Well the story that the leaked emails told hit the Democrat Convention like a nuclear stink bomb. Debbie Wasserman Schultz, the chairwoman of the DNC, was forced to resign. The entire event was falling apart at the seams right before everyone's eyes…and it was glorious. It felt a little like redemption. For months America had been seeing political violence for the first time in decades directed at one specific group...Trump supporters. Hollywood and the mainstream media were in overdrive pumping out the nasty narrative that *anyone* who supported Trump was a despicable racist – signaling to the crazies that it was open season on the MAGA crowd. Their yearlong effort paid off when just a month earlier, San Jose Trump rally-goers were pummeled bloody while news cameras and a battalion of police officers quietly stood on the sidelines...refusing to intervene. America was learning quickly that it was okay to punch right-wingers. So watching the Democrat party devolve into complete and utter chaos on the very first day of their convention was better than a day at the spa.

When I logged onto Facebook, the mudslinging from the Bernie-bots at camp Hillary had escalated quickly. The Bernie-bot commies were so livid that they were posting tirades encouraging riots on the convention floor! Angry doesn't begin to describe what I was witnessing in my feed – the insults and putdowns would easily get you banned for life from Facebook today. Truthfully, I'll never understand why people think it's appropriate to hide behind a computer screen and be rude on social media. That's just not how I roll. Personally, I prefer being rude to people's faces – so long as it's warranted. I'm old fashioned like that.

So there I was...scrolling through Facebook and *really* hoping for a laughing baby video, but all I'm seeing is DNC political venom. At the time, for the sake of our daughter, my husband Patrick and I had made a concerted effort to tone down our politics on social media. We'd been early supporters of Donald Trump. Shortly after his presidential announcement, Patrick penned an op-ed for Breitbart News entitled *GOP Trump Haters, Stop Your Free Bleeding* that was critical of what would later be called the #NeverTrump crowd who seemed bent on taking the real estate mogul down. But the environment had turned violent, and our baby girl was attending a prestigious Hollywood private school packed with elite triggered Hollywood leftists. We'd been butting heads with parents because of our right-leaning politics for years and really didn't mind the conflict personally...but now our daughter was starting to take some of the incoming fire. It felt like these people were on the verge of being unhinged. On top of that, I was still recovering from serious organ surgery. So we thought it best to take it easy on politics when posting on social media...especially Facebook where all of the parents from our school seemed to live. It was tempting to get in on the social media insult bandwagon. But Patrick and I had a plan – deescalate the political vitriol – and I had to stick to it.

So I came up with an idea. For every heated political take I saw on Facebook, I'd post a *selfie*. I snapped a picture of myself wearing sunglasses then wrote at the bottom, "...but these sunnies are bomb." It was sort of my very first attempt at a meme. To launch my good-humored campaign, I wrote a fun FB post explaining that we all needed to bring down the political temperature. The post read:

"Share your Sunshine. Focus on the positive. Be mindful of others. Think twice about sharing negative memes or long-winded posts about how much you hate 'the other side.' I have the common sense to refrain from posting beautiful 'selfies' of myself when I REALLY want to because let's be honest, I'm better looking than most of you. Also, I am courteous enough to keep my political views to myself when clearly my opinions matter WAY more than yours and the person I'm voting for is the one who is going to win - so please be respectful or prepare to get a "selfie" from me. This is Facebook - where we all haven't seen each other since high school, or have possibly met once. If you want to discuss politics, make a dinner reservation with your real friends. Thanks in advance."

I then proceeded to post my selfie meme on a select few Facebook posts that I felt were…let's say impolite. The whole thing just took a few minutes. Then I logged off of FB and went back to work. But as luck would have it, I started getting inundated with notifications. My post was getting some serious traction. Yay me! So I logged back on and saw that it had a significant amount of comments and likes. "I'm practically on the brink of becoming FB famous," I thought. "I guess those sunnies *were* bomb." The newfound attention quickly went to my head. I'd felt this feeling before, back in middle school when I walked on campus for my first real fist fight. People I didn't even know where cheering me on. I should have learned my lesson back then not to bask in the random accolades. But I didn't. The notifications kept coming in. I became drunk from the praise. From there on – it's a bit of blur. But I can clearly remember saying to myself, "I'm the laughing baby video of the day! Embrace this moment." So I proceeded to go on an epic Facebook shitposting campaign, slapping my selfie on *every* political post I saw. I had a fever and the only prescription was "more selfie." The original mission had completely gone out the door because I was blinded by the likes. As I posted selfie after selfie of myself on any and all political commentary, I remember thinking, "I'm freaking trending! Pretty soon I'm going to have to make some hard decisions, like who is going to represent me – CAA or UTA… because these selfies are breaking the damn Internet!" There was obviously a pent up silent majority that was tired of these leftist hate tirades on social media. And I took note. In fact, it was one of the first clear signs to me that Trump was going to win.

As the day progressed, I was pleased to see that my gorilla marketing campaign continued to generate favorable metrics. People seemed to get the joke. Friends who I hadn't seen in years respond with witty banter of their own. Some asked if they could share the post on their pages – I said yes, waiving my valuable copyright. For the first time in a long time I was actually enjoying Facebook, and everyone seemed to understand that I was trying to share some lighthearted humor on a particularly divisive day.

I continued to ride the wave of accolades for the next few hours – and at some point, as the notifications began to die down, I entered into a conversation with Patrick about how maybe this election cycle wasn't going to be so bad…when my phone beeps with another Facebook notification. "Wow, this thing's still going," I tell Patrick. But this time a comment with a completely different tone entered the mix. "Obviously idiots are everywhere," said a woman named Christine, a parent of twins that were elementary school classmates of my daughter. She'd left the comment on one of my selfie posts. I've known Christine since our children were in preschool together. But as the years progressed and our children had grown, our relationship had not. As fate would have it, Christine was not my favorite person in the world. She was an author that had an arrogance about her that didn't match her talents. To give you a feel of where her politics stand…a portion of the proceeds of her first book went to Planned Parenthood. She was a triggered leftist.

One of my earliest experiences with her was when our family was touring private elementary schools. The institution we were touring had a reputation for being less leftist than others in Hollywood. Its founding in the 1940s was based on the need for religion in the daily education of its students. Since its birth though, the school has been inundated with Tinseltown types. However, the school's origin story must have screamed "conservative" to Christine. At some point the tour convened in the gym and Christine was sitting in front of me as the administration presented a school video – showing an array of the children on campus. As she watched, Christine blurted out, "White kid, White kid, White kid!" Everyone awkwardly shifted in his or her seats, and a few glanced over at my husband and I with half smiles. Oddly, Patrick and I were the only Hispanics in the private school touring circuit…a fact that everyone knew. It's a small community. We didn't end up choosing this particular school because it was a K-12 institution, and we just couldn't imagine sending our five-year-old to a campus that included 12th graders. But as chance would have it, both our family and Christine's family chose the same private elementary – Oakwood in North Hollywood…and our kids ended up in the same class. As we'd later learn, Oakwood was a gateway into the Hollywood machine, and anybody looking to work in Tinseltown that had kids pulled out all of the stops to get into that specific school. The campus also doubled as practically a remote satellite office for Democrat fundraisers. The wealth of the parents lined the pockets of the "I'm With Her" campaign – so much so that many families within the school community were on Hillary Clinton's million-dollar donor list.

At Oakwood, if you were part of the Hollywood "it" crew, you were golden. As it turned out, Christine was part of that click because her husband Andrew was once the head writer for a little known show called *Friends* during its forgettable years. His old boss and the show's creator, Marta Kauffaum, was at one point the Chair of the Oakwood Trustees Board. Marta has a "POTUS peed here" sign inside one of her home bathrooms where she hosted a fundraiser in 2012 for President Barack Obama. In other words, these people were connected within the leftist cult we call Hollywood...so you get a flavor of the crowd that we roamed amongst at Oakwood.

Frankly, I never cared much about any of the Hollywood stuff. I've been around enough celebrities to know that most are not impressive. But coming from a background of very little means, it was clear to me once we unwittingly entered this cult that we weren't yet accustomed to how they operated. So when I received the Facebook comment from Christine – "Obviously idiots are everywhere" – I was stunned. Our kids were in the same small class together, they'd been sharing the same schools for seven years, and we'd likely be part of the same community through 12th grade. Christine and I may not have been chummy, but honestly I was holding out hope that we'd develop a friendship. And as far as I was concerned, we were now part of the same tribe. So you can imagine how shocked I was that this bitter bitch was publicly calling me an idiot for everyone at Oakwood to see.

Our relationship had been in decline for years. We started off friendly – sharing many of the same friends. Our husbands had developed a great relationship. Christine once told a mutual friend that Andrew and Patrick were "best friends." She hosted an annual Halloween trick-or-treat party in her fancy Larchmont Village neighborhood and would invite several of our common friends and also families from Oakwood – including ours. But when the 2012 Election came along, her husband Andrew took it upon himself to email me his election-voting guide – basically telling people how they should cast their ballot in the upcoming election. You know how people in Hollywood think they're better and smarter than us regular Americans? Well, in case you hadn't gotten the memo, I did – literally. But because I'm not a deranged leftist, I wasn't offended...just a little weirded out. Andrew and I had never discussed politics, and now he was basically telling me how I should vote and worse...he was assuming I was a Democrat. I responded to Andrew in a politically incorrect way thinking he'd appreciate it since he once had a television show canceled for what some thought was a cruel portrayal of minorities. I just thought the show sucked.

So I responded to his email with something along the lines of, "Thanks mijo, but this beaner leans right..." Given that the only Mexicans that most of the people at our school knew personally were their gardeners, nannies, janitors, and day laborers that most consider to be democrats, he was likely surprised by my admission. Christine struggled to maintain social norms with me ever since then. She unfriended me on Instagram – which was somewhat of a blessing considering she curated her feed like a Lena Dunham wet dream. Nevertheless, unfriending is a rather hostile move in this day and age – especially when it's with someone that you have to see daily. It's an act of aggression in a cold war. Our daughter never received another invite to their annual Halloween party – which was tough for her because she had to hear from her friends about all the fun she missed. However, I continued to maintain a respectful relationship with Christine because unlike her I have manners. But the birth of the Trump candidacy obviously pushed her over the edge. In hindsight, I think she was patient zero for Trump Derangement Syndrome. She'd later host a Stop Bannon play date with ten-year-olds who made artistic postcards to stop the President's Chief Strategist. Who makes leftist propaganda for arts and crafts hour with kids? That's like Rob Reiner weird.–

So I took a deep breath and read Christine's response to my selfie post again to make sure I was interpreting it correctly and didn't perceive it through the lens of my own bias – "Obviously idiots are everywhere." She definitely wasn't making a joke. Christine is humorless. She makes Rachel Maddow look incurably cheerful. "Nope, she's definitely calling me an idiot," I thought. I ran it by my husband. He agreed. I got a second and third opinion from other friends who knew Christine, and everyone concurred – she was indeed publicly disparaging me. This was a million times worse than being dumped on Instagram. So I thought I'd try a different tactic. Instead of going full MS-13 chola on her, as every fiber of my being was screaming, I thought I'd double down on the funny. I responded to her with another selfie…but this one was over the top ridiculous. I used a Snapchat filter that morphed my face into a gummy worm head, with a gummy worm coming out of my nose. What I hoped was that she would return with a comment that said something along the lines of, "LOL! I hope you didn't think I was talking about you!" I was giving her an out. Good plan right? Wrong. Instead, she responded with one word – "Yup." My heart sunk. If there was any confusion before, there was none now because she just confirmed that, "Yup, I am calling you an idiot." Thanks for clearing *that* up Christine!

This may come as a surprise to people who've never been in a conflict with me, but I am a proud ghetto-card holder. Granted, it's been a *long* time since it's seen the light of day, but in the blink of an eye I can go from zero to "oh no you didn't" hood-rat. But honestly, this was the last thing I wanted because our kids shared a class together. So I decided to move the conversation offline and email Christine privately. "As a courtesy, I'm not going to ask you this on Facebook. Are you calling me an idiot," I asked. We had a bit of back and forth. She made some excuse about Trump and Russia, and attempted to turn the tables – claiming that I obviously misinterpreted her comment and that she wasn't "interested in drama." Now

she wasn't only disparaging me in public, she was attempting
to insult my intelligence in private as well. So I responded. "If
you aren't interested in drama, why would you publicly insin-
uate that I'm an idiot? So I'll ask again, were you calling me
an idiot, yes or no?" She got a glimpse of my gangstah lean.

I've had email exchanges with Christine in the past and
you can always tell when her husband takes control of the
steering wheel because the tone in the response typically takes
a notable, more rational shift. *She* responded, "Is there something else going on that is upsetting to you? You are obviously an intelligent person. No need for public name-calling.
I will happily delete that comment with apologies if it means
this conversation can end." A few minutes later she deletes
all previous Facebook comments and inserts the simple note,
"Sincerest apologies." Problem solved.

The next morning, I woke up ready to move on from the
previous nights debacle but there's a new email in my inbox.
It's from Christine. Ugh. She declared that she feels terrible
about our exchange and that the "idiots" comment was not
meant to be about me...but when I responded with my gummy
worm selfie, she thought it felt very aggressive. Who knew
gummy worms screamed toxic masculinity. It was quite a con-
coction of half-truths and historical revision that I almost admired in its creativity. She ended by asking if we could meet at
the park outside of summer school the next day to talk about it.
I agreed to meet. I'm a big believer in hashing things out face-
to-face...something I learned about myself at an early age.
When I was a young girl in Catholic school we had to go to
confession once a week. I had the choice of confessing my sins
to the priest in one of two ways – either to sit behind a screen
which gives your confession some anonymity, or I could do
it face-to-face with the priest, looking him dead in his eyes to
confess my sins. I *never* went behind the screen. I considered

it a huge sign of weakness. I felt like God respected those who had the balls to show their mug and say, "Father Michael, I lied to my parents, even though I said I wouldn't do it again last week. I also shaved my legs without my mom's permission after she specifically told me I wasn't allowed to. That's why I'm wearing these leg warmers in ninety degree weather."

As the day progressed, the DNC leak scandal was reaching a peak. Walls had to be put up to block Bernie Sanders' followers from protesting at the doors of the DNC. But the mainstream media was largely staying away from the chaos. You had to watch people like journalist Mike Cernovich's Periscope feed to get a feel for what was really happening on the ground. To counter, Hillary's camp and her mainstream media lackeys decided to step up their rhetoric – pushing heavily the idea that the Russians hacked their email server to help the Republican nominee Donald Trump. The Democrats had released the Kraken – and if you were in a far-left enclave like my husband and I, you felt the increase in vitriol immediately. The Democrats had gotten their marching orders – find and attack all Trump supporters. This was a landmark moment for Facebook and launched what could be thought of as the "Unfriend Me Now" Movement. One mother at Oakwood, Brooke, highlighted this phenomenon well with one of her posts. It read:

"I understood why people liked Romney and McCain. I understood why people voted for both the Bushes and Reagan. But now things have turned crazy. If you support Trump, unfriend me. Because I believe that if you support Trump something is deeply wrong with you."

Notably, Brooke was buddies with The Creepies – parents at Oakwood that we called out because the dad of their family was getting in bed with other people's kids. Apparently, kid cuddling wasn't "unfriend me" worthy for Brooke, but vote for Trump...now that was just a bridge too far. But her post got me to thinking...and I began rifling through the Facebook pages of other Oakwood parents. I learned pretty quickly that many of them were openly talking smack about yours truly. It turned out I didn't even have to talk about politics. The mere fact that I posted selfies against political mudslinging was somehow an act in support of Trump. These parents weren't even trying to remotely hide their disgust for me. It was about then that I got a text message from yet another Oakwood parent – one of the few I considered a friend. Our families were slated to go on vacation together in Mexico in one short week. The text read:

> "Somehow people think you are a huge Trump supporter did you post something... Brooke just asked me after I posted something saying how I am disgusted and silently unfriend trump supporters and then she texted me and asked me if you are supporting trump that is what people told her."

Believe me when I say that the line about being disgusted and silently unfriending Trump supporters landed pretty hard. I think it's fair to say that I have thick skin and that I'm not the *feel sorry for me* type. However, everyone has limits. We'd lost a ton of friends at the school after calling out the kid cuddler Mr. Creepy. Good riddance to anyone defending that creep. But then others peeled off after his wife Mrs. Creepy began a campaign promoting that we were conservatives. The last remaining friends in our Hollywood school had been hanging on by a thread. Being a Trump supporter would likely be the straw that broke the camels back for anyone remaining. Patrick and I weren't worried about that happening for ourselves...we were concerned that our daughter would become even more excluded. We all want to be accepted...but at what costs? I ultimately came to the conclusion that I had to be true to my beliefs. These Oakwood people were not my tribe. Better to speak truth than live a lie. So I responded to what many of the school parents were saying on Facebook about Trump supporters:

"In what universe is it okay for Brooke to ask you a question like that about me? I'm SUPER fucking offended and Brooke is in for a rude awakening... So basically people think – are saying – we are racist, homophobic, xenophobic, and misogynistic? Two Mexicans who worked their way out of poverty... We are the ones people have decided to shun and target? People should think twice before going on witch-hunts. It's very hurtful. Intolerance, cultural bias, discrimination...ugly, ugly things."

Anything less than a complete rejection of Trump meant we were MAGA...and I knew that. The verdict was swift. Their family canceled their Mexico vacation with us, saying one of their kids fell sick...then quickly planned a Hillary Clinton fundraising bake sale. It looked like they wanted to show everyone they weren't with us...they were *with her*. Apparently our conservative stink had gotten on them...and they needed to cleanse themselves. News spread fast that we were MAGA...and any remaining Hollywood school friends fled faster than Ana Navarro seeking an all-you-can-eat buffet at closing time.

**

The next morning I was slated to meet with Christine. I woke up feeling a little battered and bruised but most of all I felt angry knowing that everyone on campus was talking about us being conservatives...again. But it was time to put my game face on. Because who knew...maybe this Christine woman wanted to "punch a Nazi?" I thought back to my middle school days and channeled my inner *Karate Kid*. AJ-son was ready to *wax on, wax off*. I'm always prepared for the worst.

As I walked up to greet her I notice that despite how attractive she was - she had that look of constipation. You know what I'm talking about...a deep look of discomfort. She couldn't hide her disgust of me. Christine is tall and slender with pale skin. Her dirty blonde hair was cut into a short bob that framed her face, and her lips were pursed so tightly they resemble...well, an anus. The irony was not lost on me that her personality aligned well with her looking like an asshole.

As we began our talk, she immediately interjected by patronizing me with a speech about how "regular people" have a hard time understanding her method of communication. "Uh, no bitch. I'm not a normie. I understood you were calling me an idiot," I thought. As she continued with her lies – the middle school martial artist in me was on the brink of pouncing. But I took comfort in the fact that I – who many of her ilk thinks of as "the help" – had made it into the same prestigious private school after coming from nothing while they all started on third base. I'd been disposing of people like her for years to rise out of poverty. I was standing in that spot despite elitist liberals like Christine. And now I was going to beat her using *her* rules. Christine had shown me her cards years ago. "White kid, White kid, White kid," were the words that this wealthy White leftist woman said while on tour for private schools. For all of their talk of diversity, I'd never faced more bigotry than in this Hollywood community. As I opened my mouth to respond, I knew it was time to pull the race card. "As a privileged White woman, you can't possibly understand the challenges and cultural bias I face here on a daily basis as a first-generation American of Mexican descent," I said, opening with venom. "Look around. Do you see any other parents in class that look like me? And you have the audacity to ridicule me for being different!" The look of shock on her face was priceless. A Latina was throwing identity politics right back in her face. For the record, I despise "the race card." Before I had my daughter, I though racism was a largely marginalized behavior in our society. But when I entered this community of Hollywood elites, I had an awakening. I learned that racism is alive and well in Tinseltown. If a "minority" within their circle refuses to fall in line with their leftist beliefs – they come down on them with everything they've got. So when a leftist calls you, a brown person, an idiot because of your politics… it's time to make them play by their own rules. By the time I finished with Christine, she devolved into a stuttering fool. "I am sorry," she babbled. "I can only imagine how you feel. You're right. We need more diversity around here. I couldn't agree with you more."-

I left our little encounter feeling energized. If life has taught me anything it's that if you've got one more day, then you've been blessed with another glorious opportunity. And because I live in the greatest country that the world has ever known…I have the freedom to choose not to hide in the shadows for being a Deplorable…come what may. I say live and let live, but if a leftist lunatic comes for me, I'm going to return fire.

Which brings us back to the question, how do you handle a triggered Leftist? The answer is…you make them play by their own rules. When a deranged liberal, or arrogant Planned Parenthood-loving author, tries to shame you for your beliefs, do not go gentle into the night. Fight. Claw back with whatever you have at your disposable. Use the rules *they* created against them. Shove those rules down their smug mouths. And if you feel like having a little fun…you can always mock them with a story about a selfie.

ELEVEN

Frank Talk

*How do we survive these
politically volatile times?*

Life is a game of war. It may be hard to accept, but there's
clear evidence of this fact all around us. We see it in the news
cycle...when politicians seek to impeach a duly elected president. It plays out in business...as two Silicon Valley titans
seek to sabotage a rival's new product. We even witness in action between family members...when an heir seeks to wrestle
control of the family enterprise from his siblings. This game
of war is the struggle to be heard, outlive, acquire, convince,
sell, defeat, grow, and survive. This conflict is always present.
Those that accept this fact welcome those that do not.

Although this struggle is typically subtle & measured like
a chess match – it often sheds its niceties & more resembles a
battlefield. And before you know it, you're forced into a conflict with an enemy that you didn't even know you had. Thinking of life as a game of war is an uncomfortable thought for
many. We've been conditioned to see conflict as uncivilized
– banished to the arenas of sports, the military, or the thug
class. We actually try to avoid those few unseemly characters

that relish in conflict. We call them aggressive, or troublemakers, and we throw them into a special basket thinking we've isolated the problem if we can just stay away from *that* group. But we all know it isn't as easy as that. Confrontation is often an arm's length away – whether or not we choose to accept it.

Acknowledgement that life is a game of war is captured in our oldest of text. "The life of man upon earth is a warfare," are words taken from the Book of Job, Chapter 7. This condition has survived into the modern times…and the birth of social media seems to have only accelerated this perpetual phenomenon. With that in mind, how do we survive this game of war? To find the answer, we are going to follow the story of a man who worked his way out of one of the harshest environments in America…only to find himself, as an adult, faced off with perhaps an even more formidable obstacle.

**

War zone. That's probably the best way to describe South Los Angeles in the 80s and 90s. An area bordered by the 10 Freeway in the North, and straddling the 110 Freeway all the way down to Rosecrans Avenue, South Los Angeles has long been known as one of the most dangerous enclaves in California if not the entire United States. By the early 1980s, gang violence exploded and the crack cocaine epidemic that fueled the mayhem was ripping the area apart.

Tyrone Jackson grew up in this area, near the intersection of West Slauson Avenue and Crenshaw Boulevard – almost smack dab in the middle of South Central, as the region was once called. By the time Tyrone was born, there was a desire to clean up this war zone ahead of the 1984 Olympics. Law enforcement began to sweep the area before the world's eyes descended on the city. The Games eventually ended, but the sweeps did not, reaching a height in April 1988 when, over a single weekend, almost 1,500 people were arrested by one thousand police officers. This was the place where Tyrone entered the world. "I grew up during the 80s and just gang violence was absolutely just, it was ridiculous," remembers Tyrone. He went to Horace Mann in South Central, arguably one of the most violent middle schools in Los Angeles at the time. "And you know, just people were getting shot," recalls Tyrone. "You're eleven, twelve years old people just gang violence...Someone told me that black men, we were a rare species...I mean we were rare in that it was rare for us to survive, and not be in jail or be murdered."

Tyrone has a twin sister and little brother, and they grew up without a father. His mother was absent as well. "The way it looked like for me as a child was that my mom was more interested in men and in traveling than being at home with her kids." To provide for her children, Tyrone's mother worked a lot as a caretaker – in shifts that would sometimes last for three and four days at a time. As a result, Tyrone and his siblings wouldn't see her for long stretches. For such young kids having to fend for themselves, it was an incredibly tough time. So he and his sister made up their minds that they were going to live with their grandparents. "We ended up moving out of our mom's house at ten. I remember my sister, one day she just got tired of my mom not being home...and she just said, 'I'm leaving.' And she packed up her backpack and walked out. And it helped that my grandmother lived around the corner. And so she left and I was like, 'Hey I don't want to be here by myself.' So I left about an hour later."

Their grandparent's place became their new home. But at seventy-years old, Tyrone and his sister were worlds apart from their new guardians. "So in many ways...I felt alone and that was just life growing up," says Tyrone. "I felt abandoned and alone and hurt a lot, but it wasn't something I had the luxury of having the time to complain a whole lot about, or wallow in a lot." By the time Tyrone and his sister made the move to their grandparents, the conflict between the police, gangs, and residence of South Central had reached a breaking point, and was just about to get worse.

"Now the story that might never have surface if someone hadn't picked up his home video camera," reported ABC News Peter Jennings at the time. "We've all seen the pictures of Los Angeles police officers beating a man they had just pulled over. The city's police chief said today he'll support criminal charges against some of the men." Several Los Angeles Police Officers were caught on an amateur home video camera relentlessly beating, kicking, and clubbing a black man named Rodney King. "In our review we find that the officers struck him with batons between fifty-three and fifty-six times," said Los Angeles Police Chief Daryl Gates to a gaggle of media at the time. "One officer rendered six kicks, and one officer one kick." King looked to be submitting. The beating left him badly bruised, face swollen, with a broken leg...and scarred by the 50,000-volt stun gun he endured during the incident. The video was shocking and enraged people, especially the Black community – with civil rights leaders calling for Chief Gates to be terminated. South Central became a tinderbox just waiting for a spark to set the entire place on fire. That would come in April 1992. The jury in the Rodney King case delivered its decision of not guilty for all of the police officers accused of excessive force. The verdict incensed many throughout Los Angeles. Citizens of South Central immediately took to the streets, setting fires, looting, and at times attacking innocent passersby. The LA Riots as they came to be known went on for five days. In the end, sixty-three people were dead, and more than a thousand buildings were damaged. This was the environment that Tyrone had to endure before he had even reached puberty.

When most kids were concerned about making the all-star baseball team, or riding a bike, or acing their next test – Tyrone had much more fundamental aspirations. "My basic first set of goals was to live to be eighteen. I wanted to survive pre- adulthood. And then I wanted to get out of Los Angeles. Those were my two goals. And I'll tell you I barely made the first one, to survive. And I was a kid that was as straight as an arrow." Tyrone was able to avoid joining gangs, but he became a target for bullies. He was relatively small. And he also wore glasses and never picked up what he refers to as "the ghetto accent." Collectively, these traits tend to put a bulls eye on your back in the so-called hood – and that's what happened to Tyrone.

His first fight was when someone walked up to him and punched him in the face with a cast on their arm – that's how emboldened the bully felt. "That was when I discovered my own personal power. And so when my awareness came back to me, I guess they saw I was a different person and I wasn't gonna be the person that was gonna get picked on. And so I looked at them and I was ready to fight." That caught the bully off guard, and he started running. Tyrone took chase through the playground and as he did, he spotted his cousin off in the distance. "He was coming out of a building so I called him, 'Hey Dimitri come on.' And so I turned around and I ran right into a basketball poll. And I was out for I don't know how long, maybe four or five minutes." When he came back to, he realized that his front tooth that just came in was cracked. "I remember getting up, spitting out my teeth, just in incredible pain. And I still found the dude that hit me and I gave them the beating of his life," he recalls.

For the next couple of years Tyrone developed an itchy

trigger finger. If someone just rubbed him the wrong way, he'd come out fists flying at even the slightest of provocations. It was a stretch of really tough years for Tyrone. He'd acquired an anger problem. "You grow up in that situation and you're just, you're mad. I mean…you don't have love and concern from your parents, or you don't feel like you have that. There's just a kind of a resentment, just almost a hatred and a bitterness that festers inside of you." That anger grew within Tyrone, to a point where it landed him in really hot water.

Tyrone was working in the school cafeteria on a hot Southern California day, when a classmate swiped his soda and ran away. Tyrone didn't see which direction the soda thief went, so he asked a white kid in the vicinity if he saw the soda thief take off. The kid responded snarkily. "And he was like, 'I bet you wish I would tell you where he went.' He was just sitting there teasing me, and I'm about to die of thirst," recalls Tyrone. Tyrone's trigger finger was about to get itchy. His grandmother had just gotten him eye glasses with the nylon strap that connects to both arms of the glasses and wraps around the back of your neck when you wear them – the kind that fictional character Steve Urkel wore that hold your glasses on your head. So Tyrone, irate that the kid wouldn't tell him which direction the soda thief went, grabbed the strap and wrapped it around the kids neck and somehow lifted him up. As he held the kid up off of the ground, the soda thief came back pleading with him to let the kid down. So he did. Tyrone then grabbed his soda and went on with his day – not thinking much about the incident. But the next day he heard his name over the loudspeaker summoning him to the principal's office.

When he arrived, he realized that he was in big trouble. "There [are] two police officers sitting there and the kid's parents. Turns out not only did he have this enormous burn all the way around his neck, but the kid passed out…he was laying there unconscious. I didn't even realize it." The cops turned to the parents and asked if they wanted to press charges. Even as a young boy, Tyrone sensed the gravity of the situation. The anger inside him was in danger of becoming a permanent fixture of his personality. In the moment, he contemplated his situation. "I'd never thought of myself as a bad kid or stupid kid, but I was like, 'Dude, I'm sitting here about to become *that* kid. That black kid that ends up in juvenile hall over something…ignorant.' And…at that point I realized that I needed help…and if I didn't get the help, there's a good possibility goal number one may never be made. And so I found that help. I started to really pray and ask God to help me because people said that he could heal wounds. And I realized… that I was hurt and so my relationship with God began then." Tyrone started to attend church in the heart of South Central and that relationship with God remains with him to this day.

As he began to heal, he also started to notice other things around him. Even in retirement, both his grandparents had side hustles. His grandfather converted his garage into an auto mechanic shop, and his grandmother was a babysitter. He realized that they both became entrepreneurial to make ends meet. That idea stuck with Tyrone.

In high school, Tyrone participated in a class called Upward Bound. If you are raised in a poor community anywhere in America, there is likely a similar program that works to steer kids towards college. When he graduated from high school in 1999, Tyrone ended up attending Fisk University, a historically black college in Nashville, Tennessee – majoring in Political Science. He met a student named Marcella on her first day at Fisk. They fell in love instantly. "And it turned out Marcella, she was just as God seeking as I was," Tyrone fondly remembers. "And she began to have like dreams very early on. And it turns out she was dreaming about me for years and didn't even know that I existed. And then one day like I popped up, and we never dated or anything. We just…we knew."

In just a few years they would be married. His experience with Marcella was magical, but school, on the other hand, was a bit of a let down. Tyrone considered the experience largely a waste of time. He was going down a political science path – but he felt something was missing in his education, and wanted to learn about business before graduating. But his academic career was wrapping up. So his plan was to start a hotdog cart to learn the ins and outs of business. "It seems like to me most of the principles of business are present in a hot dog cart, maybe just not as extreme," he thought at the time. So immediately after college, Tyrone and Marcella worked a few jobs in Nashville, and by 2005 in the middle of winter, they'd saved enough to begin their entrepreneurial journey by opening a gourmet hotdog stand. They set up shop in downtown Nashville on the corner of 4th and Church. People would line up to buy their products and the two had immediate success.

Business began to grow, so they acquired a second cart. They expanded into catering, then moved into night service… setting up outside of nightclubs. It wasn't long before Tyrone and Marcella lined up a gig providing all of the food for a local country club. Business was going great, but then a chance encounter changed everything. "One day [there] was a Jewish lady that came by our cart. And I saw her every day, you see the same people over and over. But she came by and…I asked her, 'Why won't you buy something?' And she said, 'You know, you're not kosher.' I was like, 'We have kosher hotdogs.' But she was like, 'Your stand isn't kosher.'" So Tyrone went home and began researching how to get kosher certification for his cart. But in his research he started to discover for the first time how meat was handled in the United States.

As he dug into the literature he became disgusted. "And I remember reading seventy percent of the ground beef in America contains ammonium hydroxide, which is literally ammonia and water. And so quite naturally I started to call my suppliers and ask them where they're getting their beef from, and what I learned terrified me." His suppliers in essence laughed at the question. They told him that one batch of beef could have meat from one hundred cows; so finding the origin of it was near impossible. At this point they were expecting their first child. "And we're doing children's birthday parties and I'm like, 'I'm feeding these people ammonium hydroxide. Oh my God!' For me, my logic was so very simple. It literally came down to this – either you are part of the problem, or you're part of the solution. There is not really a gray area. And as far as I saw I had to face the fact that I was selling hotdogs that were coming through a system that was poisoning people. There's really no other way it can be interpreted. And the reason I was doing it was for profit so I was actually as guilty as the people were making the hot dogs because I was profiting from their poisoning."

Tyrone felt something had to change. He started to lose sleep over his discovery, and slowly began to lose the desire to even continue his hotdog business. So he tried to remedy the situation by ordering organic products. But this was before the whole organic movement took hold. At the time, ordering quality organic hotdogs turned out not to be an easy task. Everything he ordered tasted crappy, and the product was expensive to boot. Tyrone decided he couldn't make money with the garbage that was out there, and if he couldn't do the business in a way that was beneficial to his customers, he didn't want to do it at all. So Tyrone and Marcella started the process of winding down their hotdog venture. But the timing of this decision was about to collide with an unprecedented event – one that would hit small business owners the hardest.

The subprime mortgage crisis hit, and the United States economy was about to take a nosedive. Tyrone and Marcella were about to have an awakening. "Every Disney movie... turned out to be an outright lie," says Tyrone. "There was no cavalry. There was no guiding angel. There was no fairy godmother. I proceeded to lose every asset that I had. At that time I had an investment property. I ended up moving into that. Everything just went to hell in a hand basket. I couldn't find a job. I was looking for a job for almost a year. It was just an absolute mess. When I found a job, I was working like three jobs just to try to keep things afloat."

And like the saying goes, when it rains it pours. After he moved into his investment property, a major storm hit that year and his roof collapsed. When he turned to his home insurance to deal with the problem, they said it wasn't covered – claiming it was a pre-existing condition. So he was stuck with a ten thousand dollar repair...and he just started working. Tyrone turned to his mortgage company hoping for some leniency, and told them that he was going to miss two months of his mortgage but by the third month he'd have all the money together. "And so I did exactly that. You know even with two weeks to spare, I sent them a check for everything that I owed them. They took my money, they held it for like three weeks, and then sent the check back to me with a note for foreclosure." Tyrone and Marcella were losing the house. It was a heartbreaking time for their young family. "If there was ever a time where my spirit was broken it was broken then," Tyrone admits.

He felt like he'd done everything right. They'd scrimped and saved to open their first hotdog stand, then when it took off...they expanded by adding another cart to their operation. Business was booming, and they made enough to buy a house.

When he learned about the poor source of his hotdog products, and couldn't find a quality replacement, he decided to do what he saw was the right thing and close the business. But that fatal decision ultimately led to him losing his property in the midst of an unpredictable storm and the biggest financial crisis in over seventy-five years. Everything was falling apart. "It wasn't even downhill. It was like I was in a seventh dungeon of hell somewhere."

They had to walk away from their home. Tyrone and Marcella took their family to Columbus, Ohio where they moved in with some of Marcella's family. Things were incredibly tough. At one point, Tyrone remembers driving down the street and they only had ten dollars left. "We were just going to buy a hamburger and die," he says laughing through the pain. But then one day Tyrone was driving down the street and a thought came to his mind – and it literally shook him out of his depression. He wasn't going to accept this defeat. "And I said, 'If I'm dealing with this problem, I can't find good quality products, I can't be the only person. I know that there's something within me that wants to do this.' And I was like, 'I'm going to restart my business if I have to raise the cow myself, if I have to learn how to make sausage myself. I will rebuild this. We will recover and we will rebuild our business.' And so from that decision I end up finding a job at Nationwide washing dishes."

Every night after work he'd come home and spend hours on a business plan to rebuild his company. Tyrone even turned to some of his coworkers in the industrial kitchen, trying to get them to join him...but he learned he was surrounded by naysayers. "And I was like, 'Look I've done this before. I've started a business before. Let's go in together. We can get this done a lot quicker, we can make more money than this.' And they were like, 'you're not gonna do nothing. You ain't gonna be nothing but a dishwasher. You running your mouth.' It's like, okay, I don't have any allies here."

So Tyrone and Marcella focused and started to figure out their own way forward. What that meant was they'd have to learn how to make their own frankfurters. "And I decided that I needed to learn to farm," recalls Tyrone. "I needed to start all the way at the beginning. And so...I saved enough money to be able to live for six months and I quit." He figured that not only did they have to learn how to make their own frankfurters and sausages; they had to learn to raise and grow their own ingredients. They found an urban farm and started there. Tyrone and Marcella's new business, The Good Frank, was born.

They started their new business actually farming – raising their own crops. Marcella learned the trade through a welfare program then developed a system to provide local businesses with fresh produce from what they grew. Tyrone did his part, volunteering at the farm. They were able to add to their six-month savings reserve, stretching it to a year and a half. But they were running out of money again fast. "We're like we need to actually learn to make sausage. We need to get this thing going or we're going to end up sinking right back to where we were." And so they did some deep research and took a class on sausage making. Next thing you know, they're buying equipment and making frankfurters. But Tyrone and Marcella took it a step further. They connected with a family of organic farmers, began raising their own cow, learned how to slaughter it – then found co-packers to process their beef frankfurters. And finally, they put those products in stores. To bring it full circle, they bought a hotdog cart and restarted that part of their business. Tyrone and Marcella had finally gotten back on track with their passion.

The family briefly moved back to Texas, learning how to smoke frankfurters and other kinds of meats. They were honing their craft. When Tyrone and Marcella shook off the defeat of losing everything...their worldview began to blossom. To get an understanding of what happened to them during the Financial Crisis, Tyrone began reading about how the banking system operated – how others profited off of the crisis, how the players that caused the chaos got off scot-free...and in many cases wealthier. They learned by building their company how the government works against small business owners. And they eventually came to the conclusion that they were conservatives.

Through this awakening, Tyrone came to the realization that the GOP was doing nothing to connect with the place where he came from...the inner city. While the Democrats were coming into these neighborhoods and pushing a victimhood mentality, the Republicans were missing an opportunity. He thought they should be spreading the message of entrepreneurship...what Tyrone sees as a critical tool in tackling the problems of poverty stricken areas like his hometown South Central. So when Trump, a successful businessman, entered the political scene, Marcella and Tyrone were ecstatic...and they posted a video to YouTube expressing their excitement. It was really their first outward political expression. Otherwise, they had largely kept their politics to themselves.

When Hurricane Harvey hit Texas, they moved the family back to Columbus, Ohio and saw it as their moment to put everything they'd learned into action. Throughout the years they'd been developing each part of their food system to ensure quality and healthy products. Tyrone and Marcella had fully developed their process. "We have a farm that raises our ingredients or raises our raw materials," explains Tyrone. "And then we process our raw materials. And then we bring them into our kitchen, and we assemble hotdogs. They go out on hotdog carts. And then we assemble some [and] they go out in the stores. And then we assemble some [and] they go directly to customers through shipping." They'd spent countless hours developing this entire system and now that they were back in Columbus, they decided to put their plan into motion. They rented space in a kitchen and began making both meat and vegan frankfurters. They created the entire product on their own, from the farming to the handmade frankfurters, and even designed the packaging themselves – branding some of their products with their faces. Their vegan franks tapped an underserved niche and they lined up a solid wholesale business selling them to a few local accounts. They also began promoting their meatless products to a Facebook page called Vegan Columbus – including images of their products and packaging to increase their brand awareness. The duo started hosting tastings in town and promoted the events through this Facebook page.

Tyrone and Marcella had finally seen the light at the end of the tunnel. The early success and joy, the excruciating suffering through the downturn, the slow rebuild, and the years of developing their new process was now paying off. Their new company, The Good Frank, was beginning to prosper. But what they didn't know was that they were about to hit another roadblock...one that they never saw coming.

"My kids love Donald Trump...When I say love, these kids they knew everything about Donald Trump," says Tyrone. "I just came home one day, they knew when his birthday was, where he'd been born. I mean just crazy, they were drawing pictures...they literally love Trump. And so I was like, 'One day if Trump does a rally here in Ohio and we have some time, we're gonna go to one of the rallies.'" That moment came in August 2018, when Trump visited Tyrone's area to support Troy Alderson, an Ohio politician running for Congress. "And so Trump came and we went to the rally," recalls Tyrone.

"And I guess, this is probably the only black advantage…but it was six of us. My family, we have four kids. And so we all came in, and we're all happy and bright. And someone pulls us in, because we were there fairly early, and…was like, 'Do you guys want to sit on the stage?' We were like, 'Yeah!' And so we ended up sitting on the stage, and we got some MAGA gear. And it was really a great experience."

The entire family was overjoyed – smiles ear to ear. They were just steps away from a man that they admired for so many reasons, a man that acknowledged as a GOP politician, the plight of inner cities…the place that Tyrone struggled to just stay alive in. They'd experienced so much hardship over the years, losing everything during the Financial Crisis, being down to their last ten dollars, then shaking it all off and rebuilding – first taking a dishwashing job, then reimagining the entire process for creating their franks. Their business, The Good Frank, was now thriving and their family was celebrating life with their president. But unbeknownst to them, trouble was brewing.

A few Columbus vegans were watching the broadcast of the rally, and it was impossible to not see Tyrone's family because they were literally right behind Donald Trump. "And I guess somebody recognized us there," recalls Tyrone. "And the one thing about vegans…a lot of the vegans are very hard left. They're very angry, kind of bitter people. And so I guess when someone saw us there at the rally they recognized us. And we were just in production and my phone started to ring and it was one of our main accounts." One of their primary customer for their vegan franks told Tyrone that they have a problem. "And he was saying that they have some people threatening his business because they're carrying our products. And they were calling me a racist and a homophobe and this and that."

Some months earlier, Tyrone had been concerned that

many of the decisions coming out of the Supreme Court had been anti-Christian. So when the court landed on the side of a Colorado baker that refused to make a custom cake for a gay couple on religious grounds, Tyrone posted something on his Facebook page in support of the decision. But his page was public. After the far-left vegans in Columbus saw Tyrone and Marcella behind Trump at the rally and recognized them from the vegan franks packaging – they began combing through their Facebook page and found his conservative leaning posts. "I never thought I said anything that's hateful or mean or stupid or anything like that," says Tyrone. "But someone was going through my profile and they saw me make a comment about the Supreme Court." And that's all the far-left vegans needed. They knew a few of his biggest accounts and began applying pressure. When their main account started feeling the heat, they contacted Tyrone to see if there was a work around. "And he said, 'you know Tyrone, people love your products but they hate you…is there a way that you can provide us with products and say that you didn't.' And I was like, 'You want me to lie… dude I don't do that.'" The radical vegans hated Tyrone and his family for being conservatives and having traditional values. Tyrone figured that there was nothing stopping them from doing the same thing in the future – and potentially jeopardizing his client's business. And so after some deliberation, Tyrone decided to severe the relationship. But his problems didn't end there.

After losing their primary account, they decided to focus all of their efforts on shipping The Good Frank products directly to customers through online ordering. However, the news was about to get worse. Word of Tyrone and Marcella's politics reached the owner of the commercial kitchen the duo rented to produce their frankfurters. "Our landlord was a far leftist too," claims Tyrone. "And he refused to renew our lease agreement." So not only did they lose their primary wholesale account, they lost their kitchen. Now they had no way to make their franks. And no product meant no money coming in. Tyrone was forced to find a job. He became a mail carrier at the post office.

These far-left vegans, at the apex of the midterm election, forced his family out of business. And these are the times that we live in – where so-called tolerant leftists target a Black man that survived one of the most violent environments in America, who without a mother or father present, worked his way through high school, graduated from college, started a small business with his wife, lost everything in the banking crisis, and rebuilt his company to become a promising, health conscious frankfurter business – only to have it taken out by bigoted leftists for the crime of supporting the president. "We had heard about leftists attacking people. But we didn't really know that it was actually happening to just regular people," says Tyrone.

Which leads us back to the question, in this crazy politically charged environment, how do we survive this game of war? The answer is you need to find your tribe – and put everything into them. "For the first time ever, it prompted me to reach out to other conservatives," says Tyrone. "We had just been quiet conservatives to ourselves up until that moment. And we reached out and we shared our story."

You may have guessed by now that Tyrone and Marcella are not the type of people to give up...ever. They are rebuilding The Good Frank – and are again open for business. They found a kitchen to make their vegan and beef frankfurters and are focusing on shipping their product direct to customers – targeting conservatives, Deplorables, and anyone else that wants healthy, handcrafted franks and sausages from out of the closet conservatives. They are also exposing inner city people to entrepreneurship through classes on starting their own hotdog stands. Tyrone and Marcella are trying to build a bridge. "When this thing happened, I realized that there was no...point of connection for the conservative movement and the Black community. And so I wanted to try to form a bridge where we can talk. Where we can actually say, 'this is what we believe. Conservatives have been portrayed by the media this way, but I am a conservative and these are all conservatives and we're here and we want to know what you need. We want to know how we can help you. We know that you want more from your life. And we want to help. We really care about you and your family and your neighborhood.'"

Their story is now front-and-center on their website – The-GoodFrank.com. They aren't hiding any longer...because they've found their tribe, and they're putting everything into them.

TWELVE

Conservatism's Fatal Flaw
How has the Left dominated every
American cultural institution?

It seems like every day when we flip on the news another conservative is being purged from a major cultural institution. Google discovers an employee is a right-winger…then shows him the exit. A college puts a professor's job in jeopardy when his conservative politics are outed. ESPN fires a famed pitcher turned analyst for sharing a negative meme on transgenderism. ABC cancels a wildly popular sitcom, just weeks after its star admits to attending Trump's inauguration. Facebook forces the resignation of a high-level executive after it's discovered he supported a republican candidate. Simon & Schuster cancels the book deal of a conservative author after he broaches a taboo gay topic. YouTube demonetizes a video creator for their unauthorized beliefs. The examples are endless. Conservative actors, professors, authors, scientists, publishers, programmers, meme makers, and journalists are constantly being purged from America's most influential cultural institutions… for their beliefs. How has this happened? How has the Left been able to dominate every American cultural institution?

And calling it domination is not hyperbole. The Left has taken over the media, Hollywood, Big Tech, education, advertising, book publishing...and are on the brink of capturing sports, the church, science, and even a long-standing conservative stronghold...audio programming. The Right has controlled talk radio for the past three decades, but the Left has now taken over the form in the realm of podcasts. The Left has infiltrated every influential institution that defines our culture and methodically eliminates conservatives from the ranks. What's going on here? To find the answer, we're going to follow the story of a scientist turned teacher whose ordeal with the Left just might have exposed a fatal flaw in the conservative movement.

**

The Left constantly complains about the patriarchy, and that the system is rigged against women – that there are just too few females in science, technology, engineering, and medicine...the so-called STEM fields. So on paper the Left should love Karen Siegemund – a woman that would become a practicing scientist for roughly twenty years. Karen grew up in Pacific Palisades, California – part of Los Angeles on the coast between Santa Monica and Malibu. As a child, she showed an incredible aptitude for learning. She could read before kindergarten, and was quick at math. "My local elementary school just couldn't handle that," recalls Karen. "They kept telling my mom, well, you know, she shouldn't be reading yet and she shouldn't be doing this math...and my mom would go and get me workbooks of more advanced math classes. And so when I was finished with my 2nd grade, 3rd grade, 4th grade math worksheets in class, I would pull out my other math worksheets that mom had gotten and they did not like that. And so mom had kind of had enough of the run around."

So Karen's parents looked around and found Le Lycée Français de Los Angeles. The school is located in the heart of the City of Angels, and is a French speaking school that is accredited in France. Karen's mom grew up in the French part of Switzerland, and spoke the language. Her father grew up in Berlin. So Le Lycée fit in with their European sensibilities. "But the French Lycée seemed to hit all those things that were important to them," says Karen. "They could handle that I was an early reader. They could handle I was advanced in math. The language piece was a bonus. The European aspect was a real plus. The rigor, just the general rigor of education seemed much better than my local elementary school." When Karen first attended the school for fifth grade, it was just a few years after Le Lycée opened. At the time, the school taught only in the French language and was just like any other school in France. The curriculum was in French. The teachers were French. The books were in French. The entire program was as if you were going to elementary school in Paris. "And so when I started there in [1969], I didn't speak French," recalls Karen. "And I cried every day. And I'm so grateful that my parents didn't say, 'Oh, poor Karin, she's so unhappy. Let's, you know, take her out.' I stuck it out. And by about Christmas time of my first year…I was pretty fluent."

Le Lycée is truly an anomaly in Los Angeles – a highly regarded private school that many former and recent European transplants choose so their kids can feel at home and carry on some of their family's cultural traditions. It now has an international section for kids that don't speak French. Karen has fond memories of her childhood time there. They instilled in her the value of a rigorous education, an appreciation of all that's great of western civilization, a love of the arts, and the history of it all. "My whole life, I felt so grateful to have gone to that school. It was a peculiar place. It was a weird little European oasis in Los Angeles...and I've always valued that part of my education...I've always been so grateful to have had that exposure to something that most American kids haven't."

For high school, Karen attended boarding school on the East Coast and then came back west to attend Revelle College at UC San Diego. The structure of the program was perfect for her. "The first two years, you don't even get to your major. You had requirement of fluency in a language. You had a year of calculus...bunch of physics, biology, [and] chemistry. You had to have humanities...So if people couldn't wait to get to college because now they could finally drill down into that thing that interested them, that wasn't for you. But it was for me because I just have really broad interests." She received her Bachelor's of Science in Applied Mathematics. And then after college, Karen worked for roughly two decades during the Cold War as a scientist in underwater acoustics. She helped develop new sonar technologies to find Soviet Union submarines for the Navy. Her work in defense sparked another interest in Karen. She wanted to understand the global dynamics that led to the obvious need for defense in the first place. "We were fighting the Cold War," says Karen. "We were fighting the Soviet Union. We won, but what I wanted to go back to school for was, how does it get to this point? What's the other side of defense? I just wanted to learn more about the whole global political situation that leads to defense issues." So in 1999, Karen enrolled in the master's program at Boston University, studying international relations. At the time, she didn't think much about whether any particular issue was on the political right or left. But getting an inside view of the Cold War helped form her worldview. Having a strong national defense was simply an obvious and necessary step to counteract the forces coming from the Soviet Union. It wasn't a pro-left or pro-right thing…it was a pro-America position. Anything else was unfathomable to her.

Through her time at Le Lycée, and her life experience in defense and now studying international relations, she began to realize that she'd developed a deep appreciation for western civilization. And as this worldview slowly began to take shape within her, Karen started witnessing an alarming trend in education - one that would eventually target her in a place she least expected.

In 2002, she became a middle school teacher in Rhode Island. At some point, kids from the eighth grade were supposed to put together presentations that they would deliver to the entire student body. So they learned PowerPoint, how to do research, and they basically got a crash course in public speaking. It all seemed like a worthwhile effort to Karen. She attended the exercise and the PowerPoint presentations looked spectacular, and the students spoke well on stage – opening with funny lines that pulled in the audience. Superficially, the activity looked like a success. "Except factually everything was wrong," recalls Karen. "Not in all cases, but in some. And I pointed this out. I said, 'Hey, he did a great job, but everything that he just told the middle school was wrong.' And the response was, 'Yes, but weren't his PowerPoint slides great and didn't he look great in his confidence?' And that's when I realized we are coming at education from such a different perspective. To him, it was the skills that they needed to learn. To me, it's knowledge. Everything else is just emotion. I didn't recognize then that it was a left-right thing, but I knew that I was on a different side."

Karen continued her studies at Boston University, working towards her doctorate in education and American culture. If she ever had an awakening moment that western civilization was being attacked from within – it was during the research for her doctorate dissertation. Her idea was to probe how kids developed their national identity – so her research encompassed looking at the educational system that helped form that identity. Again, politics wasn't the framework for how she delved into the research – whether something was on the political left or right wasn't how she viewed the world at the time. She entered the process with fresh, unbiased eyes. But what she uncovered during her research turned out to be completely about leftist indoctrination. The dissertation topic was on young adult literature. She wanted to understand what was out there for adolescents to read that would help them shape their worldview, address problems, and form their identity. "And it was so horrifying," recalls Karen. "[It was] one thing after another – the hyper-sexualization…the lack of guidance that they provided one way or another. Nobody took a stance. There [were] no values in them. And I don't mean sort of backhanded or overt, just nothing. And really, the only books at that time that really showed values, loyalty, integrity, honesty, searching to find a good answer to a complicated problem, the books that address that were *Harry Potter*."

The series of books by J.K. Rowling showed kids grappling with complex issues, portrayed some adults as good, and some as bad. Good versus evil was always a clear theme. The narrative provided guidance on how to navigate the world – showing the importance of friendship and loyalty. But the other books written for kids and young adults were void of this moral guidance. "It was all just a big miasma of chaos. And it was really profoundly depressing. There was a book about a girl with anorexia. And great…there should be books because this is a real issue. It's a real problem. She did all the right things and wound up dying at the end anyway. This isn't angst literature. This is undermining kids' selves. And it was incredibly depressing." Karen spoke to librarians and other teachers to get their take on the definition of a good book. "And the answer was, a good book is a book any kid will read, she recalls. "So I'm discovering this valuelessness – again not realizing that this is a left right thing. But eventually... it was one of the professors at the school of [education] who said, 'you're not going to like what I tell you, but everything that you found is from a conservative point of view. Your conclusions are conservative. And what you're uncovering is what the left is doing.'" Karen tended to be a very non-political person, but she was coming to the realization that everything that she'd come to believe happened to land her in camp with the Right. Her beliefs were considered conservative.

She'd now spent over a quarter of a century on the East Coast. Her career blossomed in the sciences. She got her master's, became an educator...raised a family. But a few years after finishing her doctorate at Boston University, Karen's hometown began calling her back. In 2010, she was visiting Los Angeles when a friend suggested she look into an organization called the American Freedom Alliance (AFA) because her friend thought Karen's interests seemed to mesh with the group. She was intrigued. So she looked into it, and what Karen found was that the AFA defended Western civilization, they were against bias in the media, abhorred indoctrination in schools, were opponents of globalization, valued national sovereignty, and were against the spread of both Islam and radical environmentalism throughout the West. "So when my friends told me you need to know about AFA," Karen says, "they were absolutely right because I connected on every single piece of that."

At the time, Karen still really hadn't been publicly vocal about her beliefs. However, one horrific event would change all of that. On September 11th, 2012, the U.S. Consulate in Benghazi, Libya was attacked. In the end, four Americans died, including Ambassador Chris Stevens. With less than two months before the presidential election, the attack became understandably a hot button political issue. For months before the attack, Obama had been carefully crafting a narrative that his Administration had successfully destroyed the terrorist threat in the Middle East. His biggest foreign policy surrogate, Vice President Joe Biden, was tasked with helping drive that message home with the memorable slogan – "Osama Bin Laden is dead and General Motors is alive." It was a campaign rallying call that he'd been delivering constantly for months.

On the eve of the anniversary of the 9/11 attack, the New York Times ran an op-ed entitled *The Deafness Before The Storm*, criticizing the Bush Administration for missing the warnings of the deadly terrorist attack. The article closed saying, "Could the 9/11 attack have been stopped, had the Bush team reacted with urgency to the warnings contained in all of those daily briefs? We can't ever know. And that may be the most agonizing reality of all." The media was doing its part in creating a narrative that the Republicans were weak on terror. But with the Benghazi attack, the Obama Administration and his fellow travellers in the mainstream media now had egg on their faces. Their carefully developed narrative that President Obama succeeded in fighting terror where the Republicans failed was quickly being derailed. A cornerstone of Obama's reelection strategy was now in jeopardy. So his Administration swiftly crafted a new message to explain away the attack in Libya – sending out Secretary of State Hillary Clinton to deliver the deflection. "I also want to take a moment to address the video circulating on the Internet that has led to these protests in a number of countries," claimed the Secretary of State. "To us, to me personally, this video is disgusting and reprehensible. It appears to have a deeply cynical purpose: to denigrate a great religion and to provoke rage. But as I said yesterday, there is no justification, none at all, for responding to this video with violence."

The Obama Administration suggested that the Benghazi attack was not planned. There were no warning signs that they missed. The attack was simply spontaneous, and was sparked by an anti-Islam video. The narrative was preposterous to anyone except the most partisan political players. But the media ran with the narrative anyway – hoping to dampen the scandal until after Election Day. There twisted attempt even led to MSNBC's Chris Matthews famously scolding one of his own audience members for daring to suggest that the attack was caused by more than just a video:

> **Audience Member**: "They've covered up scandals in the Middle East."
> **Chris Matthews**: "What was the scandal that was covered up?"
> **Audience Member**: "Benghazi."
> **Chris Matthews**: "What was the scandal?"
> **Audience Member**: "Well I mean."
> **Chris Matthews**: "Get to it. Nail it. What was the scandal?"
> **Audience Member**: "[Obama] said there was a video. It was not about the video."
> **Chris Matthews**: "Yeah it was about the video. Read the newspaper. Thank you. Everybody knows it's about the video. It's all about the video. Thank you."

The media misinformation on the attack was just too much for Karen to stomach. She felt as a nation we could have the right and the left, but as long as the media was the de facto PR firm of the Democrat Party, our country couldn't function properly. Karen saw the media as actively creating a false reality. "The world that everybody lives in is a fabricated one," she says. "When everything everybody knows is wrong because they've been told it through television or news or whatever, we just didn't stand a chance. So I started Rage Against the Media." She launched the organization shortly after the Benghazi attack in 2012, and became publicly political for the first time. The group was dedicated to fighting back against the lies of the mainstream media. To kick it off, she organized a rally at CBS Studios in Hollywood to speak out against media bias. "It's a travesty that our mainstream media does not do its job," Karen said at the rally. "Recognize that the truth is told through Breitbart, RedState, Townhall, Politichicks...that's where the truth is being told...not the mainstream media. And we're here today to say we've had enough of the mainstream nonsense. They don't have a monopoly on this anymore. We can stand up and say, 'We've had enough!'"

Karen continued her involvement in American Freedom Alliance, but she was doing it all from the East Coast. However, with her child now going off to Claremont McKenna College, she decided it was time to come back home to Cali. After living on the East Coast for roughly thirty years – getting married, having her kids, and building her career – she woke up back home on December 31, 2012. It wasn't long before Karen decided she wanted to return to teaching. So she looked to her childhood alma mater, Le Lycée – sending them a letter about her great childhood memories of the school, and inquired about any job openings. As luck would have it, the daughter of the people that founded it was running the school. "They called me and had a fabulous interview," says Karen. "She remembered me as being brilliant and the school was super happy to have me. And it was a coming home. It felt absolutely wonderful. I loved being there. I loved being among kids wearing the same uniform I'd worn. I loved seeing kids be picked up where my parents had picked me up. I remember…going back into my fifth grade classroom and just feeling the warm embrace of my childhood, of my parents, of such a different life. And it really…it was the best feeling ever to be part of it." So she started teaching math there in 2015.

Everything was in place for Karen. She was back in her childhood town, teaching at her alma mater. And she was still supporting western civilization values through her involvement with American Freedom Alliance. However later that year, the president and founder of AFA, Avi Davis, suddenly died. It was shocking news. The organization was largely a one-man show…but it had attracted a loyal following. So in an attempt to jumpstart it after its founder's passing, the board got together and in the end, Karen wound up at the head of the organization. In some other era, her role at the AFA might have been just considered as an activity in her private life. But these are not normal times. As the 2016 campaign started to heat up, so did her school faculty room. "My fellow faculty were heavily leftist," recalls Karen. "I heard all kinds of stuff from other students about what teachers would say about Trump, about conservatives, all of that. On free dress day, a teacher wore #Resist T-shirts and other kinds of, you know, lefty messages like that. So the faculty room was full of leftist conversation." And of course, like most elite liberal enclaves, Karen says they were talking as if everyone around them were also Leftists. They were all horrified by Trump. She found this ironic. Here was a bunch of teachers largely from France teaching at an American school. Why weren't they teaching in their home country? Was it perhaps because their economy wasn't good? Was it maybe because they couldn't get a job there? Why would they want America to be more like France, a place they left behind for one reason or another? Their whole attitude was peculiar to Karen.

Throughout the 2016 Election cycle, the temperature slowly began to increase on campus. As Trump rose in the primaries, her colleagues became more vocal. It was obvious to her, given the posters in the faculty room or stickers on their computers that they were rooting for either Hillary Clinton or Bernie Sanders to win the election. "They wanted one of those," says Karen. "The conversation in the faculty room definitely got, they were all more excitable…and I didn't engage. Why would I? You know, I talk about this stuff 24/7. I've no need to have to make enemies in the faculty room."

As many people who lived and worked in liberal strongholds may remember, walking within the community in the days following the election was like attending a funeral. There was deep sadness, disbelief, and even fear. Karen's faculty community was no different. She noticed that many of her colleagues were absent on the first day The Donald became President-Elect. She assumed they were holed up at home… sobbing. But some took their disdain for the results a step further, by bringing it into the classroom. "The day after the election," Karen recalls, "one of the teachers who was there told his students he feels like it was another 9/11 attack, which is kind of insane. So this is what the kids heard, that Trump was the worst thing to ever happen to this country. Trump is a racist. Trump is like a terrorist attack." The election of Trump made some on campus irrational…but there was one incident in particular that triggered the leftist faculty to a new level.

News broke that a woman, Christine Blasey Ford, was accusing Donald Trump's Supreme Court Justice nominee Brett Kavanaugh of sexual assault when they were both in high school. But Blasey Ford's statements were viewed by many as lacking credibility – a belief Karen shared. "Two things happened as a result of that," Karen remembers. "One, another faculty woman started screaming at me. I said, 'I don't know why you're screaming at me. Every single person who Blasey Ford cited as a witness to this said it didn't happen. She doesn't remember anything about it happening. The friends who she said were there don't remember it happening. Nobody remembers that happening. She doesn't remember where or when or what or why. And so sorry, but you know, I don't believe her.' And she said, 'Until they've interviewed every single person from that high school, I don't believe it.' I said, 'Really? Every single person? Why?' And she said, 'Remember that family that had those girls held hostage in their basement for ten years?' I said, 'Yeah.' She said, 'He could be like that.' I said, 'Really? You think Judge Kavanaugh is like that?' She said, 'Could be.' I mean...this is insane." Given her colleague's irrational demeanor, Karen decided she had nothing else to say to her on the matter. But the Trump Derangement Syndrome was spreading. Another male teacher took to marginalizing Karen to his students, claiming that because of her politics, Karen was unable to see that Blasey Ford was telling the truth. "I said, 'No, it's not because of my politics. It's because I can't imagine she's telling the truth as having been a teenage girl'... But he goes and disparages me and mocks me...to his students who are also my students. It's a small school."

It was these incidents that began to give Karen a sign that an atmosphere void of reason was brewing. Teachers were feeling emboldened to publicly challenge and mock her... even with her students. The tide was shifting. And what came next was everything that Karen had been studying for the past twenty years. But this time it was personal. This time it was about to happen to her. "It's like that wave that you see coming and all of a sudden you've lost your own footing," adds Karen.

As the end of the school year approached, Karen began to get concerned because she hadn't heard from the campus administration about her teaching contract renewal. She was on a year-to-year contract, and the contracts usually arrived as early as February, and as late as April. She emailed the school administration around the March-April timeframe asking what was up with her contract. But by the beginning of May, there was still no word. On May 5th, the organization she led, the American Freedom Alliance, held a conference on the Left's long march through the institutions. The event was a daylong affair, with two morning sessions on the education system and how the Left comes in and guts the institution of its original purpose than replaces those guts with indoctrination. So the day after the conference, Karen emailed the school administration again...wondering when she'd be receiving her contract renewal. But unlike earlier, this time they responded. "I was told we're not renewing your contract," recalls Karen. "And what they said in the email was, we're not renewing your contract because of your widely publicized views...that maybe I'd be better teaching at a college where they would be more accepting of my views...And she said that there'd been increasing complaints over the years, and she said, 'As you and I have spoken a number of times,' which wasn't true." So Karen responded saying that she wasn't aware of any complaints because they hadn't spoken about them – so she was confused by her email. "And she emailed me back, citing a speech that I gave at AFA praising Western civilization. And apparently someone had drawn the conclusion that therefore, I reject those not of Western civilization, and I am therefore a bigot. While there was no evidence of my bigotry in the classroom, clearly because I'm not a bigot, this sentence that I had said about Western civilization being an unparalleled force for good, that somehow [made me] a bigot. It was all very weird."

If you've ever lost your job, or were forced to leave a community because of your politics – you'd understand the immediate feeling of despair that Karen must have felt. It sends the message that you are so disgusting that you are no longer welcome. The feeling of anguish is significantly more acute if it happens within a cultural institution like education, the media, or Hollywood because the Left in effect has the power to completely block your ability to make a living within that community. Karen felt humiliated. Even with everyone in her social circle saying she shouldn't, that feeling of being rejected by her colleagues, and losing her job at the school she called an alma mater, naturally makes a person gravitate to a feeling of shame and humiliation. Fear settles in next – the scary feeling that now your livelihood is at stake. It was also troubling to Karen on a cultural level. This topic, the Left's gutting of cultural institutions that she addressed so often within the shelter of the American Freedom Alliance, was no longer theoretical. It was personal. "I just felt the blood drain from my face and thought, this is it," Karen recalls, her voice uncharacteristically shaky. "I talk about this with AFA. I live in this…literally the day before we are at a conference on exactly this. This is what they do because a dissenting voice can't be tolerated. This is how they advance the revolution."

The Left's early attempt at sparking a cultural revolution, their socialist campaign to get the workers of the world to unite, was widely rejected by Western civilization. So the Left came up with another tactic. Infiltrate the institutions that define American culture, take them over, purge dissenters, and force cultural change that way. "This is the way they do this," says Karen. "These are the mechanics of full on infiltration. And this is what they do…and then they did it to me." Her dismissal wasn't because of her teaching, it wasn't because she said anything inappropriate in class – she became persona non grata on campus purely because of her political beliefs. "This wasn't just a plain old school. This was my school… these were my people. These were people who knew me as me, as Karen, as smart, as funny, as a good teacher, a good math teacher, as a good representative of the school."

What perhaps was most troubling to Karen about the entire ordeal is that the Leftist infiltration of education has been so thorough, that the purge from her alma mater was almost automatic. "Nobody needed to say to do this," she offers. "If you've heard enough that conservatives are hateful white supremacists, bigot, Nazi, all those – deplorable is the least of it – if you believe that, then you really think you're doing your school good to purge it of evil people like me. And that's where it got really horrendous. That people who know me and liked me somehow because of something I said about Western civilization found it in their brains to twist that into bigotry. That was really scary." Refusing to renew her contract also sent a message, not only to any faculty member whose beliefs may teeter towards Karen's – it also sent a message to the young, easily impressionable minds of the student body. And that message is: If you speak up, if you dissent against the system, the wrath will come down on you. So shut up. But Karen sees a bright side. "The good part is that my students know me well enough to know that that was crap. They know who the bigot is, and they know it's not me. They know where the intolerance is, and they know it's not me. So I'm hopeful… and I actually know that to a great extent it backfired with the students. But overall, it really has a very chilling effect."

Karen is taking legal action against her school. And she's also pouring herself into the American Freedom Alliance, hoping to expand its membership and attract other freedom loving Americans to their events…and fight back against the Left's infiltration of our cultural institutions. Which leads us back to the question, how did this happen? How has the Left been able to take control of practically every influential American cultural institution – whether it be Hollywood, Big Tech, the me-

dia, literature, advertising, education and the like – and then
purge people from those industries that oppose their ideology?
The answer can generally be boiled down to one simple fact.
The Left has exploited a fatal flaw in conservatism. It's been
taking advantage of the Right's belief in *the virtue of pursuing
self-interest*. And the Left has done so with meticulous devotion to the long game.

"To me, it boils down to the fundamental ideological differences between the Left and the Right," thinks Karen. "The
Right says, 'I've got my freedoms. Government is there to
protect them. And we're just going to do what we do. We're
going to live our lives.'" The Left has exploited this principle
with a long-term plan – and that plan is to infiltrate and takeover the most influential cultural institutions and simply rely
on right-leaning individuals within those institutions to walk
away out of self-interest, or walk away because no one from
the Right comes to their aid…because they too are pursuing
their own self-interest. "Why are they successful," Karen
asks. "Because that was their plan, we didn't see their plan.
That was the plan – 'we're going to go into the schools'…
so they become teachers. We may become a teacher [or] may
not become a teacher. As we see the Left taking over schools,
what is it that we do? We walk away…we homeschool. They
take over. And we let them." Karen has seen this phenomenon
of conservatives walking away in every influential cultural institution. She continues, "The media – they take over, we let
them. Churches – they take over, we let them. Advertising –
they take over, we let them. Science – they take over, we let
them. We keep walking away. Why are they so successful?
They had a plan. We didn't recognize the plan. We don't want
to fight. We just go and do our own thing…and they seed, we
cede. And that's what keeps happening. They go in and we
walk away, and then we wonder what the heck happened."

The late great Andrew Breitbart once cited the same frustration with the conservative movement. "Hollywood was taken over by the Left and they've never relinquished it," Andrew once said. "And in fact I would argue that the Right has abdicated its place in Hollywood because they were told that you're not wanted here anymore, and they never fought for it. So I don't know who I have more contempt for – the Left for its totalitarian behavior towards those that disagree with them or the Right, the conservative movement, for just allowing for it to happen and not to fight back."

One of the reasons the Right always walks away when the Left takes over a cultural institution is due to the conservative movement's unwavering belief that the pursuit of self-interest always heals society's woes. There is virtue in an individual pursing self-interest. It's the cornerstone of capitalism. But this principle has its limitations. Anyone that denies this may want to look at all of the influential industries that the Left has taken over exploiting the vulnerabilities of this principle – Hollywood, music, art, Silicon Valley, media, advertising, literature, education. Every single one of these institutions that define American culture has been taken over by the Left by exploiting a fatal flaw in conservatism.

Let's face it…conservatism needs a reformation. It needs to recognize the limitations on its paramount principle – the virtue of self-interest. Because its rigid adherence to this doctrine has not only led to the loss of our cultural institutions, it's even resulted in the offshoring of American manufacturing, and with it, the destruction of the middle class. If conservatism isn't reformed now, very soon there will be nothing left to conserve.

THIRTEEN

Potty Mouth

Is honesty always the best policy?

Not so long ago, I had one of those moments where I was at a loss for words. That's a bit of a rarity for me, but it happened with my daughter. I'm sure many of you have faced this before as well, where you were conflicted on how to answer a child's question so you try to run through all the possibilities in your head before responding with something that will potentially scar them for life. I was sitting on the couch thumbing through Facebook when a video popped into my timeline that sort of stopped me in my tracks. It was of two girls fighting – one of those ugly brawls that drops your mouth open but you can't help but watch. What I didn't realize was that my daughter was looking over my shoulder. "Mommy, have you ever been in a fight before," she asked. That was the moment that I asked myself, should I tell the truth? It's a moment that all parents have faced...and for that matter, anyone that has been asked an adult question by a little one. My daughter's curiosity took me back to a moment many years before...one that I'll never forget.

**

I'm standing in the middle of a dystopian nightmare. Trapped in a concrete jungle...concrete ground, concrete benches, concrete tree planters, concrete building after concrete building... and I'm concretely fucked. My middle school quad has been transformed into what feels like a cement gladiator arena, and I'm the main attraction. I've never been in a real fight before, but here I am, all five-foot-one-and-a-half inches of me, squared off against the toughest chick on campus. As I gaze at the bloodthirsty crowd that has come by what appears to be the thousands, I'm one clench away from pooping my fluorescent pink parachute pants. Spectators seem to be spilling out of every available crevice. They're perched in trees, hoisted on shoulders, scaling light posts, and dangling out of classroom windows...just to watch me be pummeled. It's a tribal atmosphere, and the natives are getting restless.

As I scan the raucous crowd my eyes are met with an endless number of faces that are, for the most part, familiar. I take note of how many truly ugly people there are in the world. And no, I don't mean that metaphorically – I mean just plain fugly. It's as if the entire school is present...the jocks, cheerleaders, marching band geeks, brainiacs, skanks, stoners, hip-hop junkies, nu-wavers, rock-a-billies, goths, disco biscuits, dorks and nerds...you name it. And not only are they here, but they're rollin' deep. It's as if the pending fight is a mandatory school assembly, organized and sanctioned by the school, because clearly even the teachers in attendance show no sign of breaking this thing up. With all eyes on me, all I'm thinking is, "This better work or I'm screwed."

The random chatter of braces now turns more melodic, with the sound of loud foot stomping to the beat of a less than flattering anthem. Some poser is attempting to beat-box while the real hip-hop heads are spitting out some pretty dope rhymes about yours truly. "She finna get her ass kicked" is the chorus. Frankly, it's a pretty catchy tune, but I certainly can't bop my head to the beat of me getting my ass whooped. It's a beautiful Southern California day, but despite the eighty-degree weather, I feel cold. My heart is pounding so hard that my left boob appears to be waving "hi" to the audience. Then the crowd abruptly becomes so quiet you can hear a number two pencil drop as everyone turns their head towards the clock. The thunderous sound of the final seconds tick away until the moment the big arm strikes 2:50 P.M. "That's it," I think. "It's. About. To go. Down." I look at my enemy dead in her Ray-Bans, bracing myself, as a question enters my mind. "How in the world did I end up in this mess?" The quick answer...my big mouth.

It was 1984 when this Catholic schoolgirl became a public schoolgirl. Yeah, the nuns booted me from St. Christopher for having a potty mouth...that's a story for another time. But let's just say for now, my record for the most pink slips in a single year likely stands to this day. So with nowhere else to go, my mom enrolled me into Hollencrest Junior High School in West Covina, California and I didn't know a single soul. I was terrified, and making things worse were the constant "you're so tiny" comments. Yes, my stature was, and still is, what you could call borderline midget...but the fact is, I identify tall. Now in Catholic school you're told all about the terrifying perils of the public school system. According to my Mother Superior, there were hedonist bullies that steal your lunch money, pull up your skirt, shove your face into toilets, and would beat you to a bloody pulp! Ay, dios mío! It goes without saying that my early educators scared the living bejesus out of me.

I walked onto my new campus and all that was running

through my head was, "I'm going to die, that girl wants to mess with me, don't make eye contact, just keep walking, don't look up. Just keep walking." On that first day of public school I had the good fortune of meeting the person who would become my very best friend – Lisa. I can still remember the moment vividly. I was wearing a fluorescent lime green top with matching pants, cream lambskin ballet flats that tied over my foot, and a giant bow wrapped around my head. The bow was also in fluorescent lime green. I must have looked like a lady leprechaun. The other kids probably expected me to say, "Stay away from me pot of gold" in a Celtic tongue when I spoke. I had *the* haircut of the moment - with one side of my head shaved and the other side long to my shoulder. It was an exaggerated version of the asymmetrical bob that was so popular in the 80s.

My sixth period was physical education, which was being held in the auditorium so that all of the classes could be properly briefed at one-time. As I entered the room, I decided I'd sit towards the back so that the murderous pagans I'd heard so much about couldn't easily spot me. "Hurry up, come on guys, sit down, there's plenty of room," opened our gym teacher. "Welcome to sixth period P.E. Okay, let's get the hard stuff out of the way, alright – gym clothes and showering etiquette." Showering? Dear God, these people are animals. As I entered my row I stopped dead in my tracks as I noticed a girl with a strikingly fashionable hairdo entering the row from the opposite side. "Could it be? No way! My gosh…she is so cool," I thought to myself. We both arrived to the middle of the row in mutual admiration. It was my future best friend, Lisa, and we were both sporting the exact same hairdo! That moment was the beginning of a lifelong friendship together. A good haircut can do that, you know.

Lisa was already – on the first day of school mind you –

very popular. Everyone knew who she was, especially all the eighth graders! Now, to a seventh grader, that was mighty impressive. I soon came to learn that Lisa had an older sister, Tori*, who had graduated the year before. Tori was legendary, and extremely...I mean *extremely* feared. The word on the streets was that it wasn't only the girls that she could handle with one swift swing of her fist, but the boys as well. She was exactly the kind of public school kid that I had heard about! I wasn't sure if I should be happy or terrified that this notorious Tori person was my new BFF's sister. I feared for the day I'd have to meet the bruiser herself.

About two weeks later, that day arrived. To my surprise Tori was no brute at all. Sweet as apple pie was the best way to describe her. Her soft demeanor behind closed doors was something that few at school witnessed. But do not be mistaken...back in 1984, she'd cut a bitch if provoked. The one thing that perplexed me most about Tori was that she, like me, was extraordinarily short. So one day I asked Tori, from one little person to another, how it was that she became so infamous and skilled in the art of fight. She let me in on a little secret that day - she wasn't rough or tough or any of the things that everyone claimed. She just pretended to be. Now don't get me wrong, she was abnormally strong for her size, but she would *go big* at every confrontation to project fear into her targets - and perception is indeed reality for most.

Roughly a week after meeting Tori, my worst nightmare came to fruition. I'd learned that a homicidal maniac was coming for me! The butcher's name was Dora. You know how the new kid becomes the target of the big shots on campus... well that was me. Dora for some reason got it in for little ol' me. Tori's *go big* advice combined with the fact that I was my father's daughter – a story for another time – meant I'd have to shed my catholic girl plaid skirt for *Dickies* immediately, and not back down once confronted by this hooligan! The day came quickly when I ran into Dora. It was in the hall on my way to third period when I saw that she was walking straight for me. My inner dialogue was screaming, "Run, run, run for your life! Save yourself! Hurry! Go! Fast!" But in that moment, I channeled Tori and my father's DNA, then opened my mouth and said, "Bitch, you do not want to mess with me mang. My hands are registered as lethal weapons Holmes!" Listen, when people look at me they see Mexican so it's either a chola or Speedy Gonzalez, and I just didn't think that saying, "Ándale, ándale! Ariba, ariba!" was going to scare her.

It turned out chola worked, and I somehow managed to Jedi mind trick Dora and put the fear of God into her. She went running to her boyfriend Mitch, and must have exhibited complete terror because Mitch decided to come after me himself! He was only a year older than me – but middle school years are like dog years – and word had it that he'd punched a girl in the face the year before. I'm telling you, these Hollencrest kids were no joke.

I don't know what it is about being in junior high but there always seems to be an announcement as to when and where someone is going to get their ass kicked – making the build up to the beat down all the more horrifying. It was broadcasted that Mitch would be pummeling me the following day after school. "Oh my gosh, a boy is going to beat me up," I cried in immense distress to my friends. That's when Lisa decided it was time to bring in the big guns. After school we walked to her house and when Tori arrived we rushed to the front door to tell her about my impending crisis. "Don't worry, let Mitch know that I'll be there and if he wants to fight you, he'll have to fight me first," Tori declared. Now those were some comforting fighting words.

Sure enough, before second period the next day it had

spread like wild fire that Tori would be coming to the school as my back up. Lunchtime rolled around and I was feeling pretty secure when I noticed that Mitch was walking straight toward my table. "Oh my god, doesn't he know he's breaking protocol? He's not supposed to beat me up until after school!" I thought I should dive under the table, but before I could courageously take cover, Mitch was standing beside me. I closed my eyes, made the sign of the cross, and then braced myself for his infamous bone-crushing uppercut. But it didn't come. After a few seconds I heard him sheepishly say, "I just wanted to come over and say I'm sorry."

"Hmmm, wait a minute...was I going to avoid getting beaten up altogether right now," I thought. Mitch continued, "I hope there's no hard feelings." It was then that I was faced with a crossroad. Do I accept his apology and let him know how petrified I'd been? That was probably the right thing to do, but then I heard Tori's voice in my head say, "Perception is reality," and my big mouth took over...again. "You'd better be sorry. But it might be a little too late because Tori will be here after school and she's coming for you." He looked like a kid getting his first rectal exam. I'm telling you, the power that Tori wielded with the threat of *possibly* coming after you was the kind of childhood indoctrination that dictators of developing countries could only dream of achieving.

At 2:50 P.M. when the final bell rang to go home, I walked outside and there was Tori. As promised, she had come to save my butt...but was proud to learn that I had held my own. Her apprentice had grown that day, so she decided it was time for me to start growing my very own myth, like she had done when she was just a young Padawan. Being that it was the era of *Karate Kid*, she suggested I tell everyone that I was a black belt. "No, that might be too much," she said. "Let's make it a second-degree brown belt in karate." Tori coached me meticulously so that no one would ever know the truth. AJ-san, with the help of her sensei Tori, performed hours upon hours of *wax on wax off*, sand the floor, and *paint the fence* exercises so that I could fool even the most trained of eyes. I didn't learn a lick of karate, but if style was anything…I sure looked like a lethal weapon.

When school came the next day, I began working that karate myth like a fat girl eats carbs. I channeled my inner Bruce Lee and told elaborate tales of my brutal and body crushing matches, about how my sensei would work me all hours of the night – which was true if the night before counted – and that I could be imprisoned if I ever used my hands against an untrained civilian. In one class in particular, math with Mr. McKinney, I would talk about my karate skills at length. As chance would have it, there was a girl in math, Emma, who took judo – so she always wanted to talk about it. Someone who got to listen in on my mythical butt kicking exploits was cute and unsuspecting BJ Castiglioni.

BJ sat next to us so she got to hear firsthand about all of our martial arts battles. I use to say – loud enough so everyone in math could hear – that the type of karate I took was tae kwon do, which in fact isn't karate at all. Karate originates from Japan and *tae kwon do* originates from Korea. Luckily there was no Google at the time, so BJ Castiglioni and the rest never questioned my faux pas. They just stood wide-eyed as I recounted stories of my death-defying encounters. I wasn't ever really sure if people believed me or knew I was completely full of it. All I could hope for was that the word would get out, and the legend would take hold…that I was lethal so I would never be faced with getting beaten up again.

Just as I thought I would be breezing through the school year unharmed, trouble started brewing again. A girl by the name of Trista Colinger – an 8th grader – got it in for me *and* she challenged me to a fight! She was a tiny, cute little blonde who had seemed so sweet from a distance. Despite the lies I'd been spewing to the masses, this Trista chick was still willing to fight me. I was shocked and quickly thereafter afraid for my life! She clearly must have known how to take someone down otherwise she wouldn't risk her life against a legendary karate master like me. Exacerbating my predicament were the rumblings all over school about how my karate skills would soon be on full display. "Dammit! Now what am I going to do," I said to Tori in a panic. Toni's advice – "Freak her out early. Grab her by the hair, yank her face down, and then knee her in the face." Nice advice, huh?

After much consideration I decided to call my dad who was actually a black belt in what he called karate kata. Most parents aren't overjoyed to hear that their kid is gearing up for a big fight, but my dad wasn't exactly conventional. My father was a gun-carrying foreigner who…let's just say didn't abide by societal norms. He sure as hell wasn't raising a sissy girl. "Is she a giant," he asked with concern. "No. She's only an inch taller and really skinny," I answered. "Screw it then! Kick her in the ass," he advised. He then proceeded to explain the difference between all the various forms of martial arts. Aside from his obviously irresponsible advice, it was actually a pretty enlightening conversation. You see, I always thought that when my dad said he took "karate kata" he meant to say just the word "karate" but his thick accent somehow prevented him from saying it correctly. But kata was an actual term that explained karate moves. He was always running around the house demonstrating his karate kicks and punches while singing "Fatman" to the Batman tune…so I logically thought he was just being funny. Every time he showcased a karate move he would pair it with a loud "Hi-yah, muthafucka!" I hung up the phone with my dad feeling a bit more prepared, but no less petrified. There had to be a way to get out of this mess.

On the morning of the scheduled fight I exaggeratedly fake vomited in my mom's bathroom in a desperate attempt to get her to let me stay home sick from school. It didn't work. I didn't dare tell my mother the truth. I then contemplated writing a letter of confession and reading it over the loudspeaker during homeroom. Once people found out I didn't really know karate, they'd lose interest in watching me showcase my ancient Japanese art form. But the lies that I'd been spewing were so good that it seemed like the entire school was planning to attend the main event no matter what! There was no way out.

The build up to my fight was monumental – second only to Muhammad Ali's *Thrilla in Manila*. I got dressed in all fluorescent pink, and went to school knowing I'd soon be facing certain humiliation. Ironically, that day at school was the dichotomy of terrifying and exhilarating. All of a sudden I was like a mega celebrity. Kids I'd never spoken to gave me the thumbs up or walked by saying things like, "Go easy on her kid." That kind of celebrity is addicting and I sort of started to believe my own hype…a trait I've retained to this day. I'd smile and nod all the while desperately trying to hide my debilitating fear. By the time sixth period came around I was on the verge of soiling my oversized parachute pants.

As the final school bell arrived, I walked out of P.E. with my trusty companion Lisa by my side. She was pep talking me the whole way to the courtyard. We turned the corner to the main quad and there was a large group of kids, with Trista Colinger standing in the middle waiting for me. I could hear myself breathing and, despite the eighty-degree weather, I felt a cold chill. Things got a little blurry but I remember clearly that Lisa took the books out of my hands, which was my cue to get into the *Karate Kid* stance. At that point I had no choice but to fully commit to the myth I'd created. I heard rumblings in the crowd as I struggled to stand on one leg to display my awesome *crane technique*. The next thing I remember is a loud "hi-yah" coming out of my mouth as I put Tori's move into action. I grabbed Trista's hair, pulled her face to my knee, and attempted to knee her in the face! What was I thinking? That move is barely legal in the UFC today. Luckily I had no idea what I was doing and missed. The scuffle continued briefly, but poor little Trista Colinger must have gotten really spooked by my Karate Kid pose because she froze. Before I knew it, it was over and all I could hear were the *oooh's* and *ahhh's* from my adoring crowd. I was dazed and confused but apparently, through style alone, I'd won the fight!

The next day at school I was a bona fide A-list celebrity. Only the likes of Madonna could compare in public adulation. Stories of my supreme martial arts skills were being told all over campus. I heard one kid, who I'd never seen before, telling the epic story of my ninja style. "She jumped into the air and kicked her right in the face," was how the story morphed… an exaggerated version to say the least.

As time went on the story of my Jackie Chan prowess subsided, and by the time I got into high school it was a distant memory. I never talked again about training with my sensei because I dreaded ever being put to the test again – and undoubtedly being found out for the fraud I was. My close friends and I would occasionally mention the time that I "beat up Trista Colinger" but it would quickly be laughed off because of the absurdity of the event. Luckily, kids have a really vivid imagination – and with the help of Tori and my dad's coaching, I made it through those scary teen years relatively unscathed. I still, looking back, find it hard to fathom that anyone actually believed that I was a second-degree brown belt. But as I sat there, over twenty years later, staring at my Facebook timeline with my daughter asking if I'd ever been in a fight before, I noticed a *friend request* with a message from BJ Castiglioni – my sweet and unsuspecting math classmate that was there when I first planted the seed of my fighting skills. "Hey AJ, how are you? Hope all is good! Are you still taking Karate," BJ asked. That was the sign I needed.

"So mom, have you ever been in a fight before," asked my baby girl. "No honey, not really," I finally responded. "But don't worry...fighting is in your DNA. You'll be fine." Yeah, good parents often lie to their kids because sometimes the truth needs to wait until they're old enough to process the information. One day, when she's old enough, she'll read this, and she too will learn the truth.

Note: Some of the names have been changed to protect the privacy of the people involved.

FOURTEEN

Right to Try
*Is Trump Derangement Syndrome
a real mental disorder?*

We've all seen cases of so-called Trump Derangement Syndrome – where people are triggered to hysteria by the simplest show of support for the president. The first signs of the new affliction date back to shortly after the announcement of his presidential candidacy – but a full-blown outbreak has gripped the country since November 8, 2016. "America is crying tonight," claimed MSNBC's Lawrence O'Donnell on Election Night. "I'm not sure how much of America. But a very significant portion, and I mean literally crying." The virus has gone airborne ever since. A store clerk goes berserk on a customer wearing MAGA gear, demanding he leave the store. A woman is removed from a plane after chastising a Trump supporter before take off. Protesters at Trump's Inauguration seemed possessed with grief at the moment he was sworn in. We joke about this seeming affliction, but in all seriousness, is it real? Is Trump Derangement Syndrome a real mental disorder? To find the answer, we follow the story of a lifelong Democrat, a true American hero, and how baring her soul opened her eyes to a frightening new normal.

**

Ellen Bukstel was born about sixty-six years ago, and raised in Miami, Florida...the Sunshine State. She was the middle child of three – with two brothers flanking her in age. Ellen had a happy childhood. "We lived in a friendly neighborhood," she says. "My parents were very open and happy, and I would say that it was pretty normal." She had great role models. Her father was an optometrist and her mother owned her own personalized papeterie business. The matriarch of her family also had a side gig. "We had a very musical family," says Ellen. "My mother was an opera singer...she was in the Miami Opera Guild chorus and she would perform in the chorus and all of the big operas that were held at Miami Dade County Auditorium for many many years...and all of us children we got her genes, let's put it that way."

Ellen was very creative from an early age. She began singing as a child. Her and her brother performed as a duo. And she also had another passion...she had a knack for art. "When I was in high school I was always the one that would draw the pep rally signs," recalls Ellen, "and when I was [a] young child in elementary school, I was the one that was asked to do all the bulletin boards." So Ellen went to Florida State to study visual communications, what we now call graphic design. She would eventually marry, and in 1976 she started her own graphic design company. Her marriage would eventually start to falter though. But around 1981, she met a different man that would become the love of her life. His name was Doug Segal. "He was a printing broker...a super salesman," says Ellen. "A friend of mine suggested that I show him my designs and my artwork. And I went to his office, showed him my portfolio and he started giving me some business." Doug had clients that needed graphic design for things related to print design – like a brochure or logo. So he directed a lot of that work to Ellen. The two became friends. Doug was tall, roughly two hundred pounds, and handsome. When they first met, the energy was electric. "It was like sparks and people noticed, and it was something that I was not going to let go in my lifetime," recalls Ellen. "It's funny, I heard a story later on after we got together that after I walked out of his first office he said to his secretary, 'Now I'm going to marry that girl.'"

As their relationship grew, Doug shared something with Ellen that seemed minor at the time compared to the love that was blossoming. One night over dinner with printing colleagues, Doug conveyed to her that he was a hemophiliac. "I don't know that I had ever even heard of hemophilia," adds Ellen, "or if I did, I didn't pay much attention to it." Hemophilia is a blood clotting disorder, afflicting mostly men, where their blood is missing a vital blood clotting protein called factor VIII. Essentially, their blood doesn't clot. So if they get a cut or even a simple bruise, they can bleed out and die. So hemophiliacs have to take medicine that adds the effect of factor VIII to their system and allows their blood to coagulate. "He and his brother both where born hemophiliacs and grew up spending a lot of time in the hospital getting blood transfusions," says Ellen. "And by the time I met Doug, of course, it was a simple infusion into his veins of factor VIII and he would be fine." Ellen's mom was concerned about her daughter getting involved with someone that had hemophilia. But Ellen wasn't...she just thought of it as something Doug had. "When you're in love, those things don't matter," she says.

Ellen and Doug would eventually marry, and in 1982 they had their first son, Brett. Doug was a model father. Ellen quickly got pregnant again, with their second son Todd. They were a young couple on their way, bursting with happiness. They deeply loved one another. Life was good. But something was already brewing...something that would redefine their life forever. Reports of a serious new condition began hitting the newsrooms:

Tom Brokaw: "Scientists at the National Center for Disease Control in Atlanta today released the results of a study which shows the lifestyle of some male homosexuals has triggered an epidemic of a rare form of cancer. Robert Bazell now in Atlanta."

Robert Bazell: "Bobby Campbell of San Francisco and Billy Walker of New York, both suffer from a mysterious newly discovered disease, which effects mostly homosexual men, but has also been found in heterosexual men and women. The condition severely weakens the body's ability to fight disease. Many victims get a rare form of cancer called Kaposi Sarcoma. Others get an infection called Pneumocystis pneumonia. Researchers know of 413 people who have contracted the condition in the past year. One third have died and none have been cured. Investigators have examined the habits of homosexuals for clues."

The street name for the condition was called "gay cancer" because it predominantly hit the homosexual community. But the condition would soon find its way into other areas of the American population in significant numbers, enough to begin garnering wider media coverage:

CBS Reporter: "It appeared a year ago in New York's gay community...then the gay communities in San Francisco and Los Angeles. Now it's been detected in Haitian refugees, and no one knows why. And in heavy drug users, especially in New York City. No one knows way. And in some people with hemophilia, a disease that prevents

blood-clotting so the patient needs frequent blood transfusions."

Researchers were initially baffled by the cause of the disease. But by late 1982, they began honing in on the cause, and
the affliction was given a name:

Ted Koppel: "The disease has already claimed more victims than Legionnaires' disease and toxic shock syndrome combined. More than eight hundred cases nationwide…three hundred plus of those fatal. And everyday
three more cases are identified. And yet still, surprisingly
few people are familiar with the Acquired Immune De-
ficiency Syndrome, or the acronym for which it is frequently identified, AIDS. The reason for that may lie in
part on the character of its most common victims. When
AIDS first cropped up about eighteen months ago, almost
all of its victims were homosexual males who frequently
changed sexual partners. Alarming enough to that particular segment of society – but, so it first appeared, not
threatening to the public at-large. But that seems to be
changing. And the disease may be spreading."

By the time it started seeping into the news, little was
widely known about the disease or how it was transmitted. It
was still predominately in the gay community, and hadn't yet
substantially made its way into the rest of the general public. But one day in 1983, it touched Doug and Ellen's life.
"Batch 4077. I'll never forget that number," recalls Ellen. "We
got a notice from the blood company saying batch 4077 was
found to have been infected with the AIDS virus." Doug and
his brother Scott bought their blood from this blood company.
The letter said that they should not use the batch and to return

it. But both Doug and his brother had already infused themselves with that batch. However at that time in 1983, doctors and researchers were sending the message that the risk for catching the disease was very low – even for hemophiliacs. "There is some suggestion that it can be transmitted through blood. And clearly now it's a problem among hemophiliacs," claimed Dr. Harold Jaffe of the Center for Disease Control at the time. "I think it's important to recognize though that this risk at present is extremely small, and people should certainly not be refusing blood that they need because of this concern."

Ellen and Doug were learning with everyone else about this new deadly disease through news reports. "My first exposure to it was with Geraldo Rivera," recalls Ellen. "[He] was talking about that in the gay community, how so many men were coming down with this weird disease and that's where it started for us." So when Doug and Ellen went to see their doctor, knowing little to nothing about the disease, they were told that he was more at risk for something else. "I always felt that there was more of a risk of me to have a problem with hepatitis than with AIDS," Doug said at the time. "And that's what the medical community still told us." And regardless, in 1983 there was no test to check if someone had the disease. But a year later, the research community began getting closer. "The probable cause of AIDS has been found," announced the then-Secretary of Hearth Margaret Heckler. At the time, Dr. Robert Gallo of the National Cancer Institute claimed that the cause was a virus called HTLV-III. He predicted that a blood test for the virus would be ready in six months.

With the risk appearing exceedingly low, Doug and Ellen went on living their lives. They had a daughter, Margo. But all the while the disease was slowly picking up steam in the general population – and then hit a major pop icon that sent shockwaves around the world. At nine in the morning on October 2, 1985, movie star Rock Hudson died in his sleep at his Beverly Hills home. With this new death, the disease entered further into American homes.

By 1986, Doug and his brother started showing subtle signs that trouble was brewing. The two became chronically ill. Colds wouldn't go away. "High fevers that were unexplained," said Doug at the time. "I started to lose weight. I lost about 40 lbs." Then his brother Scott was tested. It came up positive for HIV. It was time for Doug to get screened, so Ellen took him to Jackson Memorial Hospital. Doug recalled the visit. "The doctor diagnosed me with having AIDS related complex, which is AIDS with the exception that I had not had an opportunistic infection yet. The reaction was, we were kinda stunned because what he told us to do was 'make contingency plans and hope for the best.'" The disease that was slowly terrorizing America had now become Doug and Ellen's reality. They were in shock...and largely helpless. There was no cure for AIDS. No effective treatment had hit the market yet. So the two took control of what they could. They decided to see their attorney to get their wills in order. It helped them somewhat diffuse the shock of their situation.

The next logical step was, and this was a tough one, they had to decide whom they should tell. "We weren't concerned about what people would think about us," Doug said at the time. "We didn't want people to start rejecting our children. So in the beginning when we decided not to tell a lot of people, it was because of the children." The fear over the disease had gone nuclear – but at the same time, the public was largely ignorant as to how AIDS was transmitted. So the fear over their three children being shunned was well founded. However in May 1987, after he developed Pneumocystis pneumonia, or full-blown AIDS, Doug and Ellen decided that the kids were just going to have to roll with the punches. Their friends' reactions were just about as good as anyone could hope for. "I have an exceptional...loving group of friends," said Doug. "Their reaction was concern. They of course were concerned with how AIDS was passed on. And they educated themselves. I have not been rejected by anybody, any of the people who were important to me. I'm just extremely fortunate."

Doug and Ellen decided that they weren't going to hide. They were going to speak out – bare their souls. They felt that in the long run, it would be better for their kids and was important for the fight against AIDS. You see, at the time in 1987, AIDS was still thought to be primarily a gay disease. Now here they were, a straight married couple, facing the exact same disease that was ravaging the homosexual community. People needed to be educated, and they took on that role. They spoke to their immediate social circle. "I know you all are curious about a lot of things, go ahead and ask," said Doug at a community Q&A. They spoke to the Presidential Commission on AIDS. "My name is Doug Segal. I'm thirty-five years old. I've been married for almost six years. I have three small preschool [age] children. I am a hemophiliac and I have AIDS." Ellen joined Doug at the Commission podium. "I'm Doug's wife. I am his friend, and his lover. I do not have AIDS, nor do I test positive for the AIDS antibodies. Our children do not have AIDS nor do they test positive." And it was in this speaking out that they found a passion.

In that same year, 1987, a promising new drug had been approved for testing. "AZT was developed in 1964 as an anti-cancer drug," reported NBC News on the announcement of the experimental drug's approval. "But in experiments a year ago, it prolonged the lives of certain AIDS patients – those who had the weakest immune systems, and those who had Pneumocystis pneumonia...a common and often fatal infection in AIDS patients." After a long stall, experimental drugs were finally being tested...but there was still no known cure. So a need still existed to educate one of the highest risk groups - the sexually active youth. That's where Doug and Ellen found their calling.

They became pioneers in their neck of the woods on educating the youth in public high schools. But the Reagan Administration was hesitant on the government getting involved in public school sex education. "The federal role must be to give educators accurate information about the disease," Reagan said at the time. "How that information is used must be up to schools and parents. Not government." And that thought trickled into local communities. Doug and Ellen were on the Speaker's Bureau for Dade County Public Schools, and the group tried to impose rules on them – restricting them from using the word "rubber." Ellen never paid attention to their rules. "There was no way I was going to give in to that rule," recalls Ellen. "I didn't work for them. I was a volunteer coming in and speaking and educating kids...and I was on a mission to make sure that people understood that...not talking about these things is the worst thing you can do."

Doug and Ellen opened up to anyone and everyone that would listen. It was cathartic for them to let it all out and not hide – to not be ashamed. There was nothing to be ashamed about. And they wanted to get that message across to whoever would listen. They felt their impact immediately. "There were people in audiences who were so closeted and so fearful," she remembers. "There were some young kids that would come up and...they wanted to tell me that my brother or my mom...has AIDS and I never told anybody. Imagine being so closeted and so fearful of the community and people's harsh judgments." Like many creative people experiencing pain, Ellen turned to art as an outlet. She wrote a poem for her husband, and the words just flowed out of her. She presented the poem to Doug and he would play a game…calling everyone they knew and seeing if he could make them cry by reciting it. The poem was about Ellen meeting Doug in another place after his passing. She recited it often at their speaking engagements:

> In solitude I close my eyes / my dreams help me to see
> The joyful and the happy way / that our life used to be
> One thing that we have learned for sure / of this I'm truly glad
> To live each day as if it was / the only one we had
> If I must live without you / and our life together unsure
> We will find another place in time / where we will meet once more

Doug's brother Scott would eventually succumb to AIDS. The day after burying him, Doug and Ellen were in court. After a long debate, Doug and his brother decided to sue the blood company for their screening practices that led to them selling the brothers AIDS infected blood. So Doug was following through on their decision. "It was devastating to Doug when his brother died, and then to have to go to court the next day and be interrogated," recalls Ellen. "Of course we lost because they couldn't prove causation. I remember the clerk reading the verdict in tears. This person was crying because it was just such an emotional experience for everyone, not only those of us involved but people who were observing there and sitting in the gallery…I never would want to go through that again." Doug was consistently sick from the time he was diagnosed all the way through the trial. But he was still able to speak about his illness to audiences to warn of the dangers. Doug, along with Ellen, was able to dispel the widespread misinformation about the disease.

But within about six months of his brother's death, the disease began to overtake him. "It soon turned from normal to Doug being in bed a lot," Ellen said...the thought still brings her to tears. The journey they shared was part amazing and part agonizing. She had to watch the love of her life deteriorate. "He was six feet tall. He was probably two hundred pounds and he had what they call wasting syndrome where he couldn't process his food intake and he ended up looking like he just walked out of Auschwitz concentration camp," says Ellen. Now bedridden, Doug quickly reduced from his healthy days of two hundred pounds to what appeared to be eighty pounds – like a skeleton, just skin and bones. Ellen remembers their last night. "And we still slept together in the same bed. And I woke up in the middle of the night. My sister in law, who had already lost her husband who was Doug's brother, she was there with me caring for Doug. And I woke up and found him dead lying next to me in the middle of the night."

Doug's greatest fear was that his three young kids would not remember him when he was gone. "Because they're so young now there stands a very good chance of them not even remembering who I am without being shown by means of videotape or pictures," Doug told a local NBC News reporter before his passing. "I think what I'm trying to do now is build memories, because that's where I'll live on...Ellen and I have always said to each other that we're going to meet in a different life, and I hope that I am someplace that I can watch over them." Doug wrote his three young children a letter just a year before he died from AIDS. The letter read:

Brett, Todd and Margo,
This is real hard for me, my babies. You three are the reasons I hung on, the foundation of my will to live and the saddest part of knowing that I was going to die.
Margo, you used to say when you were almost two,

"Watch me, Daddy," and then you'd do something silly. I watched you over and over again. I wish I could watch you now.

Pete and Repeat. You're brothers. You really can't imagine how wonderful that is. If you overlook any differences you might eventually have, your brother will be the one person in your life that will always be there for you. Don't ever let that change. It's so important.

My children - grow up, change the world, your success is measured by your integrity. Be there for your friends. Love each other. And, if you're old enough now, remember that I, your father, loved you, needed you and was so very proud to have you in my life for as long as I did.

I love you, Brett. I love you, Toddy. I love you, Margo.

Doug Segal

**

After Doug's passing, Ellen continued her AIDS activism, speaking to high-risk groups about the deadly disease. She also turned to a passion from her youth...music, and began writing songs. And in 1995, her band at the time, Legacy, published an album dedicated to her late husband and his brother Scott. She adapted her touching poem to Doug for one of the tracks. Her activism even earned her an opportunity to carry the Olympic Torch in 1996 during its travel through Florida.

Over the years, Ellen would continue writing music, many of the songs tackling important social issues, with one of her songs becoming the theme song for the National Coalition Against Domestic Violence. And she got heavily involved in the local music scene, converting her house several times a year into a concert venue – called *Shack in the Back* – that raised money for various charities. Her kids Brett, Todd, and Margo also picked up her creative gene. Brett and Todd formed a music and video production company called Segal Brothers Productions, and Margo became a make-up artist. Ellen also met a new man and he'd eventually become her live-in boyfriend.

Being immersed in both the arts and AIDS activism community throughout her entire adult life, it isn't hard to guess that Ellen considered herself a lifelong Democrat. In fact, her entire social circle – including her friends, family, and music fans – were all liberals. But her sons Brett and Todd had acquired a different worldview – conservatism. The two brothers had been making waves in their family over their political views, and it started causing trouble for Ellen – so she expressed that to Brett. "Her immediate reaction was, 'Brett you are kicking the beehive. You are just being antagonistic to the family. You're alienating me from my family.' And when the other side of the family basically banned me from the family reunion, she started seeing a little bit of what goes on behind the scenes," recalls Brett. That move opened Ellen's eyes a bit to some of the intolerance on her side of the aisle. But it was the election of Donald Trump that brought it into full view.

When the real estate mogul won the election, Brett says Ellen's friends went bonkers – posting apocalyptic memes, saying it was going to be the end of the economy, and parroting Joe Biden…that Trump was going to put us all back in chains. "They really thought that [women's] rights were being curtailed," adds Brett. "That gays were being carted off in box cars just like the Jews in the Holocaust. It was gonna be another Holocaust, right. So you know, it's really not difficult to see when you look outside that there's really no holocaust going on…you go out into the world and you actually see that people aren't being accosted on a daily basis." Ellen raised her children right, so she knew that her sons would not have voted for the racist that her social circle was portraying. Her eyes began to open to the possibility that it was not her kids that were the problem...it was her friends. Ellen was having an awakening.

So her sons began talking with Ellen more about their conservative beliefs, and why they supported the president. She began warming to, if not Trump, at least her sons' views. Brett remembers how his mom framed her feelings towards The Donald. "She said, 'Well maybe he's not that bad, but I just don't like the way he talks.'"

Then something happened. "We also believe that patients with terminal conditions, terminal illness, should have access to experimental treatment immediately that could potentially save their lives," President Trump announced. "It's time for Congress to give these wonderful incredible Americans the right to try." President Trump pushed for, and then signed the *Right to Try* Bill into law. "The law enables terminally ill patients the ability to take experimental drugs outside of clinical trials when they've exhausted all other options," reported CBS News. You see, when Ellen's husband Doug was first diagnosed with HIV in October 1986, a drug AZT had been developed over twenty years earlier. After some red tape was removed, AZT entered the trail phase in 1987 to treat AIDS patients suffering from the very same ailment that was afflicting Doug – Pneumocystis pneumonia. The drug is used to this day as part of an overall treatment to drastically extend the lives of HIV patients.

When Ellen heard about the *Right to Try* law, it struck her. "And I found out a little more about it, and I decided that I would post my story on Facebook to my friends," remembers Ellen. She told her social media friends how Doug died lying next to her in bed. Brett remembers what she wrote. "So she made a very impassioned post on Facebook in which she basically said, 'I watched my husband die...and this law might have saved his life. I watched him die and the *Right to Try* might have given him some hope at the very least.' It would have made it not a death sentence...maybe just maybe it would have given us kids some extra time with our father. Maybe a week, maybe a month, maybe years." So Ellen put her moving story out there. Her first sentence was that she wanted to applaud President Trump for signing the *Right to Try* bill into law. "And you would have thought that I set a bomb off somewhere," she remembers. "She got a taste of the vitriol," says her son Brett. "She got a taste of the blind hatred. She got a taste of the absolute derangement. She had people going on there saying, 'If I were you, I'd be ashamed to be a mother.' Things like that. Her friends of years were going on and saying, 'How could you even say anything nice about him?'"

This was a woman that had not only been through a horrific ordeal, but her activism in the face of it all helped relieve pain and educate a frantic public. She no doubt saved lives. And here she was, baring her soul again, giving very specific praise to the president – about a topic that few knew more about than her. And as a result, she was attacked on a level that shocked her. And it wasn't just her friends that dog piled on Ellen. "Her boyfriend of twenty years, when he could have just walked across the house and said, 'Hey, what's going on with your warm feelings towards Trump? What's going on with that,'" remembers Brett. "Instead what he did was he posted in public on Facebook a scathing, deriding, degrading diatribe about all the fake news that is spread about Trump and conservatives, and basically tossed her under the bus in front of all of her fans, in front of all of her friends, in front of all of her family...while she was on her way to get a neurological exam." What Ellen had experienced was *Trump Derangement Syndrome* – something so many have faced over the past few years. Her boyfriend moved out in a matter of a few weeks.

The phrase Trump Derangement Syndrome, or TDS for short, appears to have been coined by a conservative writer named Esther Goldberg in August 2015 – however the term was likely derived by the late psychiatrist and political commentator Charles Krauthammer when he cited Bush Derangement Syndrome as "the acute onset of paranoia in otherwise normal people in reaction to the policies, the presidency – nay – the very existence of George W. Bush." Esther Goldberg's original reference to TDS may have been tongue-and-cheek, but since the results of the 2016 election, some suspect it might be a serious mental condition. "What people call Trump Derangement Syndrome may indeed be some kind of mental condition which is shared by many people," says Dr. Robert Whitley, the Principal Investigator of the Social Psychiatry Research and Interest Group (SPRING) at the Douglas Hospital Research Center. In early 2019, he penned a serious article about the potential of TDS being a real mental condition. Dr. Whitley continues, "In psychiatry what we often do is we raise possibilities, we raise awareness of issues for discussion. So my intention was really to start discussion…my dream is to do a research study on this."

The phenomenon that may explain TDS is something called cognitive dissonance, a concept regularly cited in psychology. "Cognitive dissonance is a concept…whereby an individual or group hold two ideas simultaneously within their own mind which are actually contradictory or which one can say are mutually exclusive." In other words, cognitive dissonance is the tension that someone experiences when they are presented with facts that completely contradict their strongly held belief. The first person to explain Trump Derangement Syndrome in terms of cognitive dissonance, and flag it as a serious issue, is thought to be the famed Dilbert artist Scott

Adams. The way Adams sees it, Trump supporters were less likely to experience a derangement after the 2016 Election because regardless of the results, the outcome would have made sense in the mind of a Trump supporter either way. If the real estate mogul would have lost, well that's what the media and the polls were telling everyone anyways, so there would have been no mental conflict. If Trump won, as he did – well, that's what a Trump supporter expected to happen anyways. The results would have explained a world that made sense to a Trump supporter. However, the other half of the country had a completely different reality about Trump. For nearly a year and a half, almost 24/7, the media was painting Trump as the reincarnation of Hitler with no chance of winning the election. Scott Adams explained:

> **Scott Adams**: "But, if you were on the side that knew he couldn't win, that there's no way that you were living in a country that this monster could possibly become our leader. And then you woke up and he was – that's a classic set up for cognitive dissonance. It's where you rewrite the script in your head to make sense of this new information. And here's what people don't do because we're all human…We rarely write the script in our head to say, 'You know, the best way to explain this is that I was a fucking idiot for two years.' Right, nobody does that…and there's nothing wrong with that. That's normal. I don't do it. You don't do it. Nobody does that. So they have to come up with a new script that explains their situation, and so I think they've come up with, 'my god, there are more racists in the country than we knew. They voted this guy in. And he must have had help from Russia. Because there's no way this happens in a natural way, because my world wouldn't make sense if he could get elected just by having policies people like…couldn't happen.'"

So when people are met with cold hard facts that refute their deeply felt opinions, they experience cognitive dissonance and sometimes lash out, or come up with wild ideas to make sense of the world that now makes no sense to them. "But we do know that some people have difficulties resolving cognitive dissonance," says Dr. Whitley. "And…that often results in blaming other people, or in coming to false conclusions, or to having a kind of mini conspiracy theory about what's happening in life."

What we have seen since the 2016 Elections is possibly the most massive case of cognitive dissonance that has ever occurred in western civilization. And that's not hyperbole. It's what led to the reaction to Ellen's heartfelt post, a post that simply cited something irrefutably good that Trump had done – signing the Right to Vote law. Here was a person, a truly special woman, and an American hero, whose horrific personal tragedy gave her a unique perspective on Trump's action. She shared that feeling with her community, and the power of her credibility on this issue contradicted the strongly held beliefs of Ellen's social circle…so they attacked her character to make sense of their world.

Which leads us back to the question, is Trump Derangement Syndrome a real mental condition? I think Ellen's story shows us the answer is yes – but we'll have to wait for Dr. Robert Whitley to find a research grant to give us clear, data-driven evidence. In the meantime, we're faced with seeing actual CNN headlines like this: "Here are eighteen reasons Trump could be a Russian asset."

Welcome to the new normal.

Endnotes

INTRODUCTION

1. Xuan Thai, Ted Barrett, Biden's description of Obama draws scrutiny, CNN, Feb. 9, 2007. https://www.cnn.com/2007/POLITICS/01/31/biden.obama/

2. Jonathan Strong, Documents show media plotting to kill stories about Rev. Jeremiah Wright, The Daily Caller, July 20, 2010. https://dailycaller.com/2010/07/20/documents-show-media-plotting-to-kill-stories-about-rev-jeremiah-wright/

3. The Rachel Maddow Show Transcript 07/10/09, MSNBC, July 10, 2009. http://www.msnbc.com/transcripts/rachel-maddow-show/2009-07-10

4. Philip Kennicott, Obama as the Joker Betrays Racial Ugliness, Fears, The Washington Post, August 6, 2009. http://www.washingtonpost.com/wp-dyn/content/article/2009/08/05/AR2009080503876.html

5. MSNBC crops video to incite racial tension over AR-15 at Obama Rally, YouTube, August 25, 2009. https://www.youtube.com/watch?v=fvBQDHqdCck

6. Kyle Drennen, MSNBC: ObamaCare Protesters 'Racist,' Including Black-Gun Owner, NewsBusters.org, August 18, 2009. https://www.newsbusters.org/blogs/nb/kyle-drennen/2009/08/18/msnbc-obamacare-protesters-racist-including-black-gun-owner

CHAPTER ONE: DAVID & GOLIATH

1. The Takeaway. Franken Wins Minnesota Senate Race. Finally. WNYC Studios, July 1, 2009. https://www.wnycstudios.org/podcasts/takeaway/segments/6882-franken-wins-minnesota-senate-race-finally

2. Al Franken finally declared Senator. The Colbert Report, June 30, 2009. http://www.cc.com/video-clips/hy9hl7/the-colbert-report-al-franken-finally-declared-senator

3. Byron York, York: When 1,099 felons vote in race won by 312 ballots, Washington Examiner, August 6, 2012. https://www.washingtonexaminer.com/york-when-1-099-felons-vote-in-race-won-by-312-ballots

4. Monica Davey and Carl Hulse, Franken's Win Bolsters Democratic Grip in Senate, The New York Times, June 30, 2009.

5. Rachel Slajda, Teabaggers Try to Shout Down Health Care Reform At Town Halls, Talking Points Memo, August 3, 2009. https://talkingpointsmemo.com/dc/teabaggers-try-to-shout-down-health-care-reform-at-town-halls

6. Elizabeth Scalia, Obama as the Joker, Patheos, August 4, 2009. https://www.patheos.com/blogs/theanchoress/2009/08/04/obama-as-the-joker/

7. ABC News. Loud, Disruptive Health Care Town Halls. August 7, 2009. https://www.youtube.com/watch?v=w4G9RGxahTM

8. PoliticsNewsPolitics. CNN Story on the 'Obama Joker' Phenomenon.

CNN, August 4, 2009. https://www.youtube.com/watch?v=GStMLFMdRcQ

9. Tammy Bruce. Poster-Sized O'Joker Pic, TammyBruce.com, August 12, 2009. https://tammybruce.com/2009/08/poster-sized-ojoker-pic.html

10. Steven Mikulan, New Anti-Obama 'Joker' Poster, LA Weekly, August 3, 2009. https://www.laweekly.com/new-anti-obama-joker-poster/

11. Amanda Carey, WaPo: Joker Poster is Racist (And So Are You), Reason.com, August 6, 2009. https://reason.com/2009/08/06/wapo-joker-poster-is-racist-an/

12. Shepard Fairey, "Helping Obama Write the Unwritten Future," The Huffington Post, August 6, 2009. https://www.huffpost.com/entry/helping-obama-write-the-u_b_253004

13. Patrick Courrielche, The Artist Formerly Known As Dissident, Reason.com, August 7, 2009. https://reason.com/2009/08/07/the-artist-formerly-known-as-d/

14. Annual Report, National Endowment for the Arts, https://www.arts.gov/about/annual-reports

15. Patrick Courrielche, The National Endowment For The Art Persuasion?, Breitbart News, August 25, 2009. https://www.breitbart.com/entertainment/2009/08/25/the-national-endowment-for-the-art-of-persuasion/

16. Stuart Varney Show, Courrielche on Fox Business, Fox Business, August 27, 2009 [correct date listed here, date wrong on website]. https://video.foxbusiness.com/v/3894796/#sp=show-clips

17. Kerry Picket, Art for Obama's sake – The NEA pushes the White House Agenda, The Washington Times, August 27, 2009. https://www.washingtontimes.com/blog/watercooler/2009/aug/27/art-obamas-sake-nea-pushes-whitehouse-agenda/

18. Courrielche Speaks with Andrew Breitbart, The Dennis Miller Show, September 1, 2009. https://www.youtube.com/watch?v=Sf-MGsCBykU

19. Alex Beam, The art of agitprop, The Boston Globe, Sept. 1, 2009.

20. Courrielche on Glenn Beck, The Glenn Beck Show on Fox News, September 1, 2009. https://www.youtube.com/watch?v=3gftF5Uv-kM&t=406s

21. Jake Tapper, Controversial Obama Administration Official Denies Being Part of 9/11 "Truther" Movement, Apologizes for Past Comments, ABC News, September 3, 2009. http://web.archive.org/web/20090905101056/http://blogs.abcnews.com/politicalpunch/2009/09/controversial-obama-administration-official-denies-being-part-of-911-truther-movement-apologizes-for.html

22. Ryan Grim, Glenn Beck Gets First Scalp: Van Jones Resigns, Huffington Post, September 6, 2009. http://web.archive.org/web/20090907223026/http://www.huffingtonpost.com/2009/09/06/glenn-beck-gets-first-sca_n_278281.html

23. Rush Limbaugh Show, September 8, 2009.

24. Eliza Strickland, The New Face of Environmentalism, East Bay Ex-

press, November 2, 2005. https://www.eastbayexpress.com/gyrobase/the-new-face-of-environmentalism/Content?oid=1079539&showFullText=true

25. Senator John Cornyn, Art Imitates...The President's Agenda?, September 9, 2009. https://www.cornyn.senate.gov/content/art-imitates...-president's-agenda

26. Yunji de Nies, Yosi Sergant: The Next Van Jones?, ABC News, September 10, 2009. https://web.archive.org/web/20090913133525/http://blogs.abcnews.com/politicalpunch/2009/09/yosi-sergant-the-next-van-jones.html/

27. Courrielche on Glenn Beck, The Glenn Beck Show on Fox News, September 11, 2009. https://www.youtube.com/watch?v=J31sYOWffvo

28. Associated Press, Obama advisor Jones resigns amid controversy, NBC News, September 9, 2009. http://www.nbcnews.com/id/32712017/ns/politics-white_house/t/obama-adviser-jones-resigns-amid-controversy/#.Xauab-dKiRs

29. This Week with George Stephanopoulos, September 6, 2009.

30. Patrick Courrielche, Full NEA Conference Call Transcript and Audio, Breitbart News, September 21, 2009.

31. Patrick Courrielche, Explosive New Audio Reveals White House Using NEA to Push Partisan Agenda, Breitbart News, September 21, 2009.

32. Rush Limbaugh Show, September 21, 2009. http://freerepublic.com/focus/f-news/2345048/posts

33. Courrielche on Hannity, The Sean Hannity Show, September 21, 2009. https://www.youtube.com/watch?v=Pa9HvR3H_bA

34. Letter from Senator Enzi and nine U.S. Senators to NEA Chairman Rocco Landesman, Washington Post, September 23, 2009. http://www.washingtonpost.com/wp-srv/nation/documents/Enzi_letter_to_NEA_092409.pdf

35. Robert Siegel, White House Cautious Over NEA Politics Flap, National Public Radio, September 23, 2009. https://www.npr.org/templates/story/story.php?storyId=113135814

36. James Taranto, 'Artists' as Servants of Power, Wall Street Journal, September 21, 2009. https://www.wsj.com/articles/SB10001424052970204488304574427111444082906

37. Political Punch, After 'Inappropriate' NEA Conference Call, White House Pushes New Guidelines, ABC News, September 22, 2009. http://web.archive.org/web/20150711225650/http://blogs.abcnews.com/politicalpunch/2009/09/after-inappropriate-nea-conference-call-white-house-pushes-new-guidelines.html

38. Philip Elliott, White House to agencies: Don't overstep on grants, Associated Press, September 22, 2009. https://www.sandiegouniontribune.com/sdut-us-obama-arts-flap-092209-2009sep22-story.html

39. Jeff Zeleny, Agencies Instructed to Separate Politics From Grant Awards, The New York Times, September 22, 2009. https://www.nytimes.

com/2009/09/23/us/politics/23grants.html

40. Andy Barr, Administration backs off NEA call, Politico, September 22, 2009. https://www.politico.com/story/2009/09/administration-backs-off-nea-call-027456

41. Jon Stewart, America: Target America, Comedy Central, September 28, 2009. http://www.cc.com/video-clips/jvnz55/the-daily-show-with-jon-stewart-america--target-america

42. James Taranto, 'Artists' as Servants of Power, Wall Street Journal, September 21, 2009. https://www.wsj.com/articles/SB10001424052970204488304574427111444082906

43. Garance Franke-Ruta and Michael A. Fletcher, Yosi Sergant resigns from NEA, The Washington Post, September 24, 2009. http://voices.washingtonpost.com/44/2009/09/24/yosi_sergant_resigns_from_nea.html

44. Andrew Breitbart, Righteous Indignation, published April 15, 2011.

45. Quotes from Yosi Sergant, Mike Skolnik, Buffy Wicks, and Nell Abernathy from interviews on Red Pilled America episode entitled One & Done? published November 1, 2018.

CHAPTER TWO: TICKING TIME BOMB

1. THR Staff, Kelly Osbourne on Donald Trump's Anti-Immigrant Stance: "Who is going to be cleaning your toilet?", The Hollywood Reporter, August 4, 2015. https://www.hollywoodreporter.com/news/kelly-osbourne-immigrants-cleaning-toilets-813080

2. Matthew Mulbrandon, Housing Price Index for the United States 2000-2010, Design & Geography, April 27, 2011. https://designandgeography.com/2011/04/27/housing-price-index-for-the-united-states-2000-2010/

3. Wolf Richter, The most expensive housing zip codes in America, Business Insider, December 20, 2017. https://www.businessinsider.com/most-expensive-housing-zip-codes-in-america-2017-12

4. Natalie Kitroeff, Immigrants flooded California construction. Worker pay sank. Here's why, Los Angeles Times, April 22, 2017. https://www.latimes.com/projects/la-fi-construction-trump/

5. Jonathan Lansner, California No. 1 in U.S. in poverty...and No. 1 in declines in poverty, Mercury News, September 16, 2019. https://www.mercurynews.com/2019/09/16/california-no-1-in-u-s-in-poverty-and-no-1-in-declines-in-poverty/

6. Gale Holland, L.A.'s homelessness surged 75% in six years. Here's why the crisis has been decades in the making, Los Angeles Times, February 1, 2018. https://www.latimes.com/local/lanow/la-me-homeless-how-we-got-here-20180201-story.html

7. Greg Norman, San Francisco human feces map shows waste blanketing the California city, Fox News, April 23, 2019. https://www.foxnews.com/

us/san-francisco-map-shows-human-poop-complaints

8. Irvine Residents Protest Homeless Plan, CBS Local LA, March 25, 2018. https://losangeles.cbslocal.com/2018/03/25/homeless-irvine-protest/

9. Workforce data from Center for Immigration Studies analysis of the Current Population Survey public-use files from the fourth quarter of 2000 to the first quarter of 2017.

10. Hampton public school demographic data from the New York State Education Department. https://data.nysed.gov

11. Alberto A. Martinez, Trump praised Mexicans a Hundred Times, New Standard Press, January 24, 2016. http://www.newstandardpress.com/mr-trump-praises-mexicans-again/

12. Leon H. Wolf, Watch Donald Trump Say There Are Jobs Americans Won't Do, Make The Case For Partial Amnesty (VIDEO), RedState, January 19, 2016. https://www.redstate.com/leon_h_wolf/2016/01/19/watch-donald-trump-say-jobs-americans-wont-make-case-partial-amnesty-video/

13. Quotes from Tom Wedell, George Overbeck, and Dr. Steve Camarota from interviews on Red Pilled America episode entitled Ticking Time Bomb published November 29, 2018.

CHAPTER THREE: CHERRY-PICKING

1. Brit Hume, Al Gore's Claim About the Snow on Mount Kilimanjaro, Fox News, June 13, 2007. https://www.foxnews.com/story/al-gores-claim-about-the-snow-on-mount-kilimanjaro

2. Doug Hardy, Greatest Snowfall on Kilimanjaro Glaciers in Years, Glacier Hub, April 4, 2018. https://glacierhub.org/2018/04/04/greatest-snowfall-on-kilimanjaro-glaciers-in-years/

3. Barack Obama, Barack Obama's Remarks in St. Paul, The New York Times, June 3, 2008. https://www.nytimes.com/2008/06/03/us/politics/03text-obama.html

4. Ryan Teague Beckwith, President Trump won't say if he still thinks Climate Change is a Hoax. Here's why, Time, September 27, 2017. https://time.com/4959233/donald-trump-climate-change-hoax-question/

5. Camila Domonoske, Colin Dwyer, Trump Announces U.S. Withdrawal From Paris Climate Accord, NPR, July 1, 2017. https://www.npr.org/sections/thetwo-way/2017/06/01/530748899/watch-live-trump-announces-decision-on-paris-climate-agreement

6. Chris Hayes, Donald Trump Believes Climate Change Is A Hoax, MSNBC, June 2, 2017. https://www.youtube.com/watch?v=yqgMECkW3Ak

7. Michael E. Mann, Raymond S. Bradley & Malcolm K. Hughes, Global-scale temperature patters and climate forcing over the past six centuries, Nature, April 23, 1998. http://www.meteo.psu.edu/holocene/public_html/shared/articles/mbh98.pdf

8. Michael E. Mann, Raymond S. Bradley, Northern Hemisphere Temperatures During the Past Millennium Inferences, Uncertainties, and Limitations, Geophysical Research Letters, March 15, 1999. http://www.geo.umass.edu/faculty/bradley/mann1999.pdf

9. Temperature Record, Science Daily. https://www.sciencedaily.com/terms/temperature_record.htm

10. Tree Rings, Climate Data Information, http://www.climatedata.info/proxies/tree-rings/

11. TAR Climate Change 2001: The Scientific Basis, IPCC, First Published 2001. https://www.ipcc.ch/report/ar3/wg1/

12. Stephen McIntyre, Ross McKitrick, Corrections to the Mann el. Al. (1998) Proxy Data Base and Northern Hemisphere Average Temperature Series, Energy & Environment, November 1, 2003. https://journals.sagepub.com/doi/10.1260/095830503322793632

13. Stephen McIntyre, Ross McKitrick, List of Global Warming: Paleoclimate / Hockey Stick Academic Papers. https://www.rossmckitrick.com/paleoclimatehockey-stick.html

14. Stephen McIntyre, A Red Noise Spaghetti Diagram, Climate Audit, Feb. 25, 2005. https://climateaudit.org/2005/02/25/a-red-noise-spaghetti-diagram/

15. Stephen McIntyre, Ross McKitrick, Hockey sticks, principal components, and spurious significance, Geophysical Research Letters, February 12, 2005. https://agupubs.onlinelibrary.wiley.com/doi/full/10.1029/2004GL021750

16. World Meteorological Organization, WMO Statement on the status of the global climate in 1999, WMO website, Issued in 2000. https://library.wmo.int/doc_num.php?explnum_id=3460

17. 1990 IPCC First Assessment Report, Intergovernmental Panel on Climate Change (IPCC), August 1990. https://www.ipcc.ch/report/climate-change-the-ipcc-1990-and-1992-assessments/

18. Michael E. Mann, Raymond S. Bradley & Malcolm K. Hughes, Erratum: corrigendum: Global-scale temperature patterns and climate forcing over the past six centuries, Nature, July 1, 2004. https://www.nature.com/articles/nature02478

19. Rosanne D'Arrigo, Rob Wilson, Beate Liepert, Paolo Cherubini, On the 'Divergence Problem' in Northern Forests: A review of the tree-ring evidence and possible causes, Global and Planetary Change, March 9, 2007. http://web.archive.org/web/20100119083916/https://www.ldeo.columbia.edu/~liepert/pdf/DArrigo_etal.pdf

20. Antonio Regalado, In Climate Debate, The 'Hockey Stick' Leads to a Face-Off, The Wall Street Journal, February 14, 2005. https://www.wsj.com/articles/SB110834031507653590

21. Stephen McIntyre, IPCC and the Briffa Deletions, Climate Audit, June 26, 2007. https://climateaudit.org/2007/06/26/ipcc-and-the-briffa-deletions/

22. Stephen McIntyre, IPCC and the "Trick", Climate Audit, December 10, 2009. https://climateaudit.org/2009/12/10/ipcc-and-the-trick/

23. Stephen McIntyre, Willis Eschenbach's FOI Request, Climate Audit, November 25, 2009. https://climateaudit.org/2009/11/25/willis-eschenbachs-foi-request/

24. The Yamal implosion, Bishop Hill, September 29, 2009. http://bishophill.squarespace.com/blog/2009/9/29/the-yamal-implosion.html

25. Questions Surrounding the 'Hockey Stick' Temperature Studies: Implications for Climate Change Assessments, Subcommittee on Oversight and Investigations of the Committee on Energy and Commerce House of Representatives, July 2006. https://www.govinfo.gov/content/pkg/CHRG-109hhrg31362/html/CHRG-109hhrg31362.htm

26. Stephen McIntyre, D'Arrigo: Making Cherry Pie, Climate Audit, March 7, 2006. https://climateaudit.org/2006/03/07/darrigo-making-cherry-pie/

27. Anthony Watt, Breaking News Story: CRU has apparently been hacked – hundreds of files released, Watts Up With That?, November 19, 2009. https://wattsupwiththat.com/2009/11/19/breaking-news-story-hadley-cru-has-apparently-been-hacked-hundreds-of-files-released/

28. "From Limbaugh to Trump: How Climategate spread through the media," Mother Jones December 18, 2017. https://www.youtube.com/watch?v=8GZCg0K-6XI

29. Data or Dogma? Promoting Open Inquiry in the Debate over the Magnitude of Human Impact on Earth's Climate, U.S. Senate Committee on Commerce, Science, & Transportation, December 8, 2015. https://www.commerce.senate.gov/2015/12/data-or-dogma-promoting-open-inquiry-in-the-debate-over-the-magnitude-of-human-impact-on-earth-s-climate

30. Judith Curry, Statement to the Subcommittee on Space, Science and Competitiveness of the United States Senate, U.S. Senate Committee on Commerce, Science, & Transportation, December 8, 2015. https://www.commerce.senate.gov/services/files/F739759E-3F1B-447E-A1EB-D42BBE70454E

31. Quotes from Steve McIntyre, Anthony Watts, Steve Mosher, and Charles Rotter from interviews on Red Pilled America episode entitled Cherry Picking published December 6, 2018.

CHAPTER FOUR: UNITY NIGHT

1. Barack Obama's Keynote Address at the 2004 Democratic National Convention, PBS.org, July 27, 2004. https://www.pbs.org/newshour/show/barack-obamas-keynote-address-at-the-2004-democratic-national-convention

2. MTV's 2010 Sprite Step Off trailer, YouTube. https://youtu.be/tYer-jfM8J-M

3. Joseph Bufanda, A Brief History of Step, Tufts University, 2004. https://ase.tufts.edu/aso/blackout/history.html

4. Jason Whitlock, White sorority's contest win a step away from equality, The Kansas City Star, March 2. 2010. http://web.archive.org/web/20100308094332/https://www.kansascity.com/2010/03/02/1785585_the-wrong-step-toward-equality.html

5. Kristi Nelson, White Squad's Step Dance Win Draws Criticism, NBC DFW, March 5, 2010. https://www.nbcdfw.com/news/local/Controversy-Over-Winners-of-Step-Dance-Competition-86681112.html

6. Smokey Fontaine, JUST CURIOUS: Should White Sorority Have Won Sprite Step-Off, NewsOne, February 25, 2010. https://newsone.com/444342/just-curious-should-white-sorority-have-been-allowed-to-win-sprite-step-off/

7. Jemele Hill, Winners hurt by corporate bad judgment, ESPN, March 1, 2010. https://www.espn.com/espn/commentary/news/story?id=4956425

8. Neely Tucker, A step too far, The Washington Post, March 6, 2010. https://www.post-gazette.com/news/nation/2010/03/07/A-step-too-far/stories/201003070218

9. NPHC webpage. https://www.nphchq.org/quantum/

10. Torri Griffith, Greeks Unveil History of Strolling, Daily Eastern News, February 11, 2016. https://www.dailyeasternnews.com/2016/02/11/greeks-unveil-history-of-strolling/

11. Ashley Martin, Arkansas Zetas step into national spotlight, Themis, Spring 2010. https://issuu.com/zetataualpha/docs/spring2010themis/10

12. cganemccalla, UPDATE: Sprite Finds Stepping Score Was Wrong, Calls It A Tie, NewsOne, February 25, 2010. https://newsone.com/443512/white-sorority-wins-sprite-step-off-competition/

13. Neely Tucker, Sprite Step Off: In step with the times, or going a step too far, The Washington Post, March 4, 2010. http://www.washingtonpost.com/wp-dyn/content/article/2010/03/03/AR2010030303895.html?hpid=sec-artsliving&sid=ST2010030403984

14. Lawrence C. Ross, The Divine Nine: The History of African American Fraternities and Sororities, https://www.amazon.com/Divine-Nine-American-Fraternities-Sororities/dp/0758202709

15. Lawrence C. Ross, Can we at least keep Stepping to ourselves, The Root, February 26, 2010. https://www.theroot.com/can-we-at-least-keep-stepping-to-ourselves-1790878707

16. A.R. Shaw, Ciara, Top Black Fraternities, Sororities Stomp at 2011 'Spring Step Off,' Rollingout.com, Apr. 3, 2011. https://rollingout.com/2011/04/03/ciara-top-black-fraternities-sororities-stomp-at-2011-sprite-step-off/

17. Aaron Randle, White Sorority beats Black Greeks at Step Off, The Hilltop Online, Feb. 22, 2010. http://web.archive.org/web/20100616160100/http://www.thehilltoponline.com/white-sorority-beats-black-greeks-at-step-off-1.2163798

18. Don Lemon, Step Show Controversy, CNN, March 6, 2010. http://edition.cnn.com/TRANSCRIPTS/1003/06/cnr.08.html

19. Krissah Thompson, Scott Clement, Poll Majority of Americans think race relations are getting worse, The Washington Post, July 16, 2016. https://www.washingtonpost.com/national/more-than-6-in-10-adults-say-us-race-relations-are-generally-bad-poll-indicates/2016/07/16/66548936-4aa8-11e6-90a8-fb84201e0645_story.html

20. Anthony Salvanto, Jennifer De Pinto, Fred Backus and Kabir Khanna, Americans optimistic about economy, but pessimistic about country's direction - CBS News poll, CBS News, January 24, 2019. https://www.cbsnews.com/news/americans-optimistic-about-economy-cbs-news-poll/

21. Chris Isidore, Black unemployment rate falls to a record low, CNN. com, September 6, 2019. https://www.cnn.com/2019/09/06/economy/black-unemployment-rate/index.html

22. Barack Obama, Barack Obama: 'Passion is Vital, But You've Got to have a Stratgey, Time.com, May 9, 2016. https://time.com/4322786/barack-obama-howard-university-commencement-speech/

CHAPTER FIVE: MR. CREEPY

1. THR Staff, The Hollywood Insider's Guide to L.A. Private Schools, The Hollywood Reporter, August 17, 2017. https://www.hollywoodreporter.com/lists/hollywood-insiders-guide-la-private-schools-1029445/item/hollywood-guide-la-schools-westside-1030388

2. Jeanie Pyun, Lesley McKenzie, The Hollywood Insider's Guide to L.A. Private Schools 2018, The Hollywood Reporter, August 24, 2018. https://www.hollywoodreporter.com/features/hollywood-insiders-guide-la-private-schools-2018-1136526

3. IMDB.com, Chris Bender. https://www.imdb.com/name/nm0070454/

4. James Alan Astman, Letter from the Headmaster, Oakwoodschool.org, January 9, 2018. https://transition.oakwoodschool.org/letter-from-the-head-of-school/

5. Adam Scott's Kids Are Anti-Trump, Late Night with Seth Meyers, February 15, 2017. https://www.nbc.com/late-night-with-seth-meyers/video/adam-scotts-kids-are-antitrump/3471136

6. Paul Bond, Steve Bannon Declares War on Hollywood Post-Weinstein, The Hollywood Reporter, October 26, 2017. https://www.hollywoodreporter.com/news/steve-bannon-escalates-breitbarts-war-hollywood-post-weinstein-blowing-up-1051964

7. Letter #1, threatening lawsuit from The Creepies to Patrick & Adryana, June 28, 2013. Some names redacted.

By Email and Certified Mail Return Receipt Requested
June 28, 2013
Adryana Cortez and Patrick Courrielche
Re: Damage to Our Reputation

Adryana and Patrick:

It is unfortunate and disappointing that this letter must be written to you but you have left us few options.

In regards to your concern for the wellbeing of children who visit our home, while you may feel that some of the ways in which [Mr. Creepy] and I have interacted with our friends' children as seemingly "inappropriate", reasonable people may beg to differ. This is evidenced by the overwhelming support, understanding and confirmation we have received from the very parents of the children with whom we have interacted in what you perceive to be an improper manner.

When we spoke about this matter to Patrick on two separate occasions on the phone, we were clear when we said that we heard you, we respect your view point and were sorry for any misunderstanding or upset this may have caused. You, the Benders and the [third family] have acknowledged to us that nothing inappropriate happened with any children at our home. And we all agreed, that this was a private matter between our families and Patrick specifically stated that there was deliberate intention to keep this concern and conversation among this small group of four families. But despite these assurances, you have repeatedly spoken of this to others, including administrators at both [our preschool] and Oakwood and parents of other children in our shared grade. And this has now come to the attention of parents outside of our shared grade, which means that this is being discussed among others.

More significantly, what we have been told that you said is inaccurate with partial or erroneous information and this is a threat to our reputation. This is both unacceptable and slanderous, and cannot continue. We insist that you immediately stop making any statements about us to anyone. We have consulted with our lawyer, and if necessary, we will commence a lawsuit against you for defamation of character and slander. We do not want this matter to escalate further but this cannot continue.

Respectfully, [The Creepies]

8. Letter #2, Patrick & Adryana's response to The Creepies letter threatening a lawsuit, July 1, 2013. Some names redacted.

Sent via email and certified mail, July 1, 2013

[Mr. & Mrs. Creepy],

Your decision to elevate this by including your legal counsel in our correspondence is troubling on many levels. Considering that we have to coexist as part of the Oakwood community, it would have been wise to take a less aggressive posture when dealing with this issue.

At no time have we ever slandered either of you as you falsely claim in your letter dated 06/28/13 ("Letter"). We have always conveyed solely the facts, as confirmed by both of you, when addressing our concerns with your practice of sharing beds with children that are not your own. Conveying the facts, as confirmed by your family, does not constitute slander. You can be assured that we will continue conveying solely the facts whenever discussing this matter. Also, at no time has our family acknowledged that "nothing inappropriate happened with any children" at your home as you claim in the Letter. Quite the opposite - which is why our family, along with the [third family] and the Benders, decided to address what we viewed as, in fact, collectively troubling incidents of inappropriate behavior.

You mentioned receiving "overwhelming support, understanding and confirmation" from "the very parents of the children with whom we have interacted in what you perceive to be an improper manner." That is demonstrably untrue. Two of the four families involved in direct incidents confirm that they do not support your behavior, while a third confirmed with Adryana that [Mrs. Creepy] did not share any of the details of the concerns raised by the families that have confronted you. Additionally, we have not shared any details with [child #3's] family and have had no correspondence with [child #4's] family, both involved in bed sharing occurrences confirmed by you, and as a result we have not conveyed the totality of incidents that led to multiple families confronting [Mr. Creepy] on his individual and your collective behavior. These facts do not remotely constitute "overwhelming support." Please be reminded that it was you that initiated conversations with Oakwood families outside of those that have openly expressed concern for your behavior, and it was you that mentioned several of your bed sharing occasions in a room containing people not limited to the families that confronted you.

The optics of your behavior, your continued position that your sharing beds with children that are not your own is appropriate, the absence of confirmation that this type of activity will cease, along with your decision to share this matter, whether partially or completely, with persons outside of the families that confronted you, which we have confirmed, has undoubtedly helped this issue reach a wider audience within our community.

Should you choose to enter into a baseless lawsuit against our family, be aware that we anticipated this as a potential route and have been prepared in advance of our decision to join other families in confronting your behavior. Legal action would lead to an experience that all involved would no doubt like to avoid, including - your children being exposed to participating in depositions; each incident, that your family has confirmed and the details of which are sensitive enough in nature for us to intentionally not include here in writing, being corroborated by multiple families and made part of the public record; the certain involvement of the Los Angeles County Department of Children and Family Services in reviewing your admitted behavior; counter suits, legal remedies and so on – all events that we have gone to great lengths to avoid by speaking to specialists and school officials before addressing our concerns with you.

Our suggestion to you is to stop all threats of baseless lawsuits and confirm that you will terminate the practice of sharing your beds with children that are not your own. Any damage to your reputation has been caused by your actions, and your actions alone.

We've cared for, and continue to care for, your children and your family enough to have addressed our concerns with you directly as opposed to enlisting any rigid, bureaucratic remedy, that would not take your family's comfort and privacy into consideration. In the past, you've referred to us as your first "ghetto friends." Please do not misinterpret our upbringing and/or your perception of our social status as any indication that we are naïve in legal matters.

Sincerely, Patrick and Adryana Courrielche

9. Letter #3, The Creepies Response to Patrick & Adryana's Response Letter, July 3, 2013.

Adryana Cortez and Patrick Courrielche
Re: Damage to Our Reputation

Adryana and Patrick:
Thank you for your letter of July 1, 2013. We agree that the situation has regrettably escalated. The situation has been upsetting to all of us.

We have different points of view on many things. However, there are some things in which we can agree. We both do not want any child to experience any emotional or physical harm. Not yours, not ours, not anyone's.

We do not think that we have done anything wrong. No child has been harmed while at our house. All of our actions were carried out with nothing but good intentions. That being said, we recognize, however, that you are uncomfortable with our behavior and that it obviously has upset you. For that, we apologize and it will never happen again.

If you wish to sit down with us and discuss this in person, we are certainly open to doing so.

Respectfully,
[The Creepies]

10. Letter #4, from Oakwood Headmaster Jim Astman, to Patrick & Adryana, October 22, 2013. Some names redacted.

Patrick –
I apologize for the delay in getting back to you. Last week was very

hectic and I wanted to give your email, which I found troubling, very careful thought.

I'm not certain why you've directed this just to me, but I am certain, as Margo and I both made clear to you and Adryana, that the divisiveness in the grade has become intolerable. It has created palpable discomfort at school, spilled into ugly rumors about [The Creepies] children, and created an atmosphere where parents too often take second-hand information as fact.

While it's true that you have expressed concern since last spring, it is noteworthy to Margo and me that your description of those concerns has escalated considerably over time. Behavior that you initially described as "bizarre" to both of us – bizarre, you said, but not abusive – Adryana has now come to describe as "grooming behavior." As I said when we last met, if you have developed the conviction that something unlawful has taken place – a conviction Margo and I, on the basis of extensive and multiple conversations, do not share – you are free to report it. You should also know that more parents are now coming to us with deep concern not about [The Creepies] but about what they have described as Adryana's "bullying" and her "mission" to force [The Creepies] out of the school.

Margo and I were astonished and chagrined when, in response to my question about the "mediation" outcome you were hoping for, Adryana said: "We want you to throw [The Creepies] out of school." She repeated that it was her "duty to protect other children by warning parents about [The Creepies]." With such an aim, school-sponsored mediation has no constructive role to play. And other parents' descriptions about your conducting a "campaign" against [The Creepies] become increasingly credible.

We join you in wanting a school that is healthy and safe for children, and for adults as well. But we part company when it comes to understanding the role that you, yourselves, have played in the divisiveness that concerns everyone. That is why I ask you to cease immediately any lobbying against [The Creepies'] presence in the school. Its effect is to undermine the goodwill and courtesy upon which a healthy community depends.

Sincerely,

Jim

11. Letter #5, Response email from Patrick & Adryana to Jim Astman, October 24, 2013. Some names redacted.

Jim,

Disappointment does not begin to describe our family's feelings to the tone and content of the school's response to our very respectful and reasonable request for mediation with [The Creepies] As parents, we try to teach our children about safety, and the difference between acceptable and unacceptable behavior. The practice of an adult getting into bed with other people's children is unquestionably a threat to the safety of a child and the stability of our community. Yet the school has currently taken the position that this is acceptable behavior because nothing "unlawful" has occurred and that none of the incidents happened while on school campus. Respectfully, that should not be the litmus test for the school's position on parent-on-child behavior within the Oakwood community. There are multiple provisions cited in the school code of conduct that are not unlawful nor need to occur on campus for the school to be within its right to take disciplinary action.

We've sought out and received Oakwood's counsel at every point along this conflict, and that counsel has informed and been the basis for our decision-making all along the way. But in the first instance that we question the sustainability of the administration's request for all involved to no longer discuss these confirmed incidents, we receive a hurtful letter containing factually void third-party accusations, and inaccurate and out-of-context quotes.

As the school knows, we've confirmed directly with [The Creepies] their practice of getting into bed with other people's children - with [Mrs. Creepy] using "spooning" and "cuddling" as descriptors of her husband's interaction with these children in their bed - and Adryana witnessed [Mr. Creepy] completely undressing our daughter without our permission. Additionally, these incidents are not the first time concerns have been raised with [The Creepy] family, as we have confirmed and informed the school of.

At no point have [The Creepies] denied any of these incidents, which the school also conveyed to us, and at one point [The Creepies] tried to argue in writing that they had the support of all of the parents involved - an easily verifiable, grossly inaccurate falsehood that displays their capacity to perversely bend the truth to intimidate and revise history.

The whole reason for the follow up request for school mediation was because we thought, rightfully given confirmed accounts of continued chatter and misinformation by [Mrs. Creepy] dating (in this iteration) to the beginning of the school year, that the situation would likely not be resolved without mediation. We are shocked to learn that the school feels that [The Creepies] confirmed behavior is now somehow acceptable because it isn't "unlawful" and that the mere practice of conveying incidents to concerned parents is now being categorized as "bullying." At no time have we ever bullied [The Creepies], a false accusation we take very seriously.

We have never embarked on a lobbying campaign against [The Creepies] presence in the school and vehemently refute that accusation. When asked in our last meeting, what do you think the school should do to remedy the situation, Adryana responded, "Why don't you ask them to leave?" It was never a demand as characterized, was not in response to a question regarding a mediation outcome, and was a perfectly logical response to a direct question given the circumstances. We discussed that we had a goal in mind when initially confronting [The Creepies] on their behavior, which was for them to confirm that they would terminate the practice of sharing their bed with other people's children, but the question of an outcome for mediation was left completely open by us – and still is.

The fact that Oakwood is being contacted by friends of [The Creepies] and accusing our family in the manner described by the school, bolsters the argument that it is in fact the Thompsons that are campaigning against and bullying our family. This position is also strengthened by the documented fact that [The Creepies] targeted solely our family (out of three) with threats of a frivolous lawsuit – a threat that they immediately retracted once presented with the facts in writing. May we also add that we never excluded [The Creepies] from the class camping trip, a long held non-school event for which the Oakwood community participates and we were asked to co-chair. Any accusations of bullying or campaigning are third-party extrapolations at best.

Also to clarify, it was not our opinion that the confirmed incidents fell within the label of "grooming behavior." When the topic of outside officials' opinions was brought up by the school in our meeting, we stated that it was the opinion of professionals apprised of [The Creepies] confirmed incidents.

Furthermore, Adryana did not say that it was "her duty to protect other children by warning parents about [The Creepies]." She stated that she felt a responsibility to inform friends, specifically ones [The Creepies] were inviting over for sleepovers and/or play dates, of the confirmed incidents. At the point in time she was referring to, [The Creepies] were arguing that there was nothing inappropriate about sharing their beds with other people's children and gave no indication that they would stop that unacceptable and potentially unsafe behavior. Adryana's position was nothing new to the school because she stated the same exact thing in previous meetings - statements that were met with "as parents, that's understandable."

We are completely within our legal right to exercise constitutionally protected free speech in sharing truthful information. And it is completely reasonable for my wife and I to express distress and to display emotion given the nature of the incidents, especially with parents that have nothing to do with our conflict who are repeating and completely misrepresenting the context that lead to [Mr. Creepy] undressing our daughter. That said, we've refrained from speaking about the incidents whenever possible and have followed the school's advice at each turn regarding discussing these confirmed incidents, including correcting any misinformation about our family and [The Creepies] family and avoiding repeated requests for information from various Oakwood parents.

Our reputation of conduct in and around a school environment is unimpeachable. We were selected by our peers at our daughter's pre-school to co-chair the only annual charity gala – the most successful effort at it's time. We were selected by our Oakwood peers to co-head the annual camping trip, an activity based on building our community. And we are currently under a (pro bono) contract by one of the leading 501(c)(3) educational organizations working to resist curriculum narrowing in public schools nationally.

Our family has also worked to improve the environment of our national community, including creating the first-ever luxury vehicle advertising campaign featuring a prominent gay married couple; successfully convincing the White House and the National Endowment for the Arts to publicly change their policy regarding conduct between federal agencies and their potential grantees; working with Robert F. Kennedy Jr. and his Waterkeeper Alliance Foundation that helps ensure a clean drinking water supply; and helping produce one of the first efforts to incorporate environmentally sustainable practices within the luxury fashion community. Working toward a healthy community is something that we actually live and breathe everyday, and have been undeniably successful at accomplishing.

We understand and appreciate that the school has been put in an unwanted position, as has our family. But for the school to seemingly deem [The Creepies] behavior as acceptable because it isn't unlawful, then listen to third parties, that never state that we are speaking untruths, claim that our family is bullying when the documented facts clearly show the opposite, is an unfortunate misevaluation. A wider audience reviewing all of the facts would no doubt support our position.

Our family works very hard to send our one child to Oakwood and does not come from the socioeconomic circumstances that have blessed many of our Oakwood peers – so our presence at the school is a personal triumph for our family. We are minorities in more than one capacity within this community. We will not be bullied into uprooting our daughter from this school due to the actions and unacceptable behavior of [The Creepies]. If truthful incidents have caused such discomfort and instability within our community, then it would seem logical to deal with the truth itself. The "divisiveness" and "palpable discomfort" are a direct result of [The Creepies] actions, and their actions alone. We will not tolerate any attempt to shift blame in our direction.

As stated earlier, our family is open to appropriate mediation with [The Creepies] as a step towards stabilizing our community. We also respectfully submit, that we think it is in the best interest of Oakwood's children and community for the school to consider addressing this unacceptable parent-on-child behavior in the school's code of conduct so that an incident of this nature never reaches this level of instability again. We will continue to do our part to create a healthy Oakwood environment and trust that the school will take the necessary steps to help ensure that this type of behavior will not be tolerated nor repeated.

Sincerely,

Patrick & Adryana Courrielche

CHAPTER SIX: LEARNED TO CODE

1. Tim Cook: Congress needs to fix DACA, CNN.com, June 4, 2018. https://money.cnn.com/video/technology/2018/06/04/tim-cook-apple-ceo-immigration.cnnmoney/index.html

2. Jack Regan, Alfredo Alcantara, Jack Dorsey: 'We benefit from immigration,' CNN.com, January 28, 2017. https://money.cnn.com/video/technology/2017/01/28/yassin-falafel-jack-dorsey.cnnmoney/index.html

3. Ed O'Keefe, Nick Anderson, Jeff Bezos donates $33 million to scholarship fund for 'dreamers,' The Washington Post, January 12, 2018. https://www.washingtonpost.com/news/powerpost/wp/2018/01/12/jeff-bezos-donates-33-million-to-scholarship-fund-for-dreamers/

4. Mario Trujillo, Zuckerberg criticizes 'fearful voices calling for building wall,' The Hill, April 12, 2016. https://thehill.com/policy/technology/275998-zuckerberg-criticizes-fearful-voices-calling-for-building-walls

5. Immigration Act Signing Ceremony, C-Span, November 29, 1990. https://www.c-span.org/video/?15232-1/immmigration-act-signing-ceremony

6. Gabrielle Russon, Legal fight ends for Disney IT workers who trained foreign replacements, Orlando Sentinel, May 9, 2018. https://www.orlandosentinel.com/business/tourism/os-bz-disney-lawsuit-workers-20180508-story.html

7. WKMG Orlando Foreign workers on visas 'Where did the jobs go,' November 12, 2015. https://www.youtube.com/watch?v=LJlesZ9popA

8. CNN Emmons 200309241, CNN, March 7, 2019. https://www.youtube.com/watch?v=MrKTUS7v0ss

9. ABC Siemens ICN replacing American workers, ABC World News Tonight with Peter Jennings. https://www.youtube.com/watch?v=9cvFVmJlK54

10. Katie Galioto, Trump ad-libs that he wants legal immigrants in 'the largest numbers ever,' Politico, February 5, 2019. https://www.politico.com/story/2019/02/05/trump-state-of-the-union-legal-immigration-1148629

11. Graham Rapier, Self-driving cars could wipe out 4 million jobs — but a new report says the upsides will be easily worth it, Business Insider, June 13, 2018. https://markets.businessinsider.com/news/stocks/self-driving-cars-could-kill-4-million-jobs-economic-impact-worth-it-2018-6-1026937775

12. Ethan Baron, H-1B: Foreign citizens make up nearly three-quarters of Silicon Valley tech workforce, report says, Mercury News, January 17, 2018. https://www.mercurynews.com/2018/01/17/h-1b-foreign-citizens-make-up-nearly-three-quarters-of-silicon-valley-tech-workforce-report-says/

13. 23-year-old Google employee lives in a truck to save money, see inside, Today Show, October 21, 2015. https://www.today.com/video/23-year-old-google-employee-lives-in-a-truck-to-save-money-see-inside-548544067840

14. Quotes from Roger Ross, Michael Emmons, and Sarah Blackwell from interviews on Red Pilled America episode entitled Learned to Code published March 15, 2019.

CHAPTER SEVEN: THE MINORITY

1. Julio Rosas, Beto O'Rourke: 'This country was founded on White supremacy,' The Washington Examiner, July 10, 2019. https://www.washingtonexaminer.com/news/beto-orourke-this-country-was-founded-on-white-supremacy

2. Lia Eustachewich, Kamala Harris, Elizabeth Warren both support reparations for slavery, The New York Post, February 22, 2019. https://nypost.com/2019/02/22/kamala-harris-elizabeth-warren-both-support-reparations-for-slavery/

3. Joseph A. Wulfsohn, Elizabeth Warren says Trump is advancing 'environment racism,' 'economic racism,' 'health care racism,' Fox News, July 30, 2019. https://www.foxnews.com/media/elizabeth-warren-trump-environmental-racism

4. Ella Nilsen, Elizabeth Warren gives a full-throated endorsement of reparations at CNN town hall, Vox.com, March 18, 2019. https://www.vox.com/2019/3/18/18272000/elizabeth-warren-reparations-cnn-town-hall

5. Joshua Caplan, Elizabeth Warren claimed 'American Indian' heritage on Texas Bar registration card, Breitbart News, February 5, 2019. https://www.breitbart.com/politics/2019/02/05/elizabeth-warren-claimed-american-indian-heritage-on-texas-bar-registration-card/

6. Quotes from Denise and Nancy from interviews on Red Pilled America episode entitled The Minority published September 26, 2019 & October 3, 2019.

CHAPTER EIGHT: SANCTUARY

1. José Diaz-Balart, Study: Immigrant teens less likely to engage in violence, MSNBC, September 3, 2015. https://www.msnbc.com/jos--d-az-balart/watch/study--immigrant-teens-less-engaged-in-crime-518663235713
2. PBS News Hour, Truth vs. perception of crime rates for immigrants, PBS, July 10, 2015. https://www.pbs.org/newshour/show/truth-vs-perception-crime-rates-immigrants
3. Jose Ramos: More immigrants = less crimes, Fusion, October 5, 2015. https://www.youtube.com/watch?v=DK2lrvG1NlA
4. Tucker Carlson Leaves Cenk Ugyur Speechless On Immigration, Informative, November 11, 2018. https://www.youtube.com/watch?v=0zDoyLj3JPY
5. Brian Rokos, Dispatcher Killed: Other driver hat two DUI arrests, PE.com, July 16, 2012. https://www.pe.com/2012/07/16/dispatcher-killed-other-driver-had-two-dui-arrests/
6. Oakland Mayor Says She'll Go To Jail To Protect Sanctuary City Police, KPIX CBS SF BayArea, January 17, 2018. https://sanfrancisco.cbslocal.com/2018/01/17/oakland-bans-cooperation-federal-immigration-agents-braces-for-ice-raids/
7. Tucker Carlson, Tucker Reveals Some Crime Statistics Democrats Really Don't Want You to Hear, Fox News, December 22, 2017. https://www.chicksonright.com/blog/2017/12/22/tucker-reveals-some-crime-statistics-democrats-really-dont-want-you-to-hear/
8. Steve Holland, Trump vows crackdown on immigrants who overstay visas if elected, Reuters, August 27, 2016. https://www.reuters.com/article/us-usa-election-trump/trump-vows-crackdown-on-immigrants-who-overstay-visas-if-elected-idUSKCN1120SF
9. Vivian Yee, For Grieving Parents, Trump is 'Speaking for the Dead' on Immigration, The New York Times, June 25, 2017. https://www.nytimes.com/2017/06/25/us/trump-undocumented-victims.html
10. Quotes from Sabine Durden, Chris Odette, and Jessica Vaughn from interviews on Red Pilled America episode entitled Sanctuary published Jan. 3, 2019.

CHAPTER NINE: TESTED

1. Larry O'Connor, Tomorrow: The Mask Comes Off, Breitbart.com, December 22, 2009.

CHAPTER TEN: UNFRIEND ME NOW

1. Sabrina Siddiqi, Lauren Gambino, Dan Roberts, DNC apologizes to Bernie Sanders amid convention chaos in wake of email leak, The Guardian, July 25, 2016. https://www.theguardian.com/us-news/2016/jul/25/debbie-wasserman-schultz-booed-dnc-fbi-email-hack
2. Amy Chozick, Democrats Allege D.N.C. Hack Is Part of Russian Ef-

fort to Elect Donald Trump, The New York Times, July 25, 2016. https://www. nytimes.com/2016/07/26/us/politics/democrats-allege-dnc-hack-is-part-of-russian-effort-to-elect-donald-trump.html

3. Alex Seitz-Wald, DNC Chief Debbie Wasserman Shultz Stepping Aside in Wake of Scandal, NBC News, July 24, 2016. https://www.nbcnews.com/ storyline/2016-conventions/democratic-national-committee-chief-stepping-aside-after-convention-n615826

4. Sean Sullivan, Michael E. Miller, Ugly, bloody scenes in San Jose as protesters attack Trump supporters outside rally, Washington Post, June 3, 2016. https://www.washingtonpost.com/news/morning-mix/wp/2016/06/03/ugly-bloody-scenes-in-san-jose-as-protesters-attack-trump-supporters-outside-rally/

5. Patrick Courrielche, GOP Trump Haters, Stop Your Free Bleeding, Breitbart News, August 24, 2015. https://www.breitbart.com/politics/2015/08/24/ gop-trump-haters-stop-your-free-bleeding/

6. Ray Sanchez, 'Work It' Controversy: Actor Amaury Nolasco Tries to Explain ABC's sitcoms Puerto Rican Diss Amid Debate About Island's Drug Scourge, The Huffington Post, January 9, 2012. https://www.huffpost.com/entry/work-it-abc-drugs-puerto-ricans_n_1193121

CHAPTER ELEVEN: FRANK TALK

1. Leon Daniel, Cleaning up mean streets for Olympics, UPI, July 23, 1984. https://www.upi.com/Archives/1984/07/23/Cleaning-up-mean-streets-for-Olympics/9364459403200/

2. Malcolm W. Klein, The American Street Gang: Its Nature, Prevalence, and Control, Oxford University Press, published July 31, 1997.

3. Peter Jennings, Video of Rodney King Beaten by Police Released, ABC News, March 7, 1991. https://abcnews.go.com/Archives/video/march-1991-rodney-king-videotape-9758031

4. Linda Breakstone, Rodney King riot in Los Angeles, ABC News, April 29, 1992. https://www.youtube.com/watch?v=bSeCpFCS32M

5. Peter Jennings, Rodney King Case Verdict, April 30, 1992. https://abcnews.go.com/Archives/video/rodney-king-beating-verdict-9922987

6. Bryant Gumbel and Katie Couric, The Today Show, April 30, 1992. https://www.youtube.com/watch?v=1LIcBLMQOZ0

7. Maloy Moore, Los Angeles riots: Remember the 63 people who died, Los Angeles Times, April 26, 2012. https://latimesblogs.latimes.com/lanow/2012/04/los-angeles-riots-remember-the-63-people-who-died-.html

8. CNN Library, Los Angeles Riots Fast Facts, CNN, April 22, 2019. https://www.cnn.com/2013/09/18/us/los-angeles-riots-fast-facts/index.html

9. President Trump Remarks at Campaign Rally in Ohio, C-Span, August 4, 2018. https://www.c-span.org/video/?449348-1/president-trump-delivers-remarks-campaign-rally-ohio

10. Quotes from Tyrone Jackson from interviews on Red Pilled America episode entitled Frank Talk published July 11, 2019.

CHAPTER TWELVE: CONSERVATISM'S FATAL FLAW

1. Ian Schwartz, Fired Google Engineer Kevin Cernekee: Conservative Employees Mistreated, Abused, and Harassed, Real Clear Politics, Aug.5, 2019. https://www.realclearpolitics.com/video/2019/08/05/fired_google_engineer_ kevin_cernekee_conservative_employees_mistreated_abused_and_harassed. html

2. UCLA conservative professor may be fired from job, Fox News, April 19, 2017. https://www.youtube.com/watch?v=b_hcieaUKiI

3. Curt Schilling fired by ESPN for social media post on transgender ruling, Today.com, August 21, 2016. https://www.today.com/video/curt-schilling-fired-by-espn-for-social-media-post-on-transgender-ruling-670673987513

4. Lisa Respers France, 'Last Man Standing' cancellation angers conservatives, CNN.com, May 16, 2017. https://www.cnn.com/2017/05/15/entertainment/last-man-standing-boycott/index.html

5. Michael Burke, Ex-Facebook exec ousted from company sparked controversy with pro-Trump views: report, The Hill, November 11, 2018. https://thehill.com/policy/technology/416157-ex-facebook-exec-ousted-from-company-sparked-controversy-with-pro-trump

6. Elahe Izadi, Milo Yiannopolis loses his book deal with Simon & Schuster amid growing outcry, Washington Post, February 20, 2017. https://www.washingtonpost.com/news/arts-and-entertainment/wp/2017/02/20/milo-yiannopoulos-loses-his-book-deal-with-simon-schuster-amid-growing-outcry/

7. Tim Hains, Dennis Prager On Suing Google For Alleged YouTube Censorship, Real Clear Politics, March 6, 2018. https://www.realclearpolitics.com/video/2018/03/06/dennis_prager_on_suing_google_for_alleged_youtube_censorship.html

8. Devin Dwyer, Biden's 'Shorthand' for first term: 'Osama bin Laden dead, General Motors alive,' ABC News, January 31, 2012. https://abcnews.go.com/blogs/politics/2012/01/bidens-shorthand-for-obama-1st-term-osama-bin-laden-dead-general-motors-alive

9. Kurt Eichenwald, The Deafness Before the Storm, The New York Times, September 11, 2012. https://www.nytimes.com/2012/09/11/opinion/the-bush-white-house-was-deaf-to-9-11-warnings.html

10. Hillary Clinton calls anti-Muslim film, Innocence of Muslims 'disgusting and reprehensible', CNN.com, September 15, 2012. https://www.youtube.com/watch?v=9dqPQblKGHY

11. "Tingles" gets owned, YouTube.com, October 24, 2012. https://www.youtube.com/watch?v=_JhP3hbXyTU

12. Dr. Karen Siegemund Begins 'Rage Against the Media', PolitiChicks,

October 24, 2012. https://www.youtube.com/watch?v=JTWZqYWC5FE

13. Uncommon Knowledge, The Politics of Hollywood with Andrew Breitbart, Hoover Institute on YouTube, May 27, 2009. https://www.youtube.com/watch?v=0mTxpFIw-3g

14. Quotes from Karen Siegemund from interviews on Red Pilled America episode entitled Conservatism's Fatal Flaw published September 5, 2019.

CHAPTER FOURTEEN: RIGHT TO TRY

1. MSNBC's O'Donnell Claims U.S. Is 'Crying' in Fear of Trump, MSNBC, November 9, 2016. https://www.facebook.com/watch/?v=1291466777543034

2. Marlene Lenthang, Vape shop worker goes on furious rant against Trump supporter, The Daily Mail, December 29, 2018. https://www.dailymail.co.uk/news/article-6538155/Vape-shop-worker-launches-furious-rant-against-Trump-supporter.html

3. Woman kicked off flight after berating Trump supporter, CBS News, January 23, 2017. https://www.youtube.com/watch?v=4n7fd95Rujg

4. Researchers Think They Have a Clue to the Cause of AIDS, NBC Nightly News with Tom Brokaw, April 29. 1983. https://www.nbclearn.com/portal/site/k-12/flatview?cuecard=39572

5. Early CBS Report on AIDS, CBS News. https://www.youtube.com/watch?v=X23vKiBE88E

6. ABC News Nightline: AIDS, Ted Koppel, March 27, 2017. https://www.youtube.com/watch?v=5FREjnYV_aM

7. A vivid 1983 reminder of initial AIDS scare, MSNBC.com, 1983. http://www.msnbc.com/msnbc/watch/a-vivid-1983-reminder-of-initial-aids-scare-264433219509

8. AIDS Discovered, NBC News, April 23, 1984. https://www.youtube.com/watch?v=krf9LWI_OVI

9. Geoffrey Cowley, The day they discovered the AIDS virus, MSNBC, April 23, 2014. http://www.msnbc.com/msnbc/the-day-they-discovered-the-aids-virus

10. Ellen Bukstel with Doug Segal, MONTAGE, November 11, 1987.

11. HIV/AIDS Historical Time Line 1981-1990, FDA.gov. https://www.fda.gov/patients/hiv-timeline-and-history-approvals/hivaids-historical-timeline-1981-1990

12. 1982-1992 AIDS, NBC News. https://www.youtube.com/watch?v=zPO5wausim8

13. Remarks at a Luncheon for Members of the College of Physicians in Philadelphia, Pennsylvania, ReaganLibrary.gov, April 1,1987. https://www.reaganlibrary.gov/research/speeches/040187e

14. Ellen Bukstel, Legacy of Love.

15. Esther Goldberg, Trump Derangement Syndrome, The American Spec-

5

tor, August 17, 2015. https://spectator.org/63786_trump-derangement-syndrome/

16. Charles Krauthammer, Bush Derangement Syndrome, Townhall, December 5, 2003. https://townhall.com/columnists/charleskrauthammer/2003/12/05/bush-derangement-syndrome-n940041

17. Rob Whitley, Ph.D., Is 'Trump Derangement Syndrome' a Real Mental Condition, Psychology Today, January 4, 2019. https://www.psychologytoday.com/us/blog/talking-about-men/201901/is-trump-derangement-syndrome-real-mental-condition

18. Trump Derangement Syndrome & the Crumbling Media (Pt. 2), The Rubin Report, November 23, 2017. https://www.youtube.com/watch?v=4_id-hCca2XM

19. Brooke Baldwin, Columnist: 18 reasons why Trump may be a Russian asset, CNN, January 14, 2019. https://www.cnn.com/videos/politics/2019/01/14/trump-putin-russia-relationship-max-boot-intv-nr-vpx.cnn

20. Quotes from Ellen Bukstel and Brett Segal from interviews on Red Pilled America episode entitled Right to Try published January 17, 2019.

21. Quotes and letter from Doug Segal provided by Ellen Bukstel.

Acknowledgements

We first want to acknowledge our daughter. We are so proud of you honey. You are a stellar girl who stood strong while our family was under attack for the crime of wrongthink. We live in strange times and never meant for our beliefs to so drastically impact your life. Our goals were to build a stable loving family, to be exemplary role models, and provide you the best education possible. We wish to impart the importance of integrity but most of all the gift of happiness. We hope that someday the stories in this book convey to you that your mom and dad tried our absolute hardest at being the best parents possible and that we love you more than we ever knew we could love.

To our moms Nancy and Gloria, we want to thank you for being our champions and for holding us up when we couldn't stand on our own. We don't know how you were able to do it all, but you did. We love you so much.

Denise, Junior and the boys, you have been such amazing role models for our entire family. We love you and are so proud of you. Jay and Lizzette, we love you…always and forever. Casey, we love you unconditionally.

To our late grandparents, thank you for being incredible role models.

Aunt Maryann and Uncle Randy, thank you for being there for us when we needed you most. We'll never forget your kindness.

To our late fathers, thank you for giving us a sense of humor. You were not perfect, but you taught us the gift of unbridled laughter...and we thank you for that.

Lisa & Ronnie and Evie & Mark, we love you like family. Thank you for all of your support throughout the years.

To our late friend Andrew Breitbart, meeting you was quite possibly the most consequential moment of our lives. We saw a kindred spirit in your enthusiasm for fun, passion for seeking the truth, enjoyment in fighting the #war, and undying energy in protecting people from bullies. You are truly missed.

Julie Talbott, thank you for believing in our show and sticking with us as we worked to build it. We truly appreciate your attention and support.

Mike Cernovich, thank you for understanding the importance of promoting independent creators, exposing the hoax media, and for using your platform to introduce our show to the Twitterverse when there was really nothing in it for you.

Rebecca Mansour, thank you for being a thinker, championing the American worker, and opening our eyes to so many America First issues.

Christian Toto, you are one of the few selfless promoters of creative work. Thank you for shining a light on Hollywood's liberal bias.

Nick Searcy, you are a fearless voice in Hollywood. Thank you for proving conservatives are just as creative as the Left, and for making us laugh time and time again.

Ali Alexander, Andrew Meyer and everyone at Culttture, thank you for understanding that culture drives politics, and for using your platforms to promote the work of others.

Jack Posobiec, thank you for having the guts to change the way the Right fights back, and for pushing for peaceful discourse in these volatile times.

In no particular order, we'd like to thank the following for supporting and contributing to our work over the years: Alex Marlow, John Nolte, Pat Coons, Paul Gosar, Candace Owens, Diamond & Silk, Jevaughn Brown, Cathy Kwasigroch, Joseph Granda, Kiera Byrd, Tom Wedell, George Overbeck, Dr. Steve Camarota, Jessica Vaughn, Damon N., David Dubrow, Paul Hair, Steve McIntyre, Steve Mosher, Charles Rotter, Anthony Watts, Brian Kolfage, Glenn Beck, Robert Barnes, Sabine Durden, Chris Odette, Ellen Bukstel, Brett Segal, Laura Loomer, Michelle Malkin, Larry Solov, Ryan Hampton, Michael Emmons, Roger Ross, Sara Blackwell, Gavin McInnes, Larry O'Connor, Nick Di Paolo, Austen Fletcher, Chadwick Moore, Isaiah Washington, Rob Smith, Tyrone and Marcella Jackson, Andrew Klavan, Robby and Landon Starbuck, Karen Siegemund, Emma Jimenez, Scott Presler, Robin Auer, Aaron Alfred, John Binder, Ryan James Girdusky, Alfred Hopton, Sam Ryskind, Ken LaCorte, Carpe Donktum, Nabeel Azeez, Brian Amerige, Curtis Glenn Morton, Ben Shapiro, Robert Kraychik, Liz Aiello, Stephen Limbaugh, Gaston Mooney, Raheem Kassam, Rush Limbaugh, Sean Hannity, Brandon Darby, Adam Baldwin, and Nick Gillespie.

To those within the MAGA Movement, thank you for refusing to cower to the race-baiting far-left media and establishments of both parties. Your courage to speak out in the face of such powerful and vicious opposition has been an inspiration for our work.

And finally, to all of our Patrons, we respect your private patronage of our show Red Pilled America and wouldn't be able to produce this book without you. Thank you all.

Culture Warriors

Patrick & Adryana would like to thank our culture warriors for their generous support in helping this book come to life. We truly couldn't have done it without you.

Cheryl Bennett
Ron & Lisa Chairez
Brad and Regina Chapman
Jason Coons
Steve Coronado
Nancy Coons Courrielche
Dan "Magnificent" Cowper
Lezlie Michele Crane
Brandie Daniels
Alfred Hopton
Dawn Igoe
Donald Johnson
Kent Kekeis
Aaron Ledebuhr
Mandy Lynn
Carolyn McNulty
Jesse Mueller
Andrew Poling
Ron & Melissa Ralston
Elias Abu Shanab
Phillip Thielman

About the Authors

Patrick Courrielche and Adryana Cortez are the husband and wife creative duo behind Red Pilled America – a weekly audio documentary series that tells the stories Hollywood & the mainstream media don't want you to hear.

Courrielche is a writer, former applied physicist and marketer, and long-time contributor to Breitbart News covering the intersection between culture & politics. Cortez is a writer, entrepreneur, artist and creative director...collaborating with some of the biggest names in fashion and design. The two have produced an extraordinary array of creative projects including short films, long-form journalism, semi-scripted debate series, New York Fashion Week runway shows, and have even pioneered *pop-up retail* – a marketing technique that has become a global phenomenon.

They live in the Greater Los Angeles Area with their daughter and two dogs.

CPSIA information can be obtained
at www.ICGtesting.com
Printed in the USA
BVHW032316151119
563724BV00001BB/1/P